FUN WITH PATENTS

THE IRREVERENT GUIDE FOR THE INVESTOR, THE ENTREPRENEUR, AND THE INVENTOR

Kfir Luzzatto, Ph.D.

PINE 10

Pine Ten, LLC
616 Corporate Way
Suite 2-5772
Valley Cottage, NY 10989

This book is educational in nature and does not contain legal advice. Nothing of what is said in this book can be used instead of competent legal advice taken in the jurisdiction in which the reader lives or works. The intent of the author is only to offer information of a general nature. In the event that you use any of the information in this book without qualified legal advice the author and the publisher assume no responsibility for your actions. The advice and strategies contained herein may not be suitable for every situation. The publisher and the author make no representations or warranties with respect to the accuracy or completeness of the contents of this work and specifically disclaim all warranties, including without limitation warranties of fitness for a particular purpose. This work is sold with the understanding that the publisher is not engaged in rendering legal or other professional services.

First publication, February 2016

Book Cover Design by Dane Low / EbookLaunch.com.

ISBN-10: 1-938212-33-9
ISBN-13: 978-1-938212-33-8

What the experts say…

"I've worked with Kfir for many years and I'm always impressed by his insights. I'm excited he has turned his years of experience and gift for clear straight-forward prose (and a touch of irreverence) into this guide, so that the important world of patents can be better understood by inventors, investors and business people across the globe."

Larry Granatelli, Chair of the Intellectual Property Practice Group Fenwick & West LLP, Mountain View, CA, USA

"In 'Fun with Patents', Israeli Patent Attorney Kfir Luzzatto shares many reflections from his career. As its introduction says, this book will not teach you everything about patent law or how to be a patent practitioner but, ranging from the critical difference between a patent and a patent application to the reasons not to rush to plough one's life savings into an invention, it offers much practical guidance on working with inventions. I hope you enjoy as much as I did this light-hearted treatment of some serious subject matter."

Andrew Bentham, European and UK Patent Attorney, JA Kemp, London, UK

"Abraham Lincoln once said: 'The patent system added the fuel of interest to the fire of genius.'

From now on, no inventor, entrepreneur or investor shall be able to claim that protecting an invention is a far too complex maze, to justify that he did not bother patenting his creation and then cry over his wasted R&D. This long-waited guide on patents eventually sheds light on the most passionating and entertaining area of law, which purpose is precisely to enable those imaginative risk-takers to be rewarded for their work, time and investments."

William LOBELSON, Partner GERMAIN MAUREAU, Lyon, France

"I spent a whole day to read this book from beginning to end and it was well worth it! I will also recommend it to the students of the course where I teach: I am sure it will unburden my task."

Giorgio Long, Partner - European Patent Attorney
Jacobacci & Partners Spa, Milano, Italy

"In the bible it is stated, 'Many who are first will be last, and many who are last will be first', but in patent, Who files first is who will be served.

Kfir Luzzatto is among the first to use 'fun' in patent related books. You can read this book (Fun with Patents) with much pleasure. This book is easy to understand and consists of A to Z about patents. It is second to none I have seen to know and learn about patents during my thirty-plus years in the field."

Bong Sig SONG, Managing Patent Attorney
Y.S. CHANG & ASSOCIATES, Seoul, Korea

"A very well written, thorough and essential guide for inventors, entrepreneurs and for readers who are not patent practitioners. Easy to read and understand, the book summarizes the important concepts in the patenting process in a very appealing manner which keeps the reader bound to the book. And as the name suggests—a lot of fun for the readers involved."

Chetan Chadha, Head: International Department
CHADHA & CHADHA, New Delhi, India

Contents

Part II: The Inventor and the Patent

Part III: The Patent and We

Part IV: Patents and Business

Foreword

I first encountered the author of this tome back in the 1980s, when we were both considerably younger, patents were a niche area of legal practice and most members of the public knew little, and cared less, about them. The year is now 2016 and the main difference between then and now is that we have both aged considerably; the ignorance and indifference surrounding patents remain largely unscathed by our efforts to attract and retain the attention of the average citizen of Planet Earth for long enough to persuade them that patents actually matter.

Fun with Patents represents a cunning attempt to sell patents to readers by telling them the truth: patents can indeed be fun. Getting a patent is not just a bureaucratic exercise like applying for a passport or seeking planning permission for a new building; exploiting it commercially requires a variety of skills, up-to-date information and a degree of intuition too. Litigating a patent has all the ingredients of an interactive multi-actor real-time battle of wits (and occasionally half-wits), while investing in the innovation that may lead to a new patent, or to something that will render a competitor's patents valueless, combines the intimate buzz of personal and informed involvement with the apparently random spin of the roulette wheel. But for those of a nervous disposition, the easiest way to enjoy the thrills and spills of patents is to read a book like this one.

One of the most enjoyable aspects of the patent system, which patents shares with other types of intellectual property right, is that it offers the chance—admittedly not a great chance but a chance nonetheless—for the little man to succeed where the big corporations do not. An occasional flash of insight can lead to an invention so simple that people assume it must have been patented years before, just as a holiday photo, a basic tune with banal lyrics or a fortuitous brand name can suddenly capture the mind of the public at large, leading to fame, fortune and visits from the tax man.

If you are looking for a "Patents for Dummies"-type publication, providing a step-by-step do-it-yourself manual for readers who make their inventions and then set out to do all the legal and bureaucratic stuff themselves, this is not the book for you (incidentally, filing your own patent application when there are skilled, trained experts around to do it for you is not much different from choosing to perform your own appendectomy when there's a hospital around the corner with a trained medical staff waiting to do it for you). Nor is this book an investment guide for the pundits, analysts and would-be gurus whose verdicts on the innovation economy can have startling effects on stock prices, personal savings and pension funds. If however you want to enjoy, become familiar with and maybe even get to love patents, warts and all, Kfir's book is a great place to start.

Professor Jeremy Phillips
Founding editor, Journal of Intellectual Property Law & Practice; Emeritus Kat

Introduction

Before you start reading this book, you may want to read this introduction. I have kept it short in the hope that you will.

First of all, let me say what this book is not. It is not a practical guide for filing and prosecuting patent applications. Those are activities that call for practical knowledge and organization, which are best left to professional patent law firms. You will not become a patent attorney by reading this book, but you will end up having a good understanding of what the patent system is about, what it can and cannot do for you, and how you should work with your patent practitioner to maximize the results that he can fetch you.

As the title of the book implies, patents don't have to be a dry and boring subject, and you may (and should) enjoy using them to your advantage. Unfortunately, for us patent practitioners, there is no efficient way to operate without relying on jargon that makes a lot of sense to us but more often than not sounds like gibberish to you. As a result, while we enthusiastically expand on "first-to-file," "priority rights," "sufficiency of description," and other similarly boring and confusing subjects, you let your attention wander to those nice pictures we keep on our walls, and you eventually walk out more clueless than you were when you walked in. This book seeks to remedy that problem.

On a personal note: I have been dealing with inventors and entrepreneurs for longer than I care to admit and have assisted both start-ups and multinational companies with their patent needs in Israel (the "Start-Up Nation") and literally all over the world. When, at the turn of the century, I realized that small companies, individual inventors, and high-tech entrepreneurs did not have a full grasp of the meaning and importance of the patent system, I decided to do something about it. This resulted in a series of educational articles that evolved into a weekly column in Israel's financial newspaper, ***Globes***. Encouraged by the positive feedback from readers, I eventually published ***The World of Patents***, a book that presented the information that I thought was vital for the general public, in a light and readable form, which also rewarded me with highly satisfying readers' feedback.

Now, some 13 years after the publication of that book, the world has changed, and many of the ideas that we championed then are no longer valid or, at least, had to be revisited. However, the need remains for a book that introduces important patent concepts to regular people in a humanly understandable fashion, with down-to-earth, practical advice and, more importantly, which is not boring, as many patent books (including ones to which I contributed) unavoidably are to readers who are not patent practitioners. I believe and hope that this book is that book.

A disclaimer is in order here. This book is educational in nature, and its contents should not be taken as legal advice. None of the matters discussed in the book should be used instead of qualified legal counsel taken in the country where you live and operate. The purpose of this book is to help you to get better-focused advice from your patent practitioner, not to help you to skip it.

You can read the chapters of this book in any order you like, because it is organized by topic. Nevertheless, a lot of thinking went into organizing it the way it is, so I believe that reading it sequentially would provide the best reading experience.

I have added as "Appendix A" the annotated text of a (mock) patent application. Its purpose is not to teach you how to draft patent applications, but rather to explain the logic of their structure so that the next time you read a patent, you will have a better understanding of the meaning of its various sections. In the appendices, you will also find excerpts from two international treaties to which I refer in the book. Those are the most interesting parts of the treaties, but if you wish, you can read the complete texts at the provided URLs. If you do, try not to fall asleep.

One more thing: to avoid turning this book into an unreadable, politically correct exercise littered with "he (and she)" and with "his (or hers)" or similar obfuscations, I have written it in the masculine form simply because, being of the male persuasion, it comes more naturally to me. However, everything said here applies equally well (and often better) to our better halves.

That's all for now. If you feel like commenting on any matter discussed in the book, you are welcome to connect with me at www.kfirluzzatto.com. Otherwise, I hope you enjoy this read.

Kfir Luzzatto, Omer, February 2016

Part I: Basics

Egad, I think the interpreter is the hardest to be understood of the two!

[Richard Brinsley Sheridan, The Critic *(1779) act 1. sc. 2]*

The basic concepts introduced in this section provide a partial basis for understanding the patent language. Additional concepts will be introduced in later parts of the book.

CHAPTER 1
The Inventor

The inventor is an almost mythological figure. Think of Albert Einstein, Alexander Graham Bell, Leonardo da Vinci, and many others. Besides the big names in science and technology, you will find in the "inventors club" many well-known people who advance and modernize our lives and, in doing so, improve its quality. The inventor is the one who will take us to the road that leads to the development of an invention and, as a result, to a patent that protects it. It is, therefore, appropriate to start our journey to the land of patents by allowing the inventor to introduce himself and his world to us.

Simplistically, we can define the inventor as "one who contributed to an invention that is the subject of a patent application." Inventions can be made by a sole inventor or by joint inventors. A joint inventor is an individual whose contribution to the invention is substantial and without which the invention would have looked different. A patent application may name a number of inventors, who may have contributed differently to it. It is possible, as an extreme example, to have a patent application with, say, 30 claims and two inventors, in which the first inventor invented the subject matter claimed in 29 claims, and the contribution of the second inventor was limited to the single remaining claim. Regardless, they will both be the inventors named in the patent application. For example, let's assume that the invention is a novel dispensing machine and the main inventor designed all the electronic elements and the mechanical parts that make it work smoothly. Those elements are claimed in claims 1 through 29. However, the second inventor discovered that since the machine is to be located outside, it is expedient to paint it white so it doesn't heat up too much during the day. This is important because heat may cause some of the mechanical elements to malfunction. Claim 30 will claim the dispensing machine of claims 1–29, which is white in color.

Being mentioned as an inventor does good to your ego (and, in some cases, also involves remuneration). Therefore, it is not uncommon to get requests to mention a person as an inventor in a patent application because "he worked hard on the project and it would be impolite not to include him." This is common practice with scientific articles in academia, but doing so in a patent application is courting trouble for a number of reasons that will become apparent as we proceed in peeling the many layers of the patent system.

As a rule, the rights to a patent application—and to the invention—are assigned to the patent applicant by the inventors, who are the original owners of what they have invented. If the applicant and the inventor are not the same person, the rights can be assigned to the applicant by the inventor, as a matter of law, if the inventor is an employee of the assignee (more on that later) or as a result of an agreement between the inventor and the assignee. However, in some cases, the development of an invention is done by a team that includes persons who are not employees of the applicant and who, as such, are under no obligation to assign their rights to him. In such cases, it is even more important to be precise in determining the identity of the inventors.

Please make a note of this: **A corporation cannot be an inventor; only an actual person, with a brain, can make an invention.** You wouldn't believe how often this simple truth has to be repeated to people who think they have found a clever way around the need to mention an inventor.

Then we have to deal with the inevitable paperwork. When filing patent applications in different countries, the inventors are often required to sign formal papers that include declarations as to their status as inventors and deeds of assignment transferring their rights to the applicant. If, after the filing of a patent application, it turns out that the list of inventors was wrong, this may cause substantial costs and undesirable administrative complications.

Moreover, a willful false statement on the part of the inventors, omitting the name of a rightful inventor or adding someone who is not an inventor to the list of inventors for a specific patent application, may have serious consequences and should be avoided at all costs.

How, then, should we determine who is and who isn't an inventor? The answer, at least on the first level, is not complicated: as explained, an inventor is someone who made a real contribution to the invention. This contribution is not measured "quantitative" but rather "qualitative": one inventor may have invested one hour to come up with an idea and to plan how to carry it into practice, while a technician who follows the inventor's instructions may have to work for months in a laboratory to turn that idea into a practical result. In this example, only the first person is the inventor; the technician is not an inventor, because he did not make any original contribution to the invention, in spite of the long hours that he worked at the project. However, if during his laboratory work, the technician comes up with an idea that changes or substantially improves the direction in which the invention is developing, it is possible that the technician has contributed to the inventive process and that his name will, therefore, have to appear in the list of inventors on the patent.

Since the question of whether a person who participated in a project made an inventive contribution is not always a simple one and is often influenced by emotional and personal considerations, the applicant would be well advised, whenever questions arise in this respect, to place the task of investigating the names of the inventors in the hands of a neutral person, who can make that determination on the basis of professional considerations that are not tinged by foreign influences. In any case, one should not be tempted to include in the list of inventors individuals who didn't make an inventive contribution, just to avoid confrontation or to make someone happy, because this mistake may come back to haunt him in the future.

CHAPTER 2
The Inventor Who Knew Too Much

Every patent attorney is sick and tired of having his clients complain to him in these words: *"I don't understand how they gave him a patent on that. It's trivial!"* This sentence often punctuates the unpleasant discovery that we had an important invention in our hands some time ago, and while we were busy sitting on our fannies, contemplating the universe, a competitor got a patent on it. This always reminds me of John Lennon's clever saying: *"Life is what happens to you while you're busy making other plans."*

It's ironic that, in many cases, this should have happened because the speaker excels in his field. This problem, which I like to call "the experts syndrome," is a result of the lack of ability of an expert to detect the value of the intellectual property (IP) he has developed.

You don't need to be an expert in patent law to know that you cannot obtain a patent for a development (be it a product, a process, or a method) that is "obvious," because it will lack "inventive step," which is a basic requirement for patentability (more on inventive step in Chapter 4). What happens, then, is that when the expert feels that he got the result easily, or if he immediately saw the solution to a problem that was put to him, he may feel that whatever he developed is not worthy of a patent because he didn't work "hard enough" on the way to creating it. This is where the big mistake lies: the yardstick by which the inventive step—in other words, the non-obviousness—of the invention is measured is based on the difficulty encountered by "a man of ordinary skill in the art," and what is to be determined is whether such an "ordinary" man (not an expert) will view the invention as "obvious."

Defining a person of "ordinary skill in the art" is a problem in itself, because it is not a universal definition that is applicable across technologies and automatically in each case. A comparable problem would be defining the actions of a "reasonable person." For instance, would it be "reasonable" to jump off a bridge? Well, if you are a bungee-jumping instructor, it probably is, but not so much if you are a Wall Street operator who's had a bad day.

Without defining who is a person of ordinary skill in the art in respect of a specific invention—a person who is less than an expert and more than a clueless beginner—it is impossible to determine whether that invention possesses inventive step. Surprisingly, despite all the mountains of paper that were used to write about this issue by different patent authorities and courts all over the world, in most fields, there is a relatively uniform understanding of what constitutes inventive step. However, when coming to examine a specific invention, it is still necessary to apply a set of considerations and to look at the invention from different points of view. An expert, who is the inventor, cannot fairly be expected to be able to judge his own invention from a distance, at least because of three reasons: first of all, he is the inventor and, therefore, his point of view is too close to the invention. Second, he is, as said, an expert, and very few experts are able to take a step back and turn themselves, even only for a moment, into a man of "ordinary skill in the art." Third, the inventor usually lacks the experience and the broad techno–legal approach required to place the invention in the right light relative to other inventions in the same field.

Because of all these reasons, an expert in his field must abstain from judging his own invention and must place this task in the hands of someone who, from a distance, can take all the required considerations into account. In doing so, he can reduce the danger that valuable inventions will go wasted. This danger is very tangible today in many high-tech companies, be they small start-ups or established companies, that often wake up to the reality that they had the key to an important development but refrained from protecting it and, thus, allowed a competitor to reap its benefits.

From all the above, we now understand that an invention that at the time of filing a patent application would appear to be obvious to a person of ordinary skill in the art, lacks inventive step and, therefore, is not patentable. We don't want to waste resources on unpatentable inventions, so we need a way to screen them out. In theory, we have a simple solution: whenever we are in doubt as to whether our invention is patentable, we can go to a person of ordinary skill in the art and ask him. However, we will have a hard time finding such "ordinarily skilled person," who should be someone who understands the relevant field sufficiently without being an expert in it. He must be capable of functioning in the relevant technological field but must not be endowed, God forbid, with an inventive spark.

So what happens when the invention is interdisciplinary? Let's take, for instance, a computer-operated medical device that is to be used for a complex surgery. The developing team will most likely include a physician, a mechanical engineer, an electronic engineer, and a software engineer. The resulting contraption may superficially look pretty much like other existing devices, but the genius is in the integration between the internal subsystems that make the device special. In this situation, there is no single person who is able to judge the inventive step embodied in the device, because it is constructed of elements coming from different fields. Therefore, it has been ruled that the "person" of ordinary skill in the art can also be a team of skilled persons who collectively judge the obviousness (or not) of the invention.

To make this already complex equation even more complicated, beside the conclusion of our virtual ordinarily skilled person, to reach a determination, we need to also take into account legal tests based on various facts. A good example is the "long-felt need" test, according to which if it turns out that there was a need for the invention and it was not met for a long time, this is an indication of the existence of inventive step. Support for inventive step can also be found in the substantial commercial success of the invention. These are not the only tests, and each single test is not conclusive, but we need to look at the invention from different angles and weigh all factors carefully and then, perhaps, we can reach a conclusion.

In various places in the world, the question of inventive step is determined by different kinds of people, some of whom have legal but no technical education, who have learned to view the approach of the (virtual) person of ordinary skill in the art through the eyes of the technical experts. Others have a technical background and have learned with time to apply the legal tests properly. Taking into account how different the patent systems can be in different countries, it is sometimes amazing to find that in different jurisdictions with different patent cultures, in many cases, similar conclusions are reached in this complex question. It turns out that it is possible to practice and learn how to address this issue in many different cases and technical fields and, eventually, to reach an in-depth understanding of this important aspect of patent law. However, arriving at the correct conclusion requires substantial experience and a deep understanding of difficult and complex questions. This is why we must be very suspicious of opinions on obviousness and inventive steps that are expressed by hobbyists, no matter how bright and smart, because it is impossible to reach a deep level of understanding of what constitutes inventive step without dealing with it in detail for a long time.

CHAPTER 3
Who Owns the Invention?

The question of who owns an invention is a basic one but is also one of cardinal importance because an inventor will work hard on his own time and money and, naturally, will want to reap a profit from his work. Unfortunately, he may discover that his wish clashes with the law, and, therefore, to avoid disappointment and grief, it is desirable to understand the rules that govern the ownership of inventions.

In most countries of the world, an invention made by an employee, which is related to the work that the employee does for his employer, belongs to the employer. More so, of course, when the employee has signed a contract that provides for an assignment of the inventions he will make to his employer. It is a common mistake that many employees make—often powered by misguided wishful thinking—to assume that if an invention was made at home after hours, it automatically belongs to the inventor and the employer has no claim to it. However, inventions made as a direct result of an employ are "service inventions" (i.e., inventions made as a direct result of the position of the inventor in the organization in which he works), regardless of the exact time of the day or the place in which the invention was made.

Virtually every invention that is a direct result of the work that an employee does, or is exposed to (if done by others within his organization) during his employment, will belong to the employer. In contrast, totally unrelated inventions made without using any of the employer's resources and outside working hours may well belong to the inventor. Things get even more complicated when the inventor works in two places and, thus, has more than one employer. Take, for instance, a physician who works in a hospital and, at the same time, teaches and does research in a university laboratory. He may find that determining the ownership of an invention he has made in the shower at home may become an entangled mess.

Whether or not the employment contract that the inventor has signed contains a specific clause relating to inventions, an employed inventor would be well advised to reach a clear agreement with his employer regarding a private invention that he wishes to develop before starting to invest time and money in it. In my professional life, I have seen too many cases in which the failure of an inventor to be open and above board with his employer resulted in misunderstandings and mistrust, leading to confrontations that culminated in lawsuits. In most cases, it wasn't really worth it, but when the mirage of the billions that the invention will surely fetch appears on the horizon, common sense takes the back seat.

When someone comes to me and tells me that he is employed but has this wonderful idea that he wants to develop and, if successful, to patent, I always tell him the following joke: A man lies in the hospital because walking along a railroad, he was hit by a train. To cheer him up, his relatives bring him a gift of a kettle and put it on to make tea. As soon as the water boils and the kettle whistles, the man gets up from his bed, grabs his crutch, and clobbers the kettle until it is completely destroyed. *"Why did you do that?"* his relative asks. *"Because it's better to kill them when they're still small,"* he explains.

That's how I feel about the problems that a private invention may generate. Kill it while it's still small, or the problem may grow too big to kill before you know it. Talk to your employer and find out how to navigate his rules. And if it turns out that to avoid getting yourself into serious trouble, you must pigeonhole your idea for the time being, so be it.

Not all employers are honest and reasonable, so yours may be one who wants to appropriate your invention even though he understands that he has no real claim to it. If you work in the Research and Development (R&D) department of a food industry, where you develop low-sodium crackers, your employer will have a hard time staking a claim to your novel and inventive "combined wine cork popper and toilet cleaner." Nevertheless, getting into an argument with him over the ownership of the invention is not likely to do you a lot of good. That's why you want to keep the record straight and to make sure that you and the employer are on the same page. Start by having a lawyer review your employment contract. Some agreements have clauses that require you to transfer the ownership of "all inventions made during the period of your employ." Such sweeping provisions, which take away your property that you haven't even developed yet, may fly in some jurisdictions and be shot down by the courts in others, but they will be a headache for you everywhere, so you need to know what you are up against.

There is one more word of warning that I need to give you: the identity of the inventor is a fact, not a preference, and must be approached honestly. Shortcuts such as declaring that the inventor is your toddler or your great-grandmother who lives in a shack in the North Pole (or even a much more plausible individual) are unlikely to survive serious scrutiny, and any ploy that has as a purpose the appropriation of an invention that belongs to your employer is unlawful. If the invention is worthless, it wasn't worthwhile doing it, and if it is of value, you will be found out. So my advice is: no shortcuts, no tricks; make a start with the right foot.

WHO OWNS MY INVENTION AFTER I SELL IT?

That's a stupid question, right? But you would be surprised to learn how many times it is asked. Inventors and patent owners are sometimes confused as to the rights they have or don't have on an invention they owned, after it has been assigned to a third party. As a result, they may find that they are infringing the patent that they themselves worked hard to obtain.

For example, let's say that you sold your house and you are sorely missing your bedroom in which you had many refreshing night sleeps; it so happens that, in your new house, you're not sleeping so well. Needless to say, you cannot go back to your old bedroom and sleep in it. The same applies to your patent, which you have sold to somebody else; now, you cannot lawfully exploit your own invention.

Problems relating to this particular brand of misunderstanding arise in two main fields: in the first case, an inventor made a service invention on which a patent was granted to his employer. Later on, he moved to a different company or opened his own shop and continued to work in the same field, developing more advanced products based on his original invention. This inventor may be surprised to learn that these new products infringe his previous employer's patent. Having his name on the patent is of no help to him at all, because the rights to that invention and the patent granted on it do not belong to him but to his former employer.

Some inventors believe that because they were the ones to make the invention, they, at least personally, can do what they want with it. They may try to rely on the principle that knowledge acquired by an employee during his employ belongs to him because the employer has no rights to his brain. While this may be right in many cases regarding knowledge of a general nature, it does not apply to intellectual property, such as patent rights. Inherently, property belongs to somebody, and we must not lose sight of who that somebody is. Patent rights are not part of the general technical knowledge of the employee; they are the property of the employer who acquired them by various means (equipment, investments, and salaries). It follows that being an inventor does not automatically grant you any rights in an invention that belongs to somebody else whether by contract, by law, or because it was sold to him.

Life sometimes creates strange situations. One example is when an inventor has sold or otherwise assigned the rights to his invention to somebody else and now finds that the patent granted on his invention is getting in the way of his own business. In such a situation, if he is not an honest person, he may try to invalidate the patent using his special knowledge of the invention, the way in which it came about, the events surrounding the drafting of the patent application, and so on. Unfortunately, we don't have "Inventor's Rules of Conduct" to tell the inventors what is and what is not done in their world. While a patent attorney cannot argue against the validity of a patent application that he drafted, an inventor is not prevented from doing so openly or covertly. The "cure" against such an inventor is found in his duty toward the assignee of his invention, be it a result of a contract by virtue of which the rights were assigned or any other agreement between the inventor and the assignee. Therefore, it is important to take this possibility into account when acquiring rights from third parties, because although this behavior is despicable, I have actually seen this happen, and no antiemetic pill managed to make me digest it.

An additional situation that is often unclear to those who don't know patent law occurs when an exclusive license is granted to a third party. In that case, we still retain ownership of the patent, but any exploitation of our patent by us would constitute an infringement. The reason is that an exclusive license is just what it sounds like: it gives the exclusive licensee an exclusive right to exploit it. An exclusive licensee, therefore, has the right to prevent the exploitation of the patent by anybody, including the patent owner. If we wish to retain the right to use our own patent, broadly or for a specific purpose, we must grant a third party only a nonexclusive license, which will not only allow us to exploit the patent for ourselves, but will allow us to grant more nonexclusive licenses to other parties. However, what the licensee will be willing to pay for a nonexclusive license will normally be much less than for an exclusive one, if he needs it, and in some cases, a potential licensee may not be interested in a license unless he has exclusivity. Another option is to grant an exclusive license and have the licensee grant us back a nonexclusive one that serves our purpose. Tortuous as this may sound, in some situations, it is unavoidable.

In conclusion, it is important to remember that being the "father of the invention" does not give you an automatic right to use it when all or some of the rights in the invention have changed hands.

CHAPTER 4
What Can We Patent?

For an invention to be patentable (i.e., to be such that a patent can be lawfully granted on it), it has to possess certain characteristics, the most important of which are *novelty*, *inventive step (non-obviousness)*, and *utility (industrial applicability)*.

The novelty requirement is easy to understand: an invention is novel if it has not been divulged in its entirety before.[1] An invention that is not novel cannot be granted a valid patent under any circumstances.

An additional basic requirement of an invention is utility. The existence of utility (or, as defined in some jurisdictions, "industrial applicability") is not difficult to determine because, in most cases, an invention will serve some useful purpose. It is important to understand that, in judging the existence or lack of utility, we are not allowed to inject our personal preferences into the analysis. We should not take into account our view as to whether a device, which is the subject of the invention, will attain commercial success or that we find it cumbersome to use to the extent that it becomes useless and, hence, not patentable. The determination of the existence of utility must be based solely on the result that is obtained and on whether obtaining

[1] Divulgation may occur in different ways, for example, in a printed publication or by public display to persons who are not under a nondisclosure obligation—for instance, during a lecture or at a trade show.

such a result is useful in itself.

Let's take, for example, US Patent No. 5,844,996, which deals with a noise suppression system and a method for reducing snoring noise, which is achieved by creating a cancelling noise. The patent claims *"A method for attenuating involuntary snoring noise emanating from the airway of a first human being as a bed partner sleeping in a bed with a second human being as a second bed partner."* The system requirements are not hard to meet: it requires the second human being to have *"a head with first and second ears,"* which is a fair and legitimate enough requirement. However, here is where things get complicated: the system requires placing a microphone close to the snoring human being and thereby *"sensing in the vicinity of the airway of the first human being the involuntary snoring noise emanating from the airway of the first human being,"* and then placing speakers *"in close proximity to the first and second ears of the second human being and the delivery of anti-snoring noise into the vicinity of the first and second ears of the second human being."* A complex electronic system operates the elements of the system.

Even if the bed partners may manage to catch some sleep with all the complicated equipment on them, my bet is that they won't remain a couple for long. However, the level of satisfaction of those people on the morning after is not for us to judge; in the context of the utility test, what we need to know is whether, after we plug them into all the complex instrumentation, "the second human being" will hear less snoring noise than he would have heard without the equipment.

Many inventions reach the stage when a patent application must be filed before the practical elements of the system have been designed in a commercially suitable form. In most cases, the invention will be perfected, and the resulting product will be sellable and user-friendly. However, waiting for everything to be perfect from a marketing point of view clashes with the principles on which the patent system is based. We must allow, and encourage, inventors to file their patent applications as soon as possible, because an early application date is what protects their rights, on the one hand and, on the other hand, fulfills an important purpose of the patent system—making inventions available to the general public as soon as possible so as to add to the general knowledge and to provide a springboard for further developments. That's why fulfilling the utility requirement is a smaller hurdle than other requirements for patentability. It is very important for inventors to understand this issue and to avoid delaying patent protection until a time when the commercial product is ready to go on the market.

Once the noise cancellation invention has been made public, other inventors may learn from it and create technological advances in other directions. For instance, classical music lovers may hope that the direction taken by the inventors of this patent may be used to cancel the annoying coughs from the audience, which plague concertgoers. And we may even dream that a day will come when we will be able to cancel out the yelps of that lady in the fifth row, who shouts "Bravo!" at all occasions without any provocation from the performers.

WHAT IS HINDSIGHT?

One of the most important concepts in patents is "hindsight"—the fake wisdom that may turn every invention, great or small, into something obvious. When analyzing an invention for the presence or absence of inventive step, we must place ourselves in the average skilled person's shoes at the time the invention was made,[2] which, at times, may be a very difficult proposition.

Let's do a simple exercise in hindsight, and we shall see what it does to the invention of the inkjet printer. It will not be difficult for us to show that the invention of the first inkjet printer was obvious and, therefore, lacked inventive step. As is generally known, the inkjet printer generates an image on paper by spraying small droplets of ink. Placing those droplets side by side with high precision creates the required image, be it a black-and-white or a full-color, high-resolution painting. However, we all have had experience with using a fountain pen long before the inkjet printer was invented. And when using a fountain pen, we inevitably dripped drops of ink on the white page in front of us. Therefore, providing equipment that is capable of placing

---

[2] Who constitutes "the person of average (or ordinary) skill in the art" has already been discussed in Chapter 2.

drops of ink on a page is not new. But that's not all: we know that Impressionist painters—including Monet, to mention but one—created well-defined images by placing blots of colors side by side. It follows that it was obvious to combine the knowledge available to everybody, on how to create drops of ink, with a further universally known impressionistic technique and, by this combination, create the ink jet printer.

"Wait a second!" the inventor will say. *"The printer creates very small drops, and the precision it achieves is amazing, which is required in order to obtain high-quality results. What do you say about that?"*

"Really!" we will retort. *"Even a child knows that by reducing the size of the pixel, we will obtain a better resolution. That's what they did for very many years with photo films. And the precision? That argument is really not well taken. Precision is not an issue. People fly to the moon with precise motors. Don't give us* ***that****!"*

"But all that has been in existence for tens of years, and the fact is that nobody made my invention although they had the means to do it," the inventor will insist. *"That surely is evidence that nobody thought to develop the invention and that, therefore, it cannot be obvious!"*

"But ***you*** *thought of it, didn't you? This is definite proof that it was obvious to make it,"* we will say.

Hindsight is the weapon that is instinctively used by a patent infringer who tries to invalidate a patent using circular reasoning of the kind that was popular with ancient Greek philosophers. The infringer will not be ashamed of telling you that since you breathe and the goat breathes, it follows that you are a goat.

Those who deal with this subject on a daily basis and are required to make a judgment on the basis of arguments derived from hindsight need to be equipped with substantial technical understanding and with the ability to separate enticing arguments from real life. They have to take themselves back in time to when the invention was made and to look at it from that perspective. It is not easy to forget the present and to put ourselves in the past so as to forget everything we know and feel today. And once they have done that, they must decide whether the knowledge of the Impressionist techniques, together with the experience of using the fountain pen, would really have prompted a person of average skill in the art to go and build an inkjet printer; and if they conclude that it might, they would need to explain why it didn't happen.

Often inventions are made when an inventive spark gives the inventor a missing piece of a puzzle. It doesn't mean that he himself invented all the pieces, but without his inventive genius, the missing piece of the puzzle would not have been found, and the puzzle would not have been pieced together. Hindsight, conversely, is akin to taking a whole picture to cut it into pieces of a puzzle from which the whole picture can be reconstructed. It doesn't involve inventiveness or creativity. It is a cynical exploitation of the picture that was put together by somebody else, after the picture was created, to claim that we had all the pieces of the puzzle all along.

DISCOVERIES AND THEIR INHERENT MEANING

Imagine that you are sunbathing at the pool when a stranger approaches you and demands to be paid for the improvement of your health and physical well-being due to the lowering of your blood pressure.

"Are you out of your mind?" you would certainly ask.

"Not at all!" the stranger would answer. *"I have proven beyond doubt that half an hour at the pool, once daily, causes a reduction in the level of stress, which is followed by a lowering of blood pressure. By my watch, you have been here already almost an hour. Kindly pay up."*

It is unlikely that these arguments will convince you to part with your money, but a similar (though usually less extreme) situation exists when "an inventor" applies for a patent on an "invention," which is no more than the discovery—or even simply a well-organized description—of a natural event or, in other words, an inherent occurrence over which the inventor has no control or influence. It is unfortunate, therefore, that some inventors insist on trying to obtain a patent for an "invention" that falls into this category.

Let's explain the problem using a simple example. Assume for a moment that a dangerous, previously unknown bacteria exists in drinking water (let's call it ***Newbact***). Everybody knows that if you want to get rid of dangerous organisms that may be found in water, such as ***E. coli*** bacteria, you have to boil the water. The question is then, should we grant a patent to someone who has discovered that the *Newbact* may sometimes also find its way into drinking water and, furthermore, that when we boil the water, we get rid of not only *E. coli* but also of *Newbact*? The answer is, of course, negative, because by boiling the water, which is a common activity, we automatically also destroyed the *Newbact*, even though we were not aware that it was there. The mere discovery that we unknowingly obtained a positive result is not the basis for obtaining a valid patent, because the positive result is the outcome of something we do anyway, and it will be achieved whether we are aware of it or not.

The question arises, therefore, whether a discovery of this kind will never be patentable. The answer to this question is also negative. Just like for any other subject, what has to be judged is the novelty and the inventive step, although when a discovery is involved, the situation is much more complex than with "regular" inventions. Let's try to look at a case similar to the above example, which may, however, result in a patentable invention. Assume that the existence of the *Newbact* is well known, but this particular bacterium is considered to be very resilient and capable of surviving simple water boiling. As a result, whenever residents of a certain area are alerted that the water may be infected with it, they have to purify the water using different chemicals. An inventor carries out in-depth research and discovers that, in contrast to what the experts believe, it is possible to destroy the *Newbact* completely, provided that boiling is continued for a minimum period of time that is longer than typically used to boil water. Under these conditions, the process for purifying water containing *Newbact* infection may become patentable, because the result is not only surprising, but also, to accomplish it, the inventor had to overcome a clear prejudice created by the experts (i.e., that it is not possible to destroy *Newbact* simply by boiling water). The method for destroying *Newbact* in drinking water and making infected water potable became not only a novel invention but also one that possesses substantial non-obviousness (i.e., inventive step).

Nevertheless, a patent of this kind will have limited utility and will only be valuable under certain conditions. For instance, the patent will not stop anybody from boiling water at home, or from boiling water to get rid of *E. coli*, only because, at the same time, *Newbact* may also be present in the water. However, it will be possible, for instance, to prevent the commercial sale of boiling equipment that is designed to process water under conditions (e.g., length of the boiling process) specifically designed to destroy *Newbact.* In other words, a patent cannot turn a permissible activity into an infringing one only because an inherent result of that activity was not previously known. However, the patent will allow its owner to stop anybody from exploiting the invention in a way that was not previously known. Thus, the principle is maintained to reward the inventor for a useful invention while allowing the public to continue to do what it did without limitation before the patent was issued.

UNIVERSAL NOVELTY

One of the requirements for an invention to be patentable, which is sometimes particularly difficult to grasp, is "universal novelty." The question that is often asked by someone who has carried out a search and has found that his invention has already been patented by somebody else in another country is the following:

"Then I can patent it here, right?" he asks.

"No, you can't," he is told.

"But they didn't bother filing a patent application in this country, so I can do it."

And when the poor inventor is again disillusioned by his patent attorney, he makes a last-ditch effort to convince him:

"But I thought of it by myself! I didn't know about that patent when I made the invention."

All those arguments, no matter how true and righteous they may seem to the inventor, are unhelpful. The patent system is cruel where novelty is concerned and requires it to be universal. The system has no mercy for someone who made an independent invention without knowing that others had invented it before him, and it doesn't care if the patentee had not bothered to file a patent application in some countries. The same applies if the invention was published in some other way—for instance, in a scientific paper or in the general press. To destroy its novelty—and, as a result, to deny a patent on it—it is sufficient that the invention was published somewhere in the world. This principle somewhat artificially assumes that a publication made anywhere in the world becomes automatically and immediately known to everybody everywhere. Even if the invention was made public through use or display at an exhibition or in a lecture given in some obscure university located in some forgotten corner of the world, it will destroy the novelty of the invention that the inventor has made independently without knowing that such a publication ever occurred.

This is a harsh but necessary condition. Think what would happen if we wanted to be lenient with the inventors and decide that patents would be granted for inventions that have already been patented in other countries (or which have been published in some other way), provided that the inventor didn't know about it at the time of filing his patent application. Such a rule, in spite of perhaps being more just from the point of view of the inventor, would be impossible to implement because the patent authority[3] cannot know with any degree of certainty what the inventor knew or didn't know at any given time. People have been known to make false declarations (yes, I was shocked, too, when they told me), and so we can expect that such a rule would be exploited by malicious inventors. This being so, the system has no other choice but to make a cut-and-dried decision without taking into account philosophical questions.

In some cases, the system really deals cruel results. Assume, for instance, that an inventor files a bona fide patent application and, when the examination of his application begins in a couple of years, it turns out that the invention was independently described, one day before the filing date of his application, in the *Journal of the Alumni Association of the University of Nowherestan.* Whoever reads the patent application understands that it is based on serious, long-term research and that there is, therefore, no way that in the few hours that passed

---

[3] The patent authority of a country, which is responsible for examining patent applications and for granting patents, is most often referred to as the "patent office." Here, the term "patent authority" is used to indicate a generic function.

between the printing of the journal and the filing of the application, the inventor could have seen the article and used it as a basis for his patent application (even if he knew that Nowherestan and the obscure university it contains existed), also taking into account that he does not speak Nowherish. Unfortunately, this clearly true fact will not help him. What counts is that this publication happened before the filing of the patent application, and, therefore, at the time of its filing, the invention was no longer new and, thus, was already unpatentable.

Sad cases like this imaginary one happen and are not as rare as you might think. Patent authorities and courts in many countries have looked for ways to provide a solution to extreme cases in which it was possible to raise a doubt that a prior publication was sufficient to destroy the novelty of invention, but these are relatively rare and borderline cases. The principle of universal novelty must remain the cornerstone of the entire patent system. If we feel that sometimes this principle may do us an injustice, we should be consoled by the thought that it does justice on a daily basis by granting monopoly rights only to those who have taken the world one step forward.

SUFFICIENCY OF DESCRIPTION

Sufficiency of description is a basic requirement for a patent application to be patentable (or for a granted patent to be valid). In simple terms, if our patent application does not sufficiently describe how to carry out the invention in a way that an average skilled person can perform it without undue experimentation or further development, then we are not entitled to be granted a patent on it.

It is very important to understand this simple fact, because many inventors mistakenly believe that their job is to "hide" the invention cleverly so that whoever reads the patent will never be able to use the invention. Wrong! The opposite is true.

All the time, we hear inventors saying that most patents they have read do not teach how to carry out the invention. Allow me to doubt this statement, which the astute reader will not take at face value. Indeed, many patents are defective inasmuch as they lack sufficient description. In all likelihood, these patents will be found to be invalid if and when tested, but this does not mean that we want to join that brotherhood of invalidity by drafting our own patents so they will be invalid to begin with.

Like in many other areas of the patent world, the issue of sufficiency of description cuts both ways and deserves great attention. A simple example will illustrate the issue. In October 1999, US Patent No. 5,970,231 was issued, which had as the subject an "ELECTRONIC NEWSPAPER AND ELECTRONIC PUBLISHING MEDIUM." It describes an electronic newspaper that is portable, lightweight, battery operated, and has a full-color display screen, passive stylus for writing and selecting icons from menus, speech and sound reproduction, and the ability to store massive amounts of data. So now is the time to open the excellent book *Immortality, Inc.* by the well-known science fiction writer Robert Sheckley and to read the beginning of Chapter 12. This book, which was published in 1959 (and on which the movie *FreeJack* is based), tells of the hero, who "went to a newsstand and purchased a microfilm *New York Times* and a viewer." As explained before in this chapter, novelty is a basic requirement for patentability. How, if so, was it possible for a patent to be granted 40 years later?

The answer is found in the term "enabling." For a prior publication to destroy the novelty of an invention, it must describe, directly or indirectly, how to carry out the invention; it is not sufficient to state the result that it is desired to obtain. That's why, in this case, Sheckley's futuristic view (which is amazing in itself) only describes the desired results; with an uncanny vision of the future, he saw how newspapers would not be read on paper but using an electronic device. However, Sheckley was clueless as to how to actually make the device that he described, and in the late '50s the means to manufacture such a device didn't even exist. Therefore, Sheckley's futuristic description cannot be used to deprive modern inventions of novelty. This simple example answers the frequently asked question: "How come inventions that were already described in the literature are granted patents?" Many high-tech entrepreneurs make the mistake of assuming that if a patent that is an obstacle to their activity claims an invention that, in their view, was mentioned directly or indirectly in a prior publication, it must be invalid. If that were the case, we could have shut down the patent offices of all countries a long time ago and stopped granting patents, since Jules Verne, Isaac Asimov, and other writers already wrote about all possible inventions, starting with the submarine and including cloning human beings by genetic engineering.

Fig. 4-1: Jules Verne

The reality is much more complex. Not only is it insufficient to merely mention a desired invention in order to turn it into reality and destroy its novelty, but we should also remember that technologically valuable products and processes often embody more than one invention and, sometimes, a large number of inventions. That's how, at the time of writing these lines, more than 1,700 US patents and patent applications exist that deal in some way or other with electronic newspapers. One patent deals, for instance, with *"a display device including a touch screen pane"* and another with an *"apparatus and method for providing information pertaining to unread articles."* A third addresses a *"foldable display,"* and a fourth claims *"techniques for recommending media."* All these coexist and complete one another without interference.

Therefore, it would be a mistake to assume, as entrepreneurs often do, that because many patents exist in a certain area, this must be the result of clerical errors that effectively invalidate all the patents dealing with the same subject. The system does not allow us to grant a monopoly—or to prevent a rightful inventor from obtaining a monopoly—only on the basis of mere generic statements that are not based on a technological reality.

One more word of warning is needed here. I have learned over the years that inventors and entrepreneurs often do not understand the difference between a granted patent and a patent application.

Anybody can file a patent application on any subject, no matter how wild or stupid. This does not mean that a patent will be issued on such an application, but it does mean that the application will be published and will have the general outward aspect of a patent document. Therefore, the existence of a patent application does not mean that the relevant patent office of the country that published it has granted a patent on it nor that it will do so. It is dangerous to try to draw conclusions from published documents without fully understanding the rights that such documents carry with them.

CHAPTER 5
The Patent Application

The patent application (which, in due course, will hopefully be issued as a patent) contains some obligatory sections. These sections and their content, as well as the order in which they are presented, assist the reader of the patent specification to understand the invention described and claimed in it. The order and the structure are mostly preserved across patent applications in English-speaking countries, as well as in others, although changes may occur for different types of inventions in view of specific needs for their description. Structural changes are also possible, and they are desirable as long as they assist the reader in understanding the invention, which, in many cases, is not an easy task.

This chapter is not meant to teach the reader how to draft a patent application; its purpose is to assist the reader to understand the reasons behind the form in which patent applications are drafted, which, to the untrained eye, may seem cumbersome, repetitive, and, therefore, unclear. Appendix A contains the commented specification, claims, and drawings of a mock patent application to which the reader can refer for an even better understanding of the way an invention can be presented.

Fig. 5-1 is the front page of an old patent, issued in 1999 (US Patent No. 5,903,723). Drafting conventions have evolved since then, so when reading patents from different decades, there are some differences that you may note.

A typical patent application will have the following sections:

The Abstract:

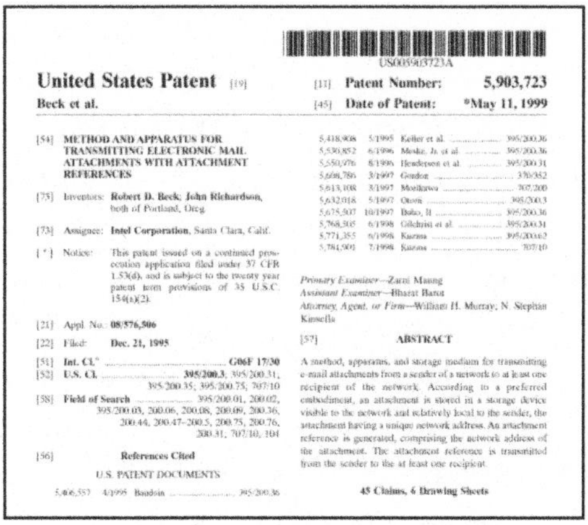

United States Patent [19]
Beck et al.

US005903723A

[11] Patent Number: 5,903,723
[45] Date of Patent: *May 11, 1999

[54] METHOD AND APPARATUS FOR TRANSMITTING ELECTRONIC MAIL ATTACHMENTS WITH ATTACHMENT REFERENCES

[75] Inventors: Robert D. Beck; John Richardson, both of Portland, Oreg.

[73] Assignee: Intel Corporation, Santa Clara, Calif.

[*] Notice: This patent issued on a continued prosecution application filed under 37 CFR 1.53(d), and is subject to the twenty year patent term provisions of 35 U.S.C. 154(a)(2).

[21] Appl. No.: 08/576,506

[22] Filed: Dec. 21, 1995

[51] Int. Cl.⁶ G06F 17/30
[52] U.S. Cl. 395/200.3; 395/200.31, 395/200.35; 395/200.75; 707/10
[58] Field of Search 395/200.01, 200.02, 395/200.03, 200.06, 200.08, 200.09, 200.36, 200.44, 200.47–200.5, 200.75, 200.76, 200.31; 707/10, 104

[56] References Cited

U.S. PATENT DOCUMENTS

5,406,557	4/1995	Baudoin	395/200.36
5,418,908	5/1995	Keller et al.	395/200.36
5,530,852	6/1996	Meske, Jr. et al.	395/200.36
5,550,976	8/1996	Henderson et al.	395/200.31
5,608,786	3/1997	Gordon	379/352
5,613,108	3/1997	Morikawa	707/200
5,632,018	5/1997	Otorii	395/200.3
5,675,507	10/1997	Bobo, II	395/200.36
5,768,505	6/1998	Gilchrist et al.	395/200.31
5,771,355	6/1998	Kuzma	395/200.62
5,781,901	7/1998	Kuzma	707/10

Primary Examiner—Zarni Maung
Assistant Examiner—Bharat Barot
Attorney, Agent, or Firm—William H. Murray; N. Stephan Kinsella

[57] ABSTRACT

A method, apparatus, and storage medium for transmitting e-mail attachments from a sender of a network to at least one recipient of the network. According to a preferred embodiment, an attachment is stored in a storage device visible to the network and relatively local to the sender, the attachment having a unique network address. An attachment reference is generated, comprising the network address of the attachment. The attachment reference is transmitted from the sender to the at least one recipient.

45 Claims, 6 Drawing Sheets

Fig. 5-1: The abstract shown on the front page of a US patent

The purpose of the abstract is to sum up the main thrust of the invention described and claimed in the patent for the reader to grasp quickly. It is only used for a quick orientation and should not be relied upon to determine the breadth of the coverage that the patent affords.

The Title:

The title of the invention is meant to convey its subject. Contrary to what some inventors believe, the title does not limit the scope of protection given by the patent (which is the "task" of the claims), and therefore, there is no need to invest tremendous effort in coming up with a title that is unique and reflects the inventor's genius.

The Field of the Invention:

The field of the invention is meant to point the reader to a greater extent to the subject that is covered by the patent. There is no need for elaborate descriptions in this section; it should be brief—one or two paragraphs—and should disclose the field to which the invention pertains.

The Background of the Invention:

This section (also often including or being replaced by a subsection titled "The Prior Art" or "Description of the Related Art") is meant to help the reader to position the invention relative to what has been done to date—that is, relative to the state of the art. In recent years, this section has lost its charm with patent practitioners because of court rulings relating to the so-called "admitted prior art," which may have a negative impact on the validity of the patent,[4] at least in the United States. But even before then, it was good practice to keep this section as short as possible and to limit it to the essential information needed to tell the reader what the starting point for the invention was.

It isn't uncommon for a patent attorney to receive long lists of published patents and articles that the inventor wants to include in this section, because he worries that if he doesn't do so, people may think that he is not knowledgeable enough in the field. Such a display of expertise is unhelpful and may certainly be harmful; therefore, inventors are advised against insisting on it. If a prior art document is essential to the understanding of some technical parts of the invention, it is also possible to refer to it in the Detailed Description section (see below).

Another common mistake made by some inventors is to insist on including many prior art references to show "the logic" of the invention, or in other words, how reading the prior art in the correct order, step by step, inevitably leads to the invention. The brilliant idea behind this appears to be that it is supposed to show that the invention makes sense to the skilled person and thereby to reinforce its value. In practice, many inventors trivialize their invention in this way and admit that their invention is obvious and unpatentable. This is a deadly trap from which there is no escape, because the inventor

---

[4] A detailed discussion of this issue is too technical to be undertaken here, so take my word for it.

himself has admitted in writing that it was obvious to arrive at the invention following the path he has outlined. Most often than not, this path is not one that would have been followed in reality and is only created using hindsight, but no examiner will argue with an inventor who so aptly killed his own invention.

The Summary of the Invention:
This section tells the reader what it is that we believe is our invention. It has to be directly related to what is claimed in the claims (to be discussed below), because it is obviously unacceptable for us to state in our patent specification that the invention is "apples" and later on to claim a monopoly on "oranges."

The Brief Description of the Drawings:
The purpose of this section is to list the figures that accompany the specification, if any, and to point out in a brief sentence what each figure shows. This list of figures is particularly important in cases in which a large number of drawings are present as an aid to the reader for a quick orientation.

The Detailed Description:
This section used to be most often titled "Description of Preferred Embodiments." However, the term "preferred embodiment" is no longer preferred by patent practitioners due to unfavorable court rulings (the discussion of which exceed the scope of this book as it would be too boring for the reader). Therefore, more fluid terms are now typically used, such as "illustrative examples of embodiments of the invention," "detailed description of embodiments of the invention," or similar euphemisms.

This is an extremely important part of the specification. In Chapter 4, we discussed the critical need to provide a "sufficient description" of the invention in each patent specification, as well as the dire consequences of not doing so.

The description has to be appropriate for the type of invention and its specific content, and it can be of any length that is required to exemplify the invention through different embodiments (i.e., different ways to carry it out or different resulting products or devices). The description of a simple mechanical device may require only a few pages since the drawings will carry the weight of much of the description, while in biotech and in chemical inventions, tens or even hundreds of pages of description may sometimes be needed to fully describe and exemplify the invention.

As said, a separate part of the patent, which is intimately linked to this section, contains the drawings. Drawings, as well as pictures, diagrams, and flowcharts may be helpful to explain what the patent describes with reference to them. However, the figures are not embedded in the description that makes reference to them, but rather they are attached to the patent specification as a separate section.

The Claims:

The claims define in a precise manner what is the monopoly that we are applying for (or in the case of a granted patent, what is the monopoly that has already been granted to us). The claims arise from and rely on the description contained in the patent specification, and the detailed description is largely responsible for the permissible breadth of the claims.

It is important to understand that because the claims represent the monopoly that we are claiming for ourselves (and not the knowledge that we are adding to the world, as represented by the specification), as long as the patent application has not been issued into a patent, we can make considerable changes to them, provided that the resulting claims are supported by the specification. It is not uncommon to see a patent that was issued with claims completely different from the set that was originally published together with the patent application. We should be aware, however, that in certain jurisdictions—for instance, in the European Patent Office (EPO)—it is not permissible to broaden the claims beyond their original scope, even if the broader claims are supported by the specification.

I often hear inventors saying that "the claims are the most important part of the patent." Well, to some extent, this statement is correct, because if the breadth of the granted claims does not appropriately cover our invention, then the patent may be useless. However, I would consider the detailed description to be, if not of greater importance, at least of comparable importance, because the claims must be interpreted on the basis of the description. While we are allowed to amend the claims in the course of the examination and, in some cases, even after the patent is issued, we cannot change the description and, therefore, if we wrote a bad or incomplete description, we are stuck with it. To emphasize this issue, we should look at the doctrine of equivalents, which allows us to expand the scope of the claims beyond their rigid letter through the interpretation of what the invention that the inventor meant to cover really is, on the basis of the detailed description. More about this in Chapter 23.

CHAPTER 6
Different Types of Inventions

Not all patents are the same in substance, in scope, and in the ways in which they came about. Different types of patents are created as a result of different situations, and it is important to understand these differences to understand why patent applications were filed in a certain way and what their purpose was. To introduce the reader to such differences, I will briefly review some examples below.

PIONEERING INVENTIONS

What is the scope of protection that we can claim in a patent? A similar question is "By how much can we stretch a polyethylene film on a pot?" and the answer is "It depends on the quality of the polyethylene film." The available scope of protection, indeed, depends on the quality of the invention.

Giving the correct answer to this question is critical to plan a realistic scope of protection that a patent may provide for our invention. Therefore, we must learn to differentiate between different kinds of inventions and to understand their respective limitations. For instance, if we invented a new material that did not exist before, we will be able to obtain broad protection for it regardless of the specific use that will be made of it. If it should be found, in the future, that the material we invented is useful as a coating for electronic components but also as a pesticidal material, although we were not aware of those potential uses at the time the invention was made and the patent application was filed, our exclusive rights to the material will in no way be diminished, and to use it for any application of any kind, a license will have to be obtained from us. However, if, conversely, the material itself was known and what we invented was its use as a coating for electronic components, we will not be able to rely on our patent to stop somebody else from using this material in a pesticidal composition.

This simple example illustrates the concept of "inventive level" (or, as it is sometimes termed, "inventive height"). This concept is related to the principle according to which different inventions deserve different levels of protection, according to their importance. An invention that is "pioneering" because it opened up a new field of technological importance will give its inventor a much broader protection than is afforded to an inventor of a small improvement of a known device or process. Moreover, the level of description that is required of the pioneering invention, in order for it to provide broad protection, is lower than that required of an invention that is only an improvement of a previously developed invention. When we improve on an existing technology, we are working in a narrow space and are required to focus on the improvement that we are providing. Attempting in this context to cover potential inventions that are only based on speculation and are not directly connected to the real and specific improvement that we made will usually not afford real and valuable protection.

Conversely, a pioneering invention is inherently much more general. Because it opens up an entirely new field, it would be unfair to require the inventor to describe in minute details all its possible applications as a condition for broad protection. Accordingly, where pioneering inventions are concerned, it is necessary to find a suitable way to grant the inventor a protection that is commensurate with the contribution brought by his invention while keeping the description requirements to a level that is low relative to the scope of the invention and its potential applications.

A correct understanding of the invention relative to its field is critical in order to provide suitable protection for the invention. Because the world of patents is dynamic and has very little black and white in it, most inventions are found between the two extremities, such that they are not pioneering inventions but embody much more than a small improvement of an existing technology. Here is where substantial effort must be invested in analyzing the invention and in understanding it in depth so as to position it in the appropriate place between these two extremities. If we do not understand the proper position of our invention, we will also not be able to present it correctly in our patent application; it will not be surprising, therefore, if the relevant patent authorities, when determining the scope of the monopoly that they are willing to grant us, will give us much less than we deserve.

A NEW USE OF A KNOWN PRODUCT

It is well understood that a new, useful product has a good chance of being granted patent protection. However, the public is not as much aware of the potential benefits of a new use of a known product. In such cases, the invention is found in the inventor's realization that a product used for one purpose can be exploited for an altogether different one.

Inventions of "second use" are better known in the field of pharmaceuticals. One well-known example is the use of aspirin to prevent heart disease. In this case, the dosage used for the second medical use is different from that conventionally given for decades for treating headache or reducing fever. Another example is the use of hashish, and of a variety of cannabis components, for medical uses.

However, second use inventions are not limited to the field of pharmaceuticals and are not limited to chemical materials, although identifying a second use invention may be more difficult in other fields. For instance, it is possible that a pin that was designed to keep together some parts of a spacecraft will be useful to treat a splintered fracture of a human bone. In such a case, we will debate with ourselves whether all we did was to make use of well-known technological facts for a similar purpose, or whether an inventive spark (or, in the legal term, an "inventive step") was needed to carry this solution from one system to the other.

We should not shy away from addressing these questions. The tests that an invention based on a "second use" must pass are the same tests that apply to every invention, with appropriate changes dictated by the nature and the field in which the invention is made. In this situation, the concept of "novelty" acquires some "localized" character because it is analyzed with reference to the field in which the invention was made. This approach (which is usually correct when examining every invention) looks at our world as if it were a collection of technical micro cosmoses, which are completely unrelated. According to this approach, an inventor who develops orthopedic medical devices will rely on prior knowledge available in his field and in closely related ones, but he will not rely on information that can be derived from unrelated fields in which he will not look for solutions. Therefore, finding a solution for the fixation of a bone that relies on research done by scientists operating in the field of space travel does not detract from the novelty of the proposed solution. Even though the pin (in our example) is not novel as a device, and it will not be possible to obtain an unlimited monopoly on it, it will be possible to obtain a monopoly on the new use; for instance, we may be able to claim in a patent the use of the pin as an "orthopedic pin." Other elements that may help us in this case are, for instance, the materials of which the pin is made, because it is likely that the requirements, in terms of biocompatibility, strength, and so on, will be different for different applications.

The test of inventive step, on the other hand, relies on the conventional approach according to which an invention is not obvious if the average skilled person (or "the man of the art") would have not naturally looked for a solution to the orthopedic problem in the field of space travel.

The result, therefore, is that when we use ideas and technologies that were developed in fields that are far from the one in which we operate, or when we come up with a very different use for a conventional product, even if in the same technological field, it is possible that the process required an inventive step and that we have a patentable invention based on a "second use." Inventions of this kind are often very valuable, and we should not likely give up on the attempt to obtain a patent on them.

SELECTION INVENTIONS

Quite often, we find that after a technological invention or process has been implemented, published, and even patented, we may obtain substantial improvements in the product itself, or in the process for its manufacturing, by selecting parts or operating conditions different from those we used in the past from among the very many options that are available to the developer. The question then arises regarding how we can protect this selection and its results.

In such a situation, we must determine whether the developer has made a so-called "selection invention." A selection invention is just what it sounds like: an invention to which we have arrived by making the right selection within a very broad field of possibilities that in itself was known. For such a selection to qualify as an invention, it must comply with stringent requirements in addition to those applicable to a regular invention. First of all, if the selection we made was mentioned anywhere in the literature in even the faintest connection with our invention, novelty is lost and the invention is not patentable. Second, the improvement resulting from the invention must be unpredictable and substantial, as compared to the existing product or process. A "just as good" result will not float your boat here.

Good examples of selection inventions can be found in the pharmaceutical field, in which it is not uncommon that one chemical compound from among the family of similar compounds that may contain millions will have pharmaceutical characteristics that are improved by orders of magnitude, as compared to very similar molecules with similar activity. Finding the "winning" molecule within such a broad field is a typical selection invention.

However, selection inventions are also made in other fields. For instance, selecting a coating material for a given product that will give it improved appearance or longer service time, or selecting coefficients for an equation used for image compression, or a mixture of flavors that are known in themselves, which will impart great taste to a synthetic food—all are examples of potential selection inventions.

Selection inventions are particularly important for those who are not one-off inventors but constantly invest in developing and improving their products. In these situations, it is expected that new-generation products will rely, to some extent, on selection inventions, whether patentable or not. Some developers believe that they can rely on existing basic patents, which do not address their selection inventions; but this is a bad idea because the protection granted to a selection invention is often the protection for the most important commercial product, and a patent on a selection invention, if obtainable, may extend the effective monopoly on the product, sometimes by a substantial length of time.

We should also remember that selection inventions derived from earlier inventions are also made by our competitors, and we may discover that our most important commercial development was lost to a competitor simply because we failed to recognize the invention embodied in it, while our competitor made the same invention, recognized its importance, and blocked our road to the improvement with a patent of its own.

"SMALL" INVENTIONS

The patent system is here to serve the needs of the industry and must adjust itself to its evolving needs. The need exists in all branches of industry, and the patent systems in most countries of the world moved quite some time ago away from the old perception of what was patentable, which mostly viewed the question through mechanical and chemical spectacles. Each and every useful invention, which is new and inventive, must be afforded suitable patent protection.

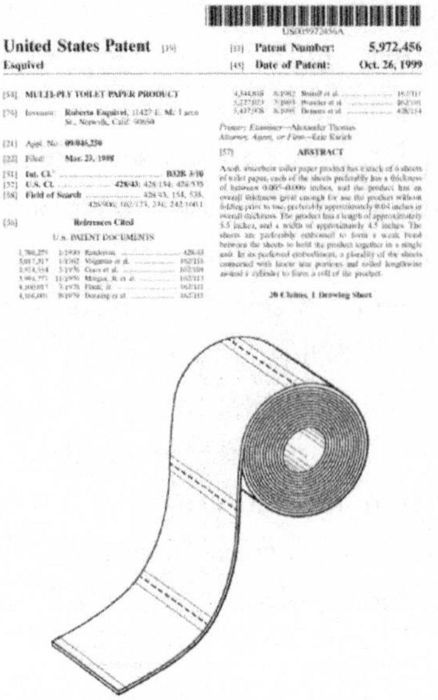

Fig. 6-1: US Patent No. 5,972,456 for "Multi-Ply Toilet Paper Product"

Another way of looking at it is to understand that virtually every novel result that has substantial industrial utility must embody a patentable invention, and the difficulty only lies in finding it. Thus, those who thought that decades ago we were done making inventions relating to toilet papers didn't take into account the inventive drive of people working in the field. A quick search shows that in the period beginning January 1998 and until the writing of these lines, the US Patent Office issued about 690 patents somehow related to toilet paper. For instance, in October 1999, US Patent 5,972,456 issued covering "Multi-Ply Toilet Paper Product." The patent claims "a toilet paper product comprising 4–10 sheets of toilet paper forming a stack, each of the sheets having a width of between 3.5–5.0 inches and a length of between 5.0–6.5 inches, the stack having an overall thickness of between 0.02–0.06 inches."

One could ask whether the system that grants patents on toilet paper should be the same that grants patents on semiconductors or on satellite propulsion methods. The answer, of course, is positive. There is no difference between the rights of patentees operating in different fields and, as far as the patent system is concerned, a toilet paper invention is not a lesser one than the invention of a sophisticated electronic system. The only difference between them is in the "language" spoken by the people in those different fields, because the more complex the technological area, the more abstruse the jargon that is used to communicate in it. However, the basic principles of the patent system are the same for all inventions, and all inventions must fulfill the same requirements for patentability.

Even those who operate in the patent system sometimes forget such basic facts and tend to place more importance on inventions that are made on a higher technological level. It is not at all certain that the inventor of a particularly soft toilet paper will make less money than a high-tech inventor who developed a piece of equipment that will fly to the moon. The importance of a patent is determined by a commercial test, not by a scientific one. Therefore, we shouldn't belittle toilet paper inventors, who develop improved products that are found in every home. From our point of view, they may turn out to be more important than those that fly to the moon.

MULTIDISCIPLINARY INVENTIONS

The patent system does its best to update itself to meet the needs of new technologies, but sometimes it still feels like it's been left behind. The rate of change that takes place in some technological fields is no longer comparable to that of a few decades ago, and the professional level needed for safekeeping our intellectual property is also higher than it used to be.

In the not-so-distant past, most of the work in the patent field had to do with developments that took place in "conventional" areas. Every now and then, a new, unconventional field evolved, such as genetic engineering or the Internet, but they swiftly became familiar, understood, and conventional. The ways of dealing with them also crystallized quickly and fairly easily because those who work in patent law are usually pretty knowledgeable people who understand technology. So, what we did when we had a computer-related invention was to approach a patent attorney with a background in electronic engineering with whom the inventor was able to have a fruitful one-on-one discussion. Of course, an inventor of a computer invention never thought to consult with an expert in molecular biology whose understanding of electronics could easily only slightly exceed that which is required to operate a TV remote control. Conversely, the inventor of a process for making a new antibiotic by genetic engineering naturally sought to consult with an expert in biology.

No more. R&D has grown in many fields to be interdisciplinary in a way that, just a few years ago, could have been considered science fiction. The trend started to be really felt at the turn of the century, and a good example is US Patent No. 6,046,925, which was granted in April 2000 to the University of California, which relates to "optical memory devices using photochromic fluorescent protein moieties." In other words, proteins made by genetic engineering were proposed to be used as elements of memory devices. In a case such as this, to maximize the chances of obtaining a good and valuable patent, interdisciplinary work is also needed from the patent attorneys, which will typically require two of them to work together. This is a somewhat unnatural arrangement for patent attorneys, if they have no experience in this kind of research and development (R&D). For two professionals, each with his own approach, cooperating on a patent application has some hurdles, but it also holds the promise of mutual pollination.

The field of biological computers is not the only interdisciplinary one. Many other areas exist, such as medical devices that combine electronics, optics, mechanics, and medicine, which require different scientists to achieve a complex result.

A patent attorney is not required to be an expert in the specific invention that he needs to protect, but he must possess the technical tools needed to properly understand it. Only after he invests the time and effort needed to understand the invention in depth is he ready to use his special expertise in the patent field and to plan the best possible protection for the invention.

Sometimes, an inventor is willing to skip the step in which the patent attorney understands the invention, and this is a really bad idea, because then the inventor will not profit from the patent attorney's expertise in patent law. The inventor's impatience in this respect is most often motivated by thriftiness, because the time the patent attorney takes to understand what the invention is costs money and may also require the time of a team led by the patent attorney, including people with specific, relevant technical expertise who can complement the patent attorney's own technical knowledge. Drafting a patent application with only a superficial understanding of the subject is akin to groping in the dark for the exit door—you can expect to bang your head on the wall at the end of the corridor.

DIVISIONAL APPLICATION

There are various reasons why we would want to file a divisional patent application, which essentially means that we are taking some subject matter that is in our original application and prosecuting it in a separate application that maintains all the rights derived from the original filing. In some cases, the motivation for filing a divisional application can be fairly complex, but in most cases, it will be the result of a "lack of unity" of invention—a situation in which more than one distinct invention is claimed in the original patent application, which is not permitted by law, since one patent should be granted for one invention only.

Once the divisional application issues as a patent, it is no longer important that it was divided from another application, or why it was divided; the scope of the patent will be determined solely by its claims.

PROVISIONAL PATENT APPLICATION

The USPTO's[5] web site has the following explanation:

"A provisional application for patent (provisional application) is a U.S. national application filed in the USPTO under 35 U.S.C. §111(b). A provisional application is not required to have a formal patent claim or an oath or declaration. Provisional applications also should not include any information disclosure (prior art) statement since provisional applications are not examined. A provisional application provides the means to establish an early effective filing date in a later filed nonprovisional patent application filed under 35 U.S.C. §111(a).

---

[5] United States Patent and Trademark Office

It also allows the term 'Patent Pending' to be applied in connection with the description of the invention.

A provisional application for patent has a pendency lasting 12 months from the date the provisional application is filed. **The 12-month pendency period cannot be extended.** *Therefore, an applicant who files a provisional application must file a corresponding nonprovisional application for patent (nonprovisional application) during the 12-month pendency period of the provisional application in order to benefit from the earlier filing of the provisional application. However, a nonprovisional application that was filed more than 12 months after the filing date of the provisional application, but within 14 months after the filing date of the provisional application, may have the benefit of the provisional application restored by filing a grantable petition (including a statement that the delay in filing the nonprovisional application was unintentional and the required petition fee) to restore the benefit under 37 CFR 1.78."*

Provisional patent applications serve some useful purposes both for large corporations and for independent inventors, particularly, but not only, for US-based ones. Unfortunately, this procedure has become the subject of some urban legends over the years. We can find, for instance, inventors who extrapolate the USPTO's statement that "*A provisional application is not required to have a formal patent claim*" to the conclusion that it doesn't even have to contain a decent description. So, they throw together a few words, an improvised chart, and perhaps a list of things they plan to do when they grow up, and they file it as a provisional application. Why bother describing the invention, they wonder, if you can get patent rights without spending time and effort on it?

Having accomplished this, they start blabbing their invention everywhere on the assumption that they have a priority date. Unfortunately for them, priority is established on the basis of the written description of the patent application, which, in their case, has no real substance. So when they file their nonprovisional application all over the world, a year later, they are in for a shock when they learn that their own divulgation of details of the invention deprived their nonprovisional application of novelty because their priority claim was worthless.

If you decide to file a provisional application for any reason, therefore, don't be tempted to take fatal shortcuts with the description of your invention. And if your patent attorney insists that it is okay for you to do so (I've met a couple who think so), get a new one.

CONTINUATION APPLICATIONS

This subject applies to the USPTO only. A continuation application is a second application for the same invention claimed in a prior nonprovisional application and filed before the original prior application becomes abandoned or patented. In practice, it is a path to continuing to prosecute subject matter that was included in the originally filed application in a separate one. You may have to do so for a variety of formal and practical reasons that are too tedious to be included here, and for the purposes of this book, it is sufficient that you know that such a path exists. There is no limitation to the number of continuation applications that you may file, but it costs money, so you should only do it if it brings a benefit.

A continuation-in-part (CIP) application is an application filed during the lifetime of an earlier nonprovisional application, repeating some substantial portion or all the earlier nonprovisional application and adding matter not disclosed in the said earlier nonprovisional application. The original parts will carry with them the priority date of the original application, while the added subject matter will have the date of the filing of the CIP application. Here, again, there may be many scenarios under which you may find it useful to file a CIP application—too many and too specialized to be discussed here.

PATENT OF ADDITION

Patents of addition exist in a few countries. In regard to the need that they fulfill, they are similar to the CIP application existing in the USPTO, although the concept is different. A patent of addition allows an inventor to file a patent application covering an improvement of an invention for which a patent has already issued or a patent application has been filed. The improvement must be novel, but it is not required to possess inventive step relative to the previous invention.

A patent of addition will typically be dependent on the main patent. This is a tool that, where existing, should be used at all only when the situation really requires it.

UTILITY MODELS AND INDUSTRIAL DESIGNS

The "utility model" (also sometimes referred to as "petty patent") presents some similarities to a patent. In fact, it is a "small patent" granted for an invention (mostly a simple mechanical one) that is new and useful but that only presents a low level of inventive step. Several countries offer this kind of protection, including, for instance, Germany and Japan, and although a utility model has a shorter life than a patent (typically 15 years instead of 20), it is a convenient way to protect certain inventions.

The utility model should not be confused with the "industrial design," also known in some countries as "ornamental design," which is an altogether different kind of protection with virtually no common ground with utility models. The industrial or ornamental design is essentially a copyright protection designed to protect industrial products (which are not covered under regular copyright laws that are intended to protect artistic output, such as pictures, music, books, and movies). The shape of a new faucet, if it has aesthetic value, can be protected by an industrial design in the same way that it can protect the new design of a chair. However, to be eligible for protection, the shape cannot have any functional purpose. Products that are shaped in a certain manner due to functional reasons can only be protected by regular patents if they fulfill the requirements for patentability. In contrast, a utility model can protect functional improvements, even small ones, and sometimes those are only protectable in this way because they do not reach the required level of inventive step for a patent to be granted on them.

CHAPTER 7
The International Patent Application (PCT)

Let's start by making something absolutely clear: **There is no such thing as an "international patent."**

The PCT is an international treaty with 148—and counting—contracting states.[6] The PCT makes it possible to seek patent protection for an invention simultaneously in a large number of countries by filing a single "international" patent application instead of filing several separate national or regional patent applications. The grant of patents remains under the control of the national or regional patent offices in what is called the "national phase."

The PCT procedure includes the following:

Filing: You file an international patent application with a national or regional patent office or with the WIPO[7] in Geneva, Switzerland, complying with the PCT formality requirements in one language, and you pay one set of fees.

International Search: An International Searching Authority (ISA) (one of the world's major patent offices) identifies the published patent documents and technical literature ("prior art") that may have an influence on whether your invention is patentable, and it

---

[6] The list of PCT contracting states can be found at http://www.wipo.int/pct/en/pct_contracting_states.html.

[7] World Intellectual Property Organization.

establishes a written opinion on your invention's potential patentability.

International Publication: As soon as possible after the expiration of 18 months from the earliest filing date, the content of your international application is disclosed to the world.

Supplementary International Search (optional): A second ISA identifies, at your request, published documents that may not have been found by the first ISA, which carried out the main search because of the diversity of prior art in different languages and different technical fields.

International Preliminary Examination (optional): One of the ISAs at your request carries out an additional patentability analysis, usually on an amended version of your application.

National Phase: After the end of the PCT procedure, usually before the expiration of 30 months[8] from the earliest filing date of your initial application, from which you claim priority, you start to pursue the grant of your patents directly before the national (or regional) patent offices of the countries in which you want to obtain them.

The Patent Cooperation Treaty (PCT) assists applicants in seeking patent protection internationally for their inventions, helps patent offices with their patent-granting decisions, and facilitates public access to a wealth of technical information relating to those inventions. By filing one international patent application under the PCT, applicants can simultaneously seek protection for an invention in all countries that are signatories to the PCT.

For a detailed graphic explanation of the PCT process see http://www.wipo.int/pct/en/faqs/faqs.html.

---

[8] Some countries and regional authorities have longer deadlines. For instance, the EPO's deadline is 31 months.

CHAPTER 8
When Will a US Patent Expire?

The purpose of this chapter is not to turn you into someone who can easily tell us when a given US patent will expire; it is to show you how that determination may be complicated, confusing, and often wrong.

A multiple-choice test would look like this:
Q: When will this patent expire?
Select the correct answer:
1. 20 years from the filing date.
2. 17 years from the issue date.
3. Sometime before the end of 25 years from the filing date.
4. Sometime before the end of 22 years from the issue date.
5. All answers are correct.

Well, not all answers are correct, but all answers 1–4 are possible. Following the Uruguay Round of the General Agreement on Trade and Tariffs (GATT 1994), the United States changed its law and rules on the expiry of patent life and harmonized it with the rest of the world, and as a result, it created a situation in which we must break our teeth to determine when a patent will expire. For instance, a patent application that was originally filed before the end of six months from the date in which GATT came into effect (i.e., June 8,

1995), but for which a patent was granted after it, will have an expiration date that is the latest between 17 years from the issue date and 20 years from the filing date. This sounds simple enough, but of course, it is not so. For instance, if a patent was issued on an application filed in January 1999, we would expect it to have an expiry date in January 2019. However, if we see that this application is, in fact, a continuation application of an earlier application filed in May 1997, then we will expect it to expire in May 2017. As simple as that, right? Wrong.

Many patent applications are issued late due to administrative delays caused by the US Patent Office. To make up for this, patent terms can be extended to take into account those delays, and the extension can be substantial—up to five years. Thus, the patent of our example may expire in 2017, or at any time between 2017 and 2022. The information is available in small print on the patent itself, but it has to be recognized and taken into account.

And this is not the only reason for extending the term of a patent. Patents for pharmaceutical products that underwent extensive regulatory processes that delayed the grant of regulatory approval, which is needed to be able to market the drug, may obtain a patent term extension (abbreviated as "PTE") of up to five years. These will not be reflected on the front page of the patent and must be discovered via the USPTO website.

And here is something else that you will not find on the front page of the patent—annuity payments. A patent for which the annuities due have not been paid expires. It doesn't matter that the front page of the patent says that it will expire 10 years from now: if you didn't pay, it's dead.

In short, we should never assume that we can automatically and safely determine when a patent will expire just by looking at it. US law has made that determination an interesting intellectual exercise for us all.

CHAPTER 9
A Short Patent Lexicon

Like in many other fields (and perhaps more than elsewhere), it is extremely important to use technical terms correctly to avoid misleading anybody into believing that the factual situation of your IP rights is different than what it is. Moreover, clueless people have contributed to the creation of statements that are not rooted in reality.

Take, for example, the simple statement, **"I have a patent!"** That is what someone who has just thought of an idea will openly tell you. He doesn't have a patent; however, he has an idea, and years may pass before he is granted a patent on something related to that idea . . . if ever. Making a statement like this without thinking may have dire consequences. In one case, for instance, a small company was sued by another with which it had held negotiations, because it misrepresented its proposed technology as being patented, while all it had was a recently filed patent application.

The following list of terms will illustrate the point:

"Patent" – A patent is a document defining the exclusive rights of its owner to an invention. A patent is granted on a patent application after it has been examined and found to be patentable.

"Patent Application" – A patent application is a technical–legal document that describes the invention and the monopoly that the applicant is applying for. It is submitted to the relevant patent authority[9] (for instance, to the USPTO in the US, to the JPO[10] in Japan, or to the EPO in Europe).

"International Patent" – This is something that does not exist (see Chapter 7), but the term is used extensively both to willfully confuse the public and simply out of ignorance. On the other hand, the International Patent Application (according to the PCT) allows a single preliminary review of a patent application by a selected authority acting for all the countries that are members of the PCT. Some misleading individuals also use the term **"World Patent,"** which is as much a fantasy as "international patent."

"Claims" – The patent claims are the section of the patent document that define the scope of protection (or, in other words, the monopoly) granted by the patent to its owner. The claims are typically the result of negotiations held during examination between the relevant patent authority and the applicant on the basis of the claims that were originally submitted. The allowed and then granted claims are often narrower than what the applicant originally hoped to obtain, and their scope may vary from country to country for a patent in the same family (i.e., with a common priority claim).

"Commissioner of Patents" – This is the person who heads the patent authority that has the power to issue patents to applicants. The role of the commissioner may differ very much from country to country. It may be purely administrative or also judicial.

Every now and then, the phone rings in the office of a patent

---

[9] **Reminder:** The generic term "patent authority" is used here to refer to the central patent office of a country and is not to be confused with a patent law firm, which is also sometimes referred to as a "patent office."

[10] The Japan Patent Office

attorney, and from the other end, this is what he hears[11]: *"Listen, I have a patent, and I need a patent lawyer who will make it a world patent. But I need to make sure that there will be no claims on my patent. Can you do it?"* That is enough for an average patent attorney to give up, call it a day, and go to the beach to cool down.

DANGEROUS RUMORS

Let's say that I told you that "I have heard that it is healthy to have your appendix removed at 20," or "If a dental caries is discovered in one of your teeth, you need to have all neighboring teeth removed to avoid the spread of the disease." It is unlikely that the discerning reader will immediately run to the nearest operating theater or dental clinic based on information of this kind revealed to him by chance while chatting with an acquaintance.

Suggestions given freely by "knowledgeable" persons, who have already had that experience (or, to be more precise, mean to have it in the future, when they can make time for it, but already know how it will be and are willing to share this insight with you) should be treated with suspicion. Strangely, when the matter at hand is one of great importance to us, such as when our intellectual property is at risk, we tend to rely much on rumors and even make important decisions on the basis of these rumors. Let's look at a few examples (out of a very long list):

The rumor: ***"We know that we haven't made an invention here, but we will always get 'something' if we file a patent application."*** No, you won't! Sometimes you'll get nothing, and sometimes, we will know beforehand that we don't stand a chance to get anything. If we get lucky, or we draw a gullible examiner and we get "something," in all likelihood, it will be worthless. Therefore, stubbornness does not necessarily lead to success.

The rumor: ***"The international examiner decided to give us a***

[11] Based on a true conversation.

patent." As explained before, the international patent does not exist. The international examiner delivers a nonbinding opinion and nothing more. Therefore, even if his opinion is positive, he cannot decide "to give us a patent." Representing that a positive international preliminary examination report is tantamount to a decision to grant us a monopoly (like it is sometimes presented by an entrepreneur to a potential investor) is wrong and misleading. Unless the potential investor is experienced and understands the process, such a representation may have dire consequences if the relations between the investor and the entrepreneur turn sour, as they sometimes do.

The rumor: ***"I've seen something exactly like your invention on sale in a shop."*** This is a particularly deadly rumor that does not require proof, which, when spoken, is sufficient to undermine the self-confidence of the inventor. I am always amazed when an inventor tells me that he has abandoned his idea at an early stage simply because an acquaintance in whom he confided told him that it was an old one. Inventors like him often come to me to resurrect their idea after one or two years, during which they realized that it hadn't been commercialized by others. They didn't go to the trouble of verifying the information that took the wind out of their sails, and they reached conclusions on the basis of an instinctive belief that it was true. Strange? Strange indeed but quite common.

To create something of value requires substantial effort, but a good rumor can spoil it easily. I will give you some good, free advice: Beware of free advice givers.

CHAPTER 10
A Few Things Worth Knowing

The purpose of this chapter is to bring to the reader, in a completely non-methodical manner and in no particular order, a number of particularly important subjects worth knowing if we want to understand the rationale behind the patent system and avoid making common mistakes.

DUTY OF DISCLOSURE

Many countries do not require the patent applicant to disclose to the examiner prior art known to him, which is relevant to the invention. The term "prior art" refers to any publication of any kind that predates the priority date of the patent application. In those countries, it is the job of the examiner to find prior art and to cite it against the patent application (in a correspondence typically called an "office action" or "examination report" or in a "search report"). On the other hand, some countries (the USA, for instance) make it a duty for the applicant to make a full disclosure of the prior art known to him.

It is important to understand the direct connection between the fulfillment of the applicant's duty of disclosure and the validity of the patent that would be issued to him. If, for instance, the applicant concealed a relevant publication that was known to him, his patent may be held invalid. A failure to disclose a relevant application is a basic violation of the applicant's duty of candor. Therefore, one might conclude that to avoid being accused of lack of candor, the way to go is to disclose to the examiner each and every publication that ever crossed our desk. Unfortunately, nothing is ever so simple.

For instance, in the US Patent Office, prior art is disclosed by submitting an Information Disclosure Statement (IDS), and what is not in the IDS is not considered as having been submitted to the examiner. In the past, some applicants submitted inordinately long IDSs and used this as a technique to "bury" a relevant piece of prior art in a heap of irrelevant publications, hoping that the examiner would not be able to read it all. Nowadays, however, excessively long lists of prior art references are considered unacceptable, and the applicant who cites too many irrelevant references runs the risk of being considered noncompliant with his duty of candor. The ball, therefore, is back in the applicant's yard. In the US, the applicant has to submit to the examiner any prior art reference known to him or to his attorney, which "a reasonable examiner" would have considered as relevant to the claims. However, there is no duty to submit references similar to one that has already been cited, if it is a reference of the same kind that is not more relevant to the one already cited. Confused? Sure you are.

Who is "a reasonable examiner" and what he would have considered to be relevant to the claims on record is a question that doesn't have a clear answer, and the applicant has to deal with it and make a decision. The reasonable rule of thumb is, of course, that when in doubt regarding the need to include a reference in the IDS, it should be included; on the other hand, when it is obvious that a reference is utterly irrelevant, it should not be included. Obviously, there is a large gray area that calls for quite a bit of head scratching by the applicant and his attorneys. This gray area can be slightly reduced if we make sure that all references cited by examiners in other countries are submitted to the US examiner on the assumption that those are "reasonable examiners" (an assumption that, unfortunately, often has no basis whatsoever). Any other prior art reference of which we have knowledge (for instance, through prior art searches that we carried out before filing the application) will have to be reviewed with specific reference to the pending claims, and decisions will have to be made as to their level of relevance.

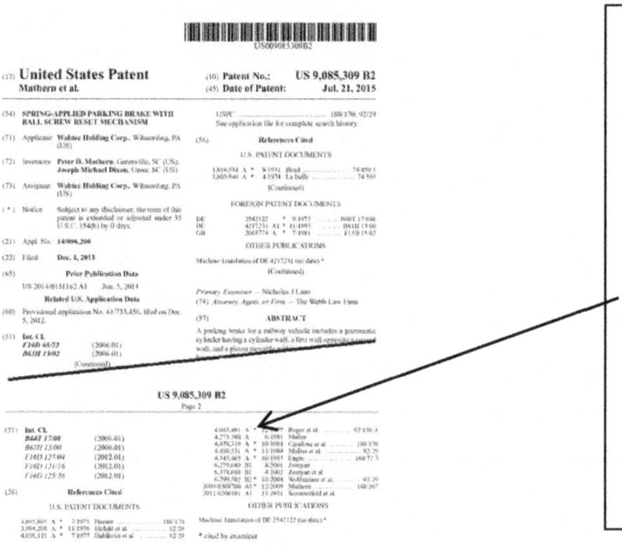
United States Patent
Mathern et al.
Patent No.: US 9,085,309 B2
Date of Patent: Jul. 21, 2015
US 9,085,309 B2

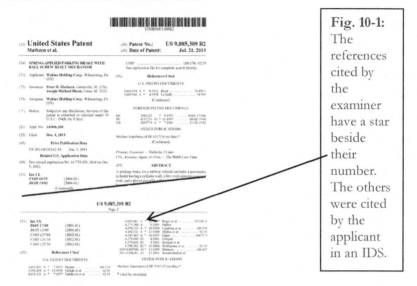

Fig. 10-1: The references cited by the examiner have a star beside their number. The others were cited by the applicant in an IDS.

There is an additional importance to the IDS because references that were not included can more easily be used against our patent in any future litigation in which it may become involved. Accordingly, we want all potentially problematic references to be considered by the examiner during examination, when we can more easily deal with them—for instance, by making appropriate claim amendments—than we may be able to do during contentious proceedings.

OPPOSITION AND CANCELLATION PROCEEDINGS

Patents are issued after a more or less thorough examination by a patent examiner (with the exception of a few countries where no examination exists) with little or no intervention of the public (see "observations" below). However, anyone who believes that a patent was granted by mistake may take action against it, and different countries have different opposition and revocation processes. It is not the purpose of this book to analyze in detail the procedural options available in different countries (which would be tedious and would distract the reader from the more important general principles);

therefore, I will outline those options and their general merits only briefly.

The basic question is, why is it appropriate to allow the general public to oppose or try to invalidate a patent that was thoroughly examined by a qualified examiner? The answer is simple: opposition and cancellation proceedings are not a replacement for the examiners' work but, rather, are a remedy for cases in which a patent was granted by mistake either because the examiner didn't do a proper job or because he didn't have all the information needed to do it. For instance, patent examiners do not carry out laboratory experiments to verify claims made by the applicant in his patent specification. Therefore, he must accept that reported experiment results are correct, unless they are wrong on their face.[12] Someone who is seeking to invalidate the patent, on the other hand, may carry out experiments, the results of which may have an impact on the validity of the patent.

Moreover, the examiner works according to information that he himself obtained, as well as that which has been submitted by the applicant. However, information may exist that is critical to the determination of whether an invention is patentable, to which the examiner does not have access. For instance, if the applicant displayed his invention at an exhibition two years before filing his patent application, or even sold products embodying his invention, this information may not reach the examiner unless the applicant discloses it. On the other hand, an opponent, who is a competitor, may have attended the exhibition or may have purchased a product embodying the invention and would, thus, be able to produce reliable evidence that the invention was not new at the time the application was filed, which renders the patent invalid.

There is, therefore, a public interest in providing good opposition and cancellation options, but this is important not only for the interest of the general public but also from our very private point of view. We should understand that a granted patent carries with it an assumption of validity, as long as it has not been proven otherwise. Therefore, our

[12] One example of obviously wrong experimental results are those provided to prove that the invention is powered by *perpetuum mobile*.

competitor who owns a relevant patent may use it to interfere with our manufacturing and/or marketing, regardless of whether, in the final analysis, the patent may be found to be invalid. But if we are aware of our competitor's attempt to obtain a preposterous patent, we may be able to take timely action against it. That is why it is important to keep an eye out for such dangers and not to limit ourselves to confront them when they are sprung on us without prior warning. Performing periodic patent searches entails little effort and may, therefore, provide substantial benefits.

Opposition proceedings are available in many countries and are of two types: pre-grant oppositions, where the patent authority advertises the intent to grant a patent, and the public is given a period of time—typically three months—to oppose the grant of the patent. Post-grant oppositions, on the other hand, take place after the patent is issued and are more akin to revocation proceedings. An example of such a system is that existing in the EPO, which allows a period of nine months for opposing the granted patent.

Other options for revocation include various types of reexamination proceedings (different ones are available, for instance, in the USPTO), according to which the authority that issued the patent performs a new examination that may lead to a reissue of the patent without change, in a more limited form, or to a total cancellation. The same may happen in legal proceedings before a court, for instance, if a patent is used to sue for infringement, and the defendant is able to show that the patent is fully or partially invalid.

Another option available in some countries is the so-called "observations" that can be submitted to an examiner by an interested party during the examination of a patent application. This is done on the assumption (which is often no more than wishful thinking) that the examiner will take serious notice of the material submitted to him. Experience shows that it is wise to submit observations only if and when the submitted material clearly and unequivocally shows a lack of novelty in the invention. Otherwise, submitting observations may be squandering useful ammunition that will lose its efficacy in later opposition or cancellation proceedings because it was already "considered" by the examiner.

In conclusion, many different options exist to deal with a competitor's patent that was mistakenly granted. However, some options are better than others and, particularly, less expensive than others. Like with medical conditions, an early detection of the problem may make a great difference to the options available to deal with it.

R&D'S ACHILLES' HEEL

Every protection system, even the best of them, has weak spots. Our aim for a given system should be to have the minimal possible number of weak spots and to make sure that if one of them is hit, the damage would not be incurable. Our smart competitor does not waste his time and effort trying to find ways to penetrate our hard armor and instead will look for those weak spots through which he will be able to pass with minimal effort. In his Greek epic, *Iliad*, the poet, Homer, tells us how the Greek god Apollo killed Achilles—whose entire body, except for his heel, was impenetrable—by directing Paris' arrow to Achilles' heel. All the divine protection was not enough to save Achilles, and there is much to be learned from this ancient story.

But here is a modern example: a start-up company designed and built a prototype of an advanced invasive medical device, which combined intelligent electronics with advanced mechanics. Because the developers came from the fields of mechanics and electronics, they obtained good patent protection for several important inventions relating to the novel joints they developed, as well as to efficient signal-processing methods. They learned the field in depth and made fast progress in their practical development, as well as in the patenting process. They only omitted to deal with one detail—to be able to use their device inside the human body, it had to be made up of biocompatible material that could withstand the mechanical forces resulting from its operation without breaking. However, a competitor had patented the use of a suitable material, which was, unfortunately, the only one that had regulatory approval for that use. It so happened that the company found itself at the end of a long and expensive development process with a lot of good IP but unable to market its device without infringing a competitor's patent. And because the competitor would not license the relevant patent to the company, they had to go back to the drawing board and come up with a different solution. This resulted in substantial delays and costs that eventually killed the company altogether.

An Achilles' heel is not something we necessarily have to put up with when planning an R&D project. But to be able to protect ourselves against this kind of problem, we shouldn't be looking for solutions while keeping our eyes on only our project without expanding our horizons to the world outside. Unfortunately, the approach taken by the developers in the example given above is not a rare one for a number of reasons. First of all, some people tend to view subjects relating to their own technical discipline as the most important subject, if not the only one deserving to be taken into account. Second, some developers shy away from dealing with technological fields and disciplines that are not close to their own. An electronic engineer will usually not like to hear about chemistry and materials engineering, just like the physician will be impatient when being lectured to about software engineering. But we live in an interdisciplinary world in which it is a severe mistake to ignore a component of the project.

Taking the above into account, our first step, before starting to actually research and develop, must be the determination—as precisely as possible—of the critical points through which the project must pass. If such critical points are located far away from the area of expertise of the persons conducting the analysis, he would be wise to bring into the project an expert in that field whose task would be to pave the road, build a protective shield around the part of the project pertaining to his field of expertise, and make sure that no Achilles' heels remain.

THE DANGER OF GIVING UP PRIORITY RIGHTS

A person or an entity that files a patent application in one of the countries that is a signatory to the Paris Convention[13] is entitled to a priority right for a period of one year, during which his patent application will have precedence over competing applications filed after his filing date by others in the same country or in other countries. This will be so even if, in a particular country, a competing application was filed before the right of priority was invoked. This right automatically expires at the end of 12 months from the day that the first application on the subject was filed and will be lost in all countries in which the right was not exploited.

However, exploiting the priority rights requires investing some money to file an international patent application or national applications, and it often happens that at the end of the 12-month period, the entrepreneur has not yet raised the money needed to further the project and to exploit the priority right. On the other hand, the entrepreneur still believes in the project and is convinced that he only needs some more time to raise the money to pursue it. At this point, he often elects to "renew" his priority right by withdrawing his original application and refiling it. It is extremely important to appreciate the dangers involved in selecting this option and the conditions under which it can be pursued.

First of all, it must be understood that, contrary to common belief, this option does not "renew" the priority right. In fact, the entrepreneur gives up totally and irreversibly all rights accrued in the invention until its withdrawal, and the clock is reset at the time of the new filing. There is no way that any rights of any kind can be transferred from the original, withdrawn application to the new one. After its withdrawal, the original application is considered as never having been filed.

Second, in order for the new application to give rise to new priority rights, it must fulfill certain conditions. The first condition is that the new application must be filed in the same country where the first one was originally filed. The second condition is that the second application must be filed only after the first one has expired or has

---

[13] Most, but not all, industrial countries of the world have signed the Paris Convention. See more about the Paris Convention in Appendix B.

been withdrawn. The third condition is that the original application was not published. The fourth condition is that the first application did not leave any outstanding rights, and the fifth condition is that the first application was not used to claim priority in any further patent application. The rationale behind these conditions is that you can enjoy priority rights only once and are not allowed to take a second bite at the apple. Should you do so, the second priority will become invalid with potentially catastrophic results for patents that claimed the benefit of that priority date.

An inventor who fulfilled all the above conditions is entitled to a new priority date but is running a nonnegligible risk. It is not uncommon for an entrepreneur who has filed a patent application (and, therefore, feels "protected") to meet a lot of people and talk a lot about his invention with a view to raising money for the project. Experience shows that the level of secrecy maintained by entrepreneurs at this stage is often not very high. Information leaked by people who heard about the project without proper secrecy agreements may find its way into the public domain, thus causing the invention to lose novelty and become unpatentable. Moreover, one year is a very long time in high-tech fields, and in many areas, competition is fierce, and it is not always possible to know who is breathing down the entrepreneur's neck. Giving up a priority date may turn a patent application that was filed by a competitor after our original filing date into an application that has priority rights over us. Because patent applications are typically only published on, or shortly after 18 months from their filing date, there is no way for us to know at the time when we need to make a decision to withdraw our first application whether a competitor may have filed a competing patent application.

Keeping all the above in mind, it is now clear that refiling a patent application while giving up the earlier priority date is not, as some people think, a brilliant way to "extend" our priority rights for another year. It is something you do when you have no choice as a calculated risk that may lose you important rights.

PATENT INFORMATION SOURCES

Twenty or so years ago, getting information on patents was hard work. The sources were limited, and the information was difficult to get at and not always reliable. But, nowadays, it is easy to gather that information from free sources, such as www.uspto.gov (the website of the USPTO), patentscope.wipo.int (the database of the World Intellectual Property Organization), register.epo.org (the European Patent Register), Google Patents, and so on. The importance of these sources is that they are readily available and allow anybody to run quick checks for things that matter to them without the need for long waiting periods. It is very important that inventors and entrepreneurs make it a habit to use these sources, but it is also important to understand their limitations and to use them properly.

In spite of all the many free resources of patent information, professional databases are still needed and thrive. For professional searches, these databases provide enhanced search capabilities and features that are not available in free services, which are needed in many cases to fine-tune a search. Moreover, the level of secrecy afforded by some free services is unclear, and in some cases, even the knowledge that someone is searching in a particular space may have a meaning for whoever is listening.

In conclusion, free patent information resources are useful and important for quick checks and for gathering background information, but they cannot be compared to the quality of the search results that can be achieved by using professional databases. It is useful for an inventor who initiates a project to learn his way around the subject by using free patent information services, but these should not be expected to provide the level of information required to make critical decisions.

Part II:
The Inventor and the Patent

"But we teach

Bloody instructions, which, being taught, return

To plague the inventor."

[William Shakespeare, Macbeth *(1606), act I. sc. 7, l.8]*

This part deals with the relationship between the inventor and his patent application and the pitfalls that this relationship may create.

CHAPTER 11
The Inventor–Invention Relationship

Inventors tend to develop a relationship with their invention, which often exceeds the dry and detached approach to it and to its limitations, which is needed to deal with the many hurdles of patent prosecution in the most efficient way. This is natural and human, and as long as we appreciate that it exists and take steps to make sure that our emotional attachments will not get in the way of making good decisions, there is nothing wrong with it. This chapter will address a number of ways in which the inventor's attachment to his invention may create problems.

TOO BROAD A VIEW

Patent applicants want to obtain broad protection from a patent application they file. This is a natural and positive tendency, as long as it is reasonable and does not end in covetous claims. However, patent applicants sometimes feel that they have not exploited all the available options if they didn't try to claim a monopoly as broad as their imagination allows. Some inventors do not understand why they should limit themselves of their own accord instead of claiming everything that comes to their mind and then leaving the narrowing work to the patent examiner. These inventors should understand that a patent application with claims that are obviously too broad is going to run into trouble. The laws of most countries clearly define how the limits of the monopoly granted to an inventor by a patent should be determined. The breadth of the monopoly is essentially in the hands of the inventor because it will be determined by the scope and the quality of the technical information that he has included in his application. In other words, there is a direct connection between the contribution of the inventor to the state of the art by his disclosure of new knowledge in his patent application and the recompense given him by the law in the form of a monopoly on his invention. Since this is a strong connection, the inventor should not be compensated to an extent greater than his contribution, and an attempt to obtain a monopoly greater than the contribution is likely to fail at some point in time.

But there is an even greater danger for the applicant who is getting above himself: he may get less than he is entitled to. The reason for this is that broadening the definition of the invention beyond what is supported by the specification may cause many prior art references to overlap fully or partially with the claims of the patent application, rendering them nonnovel. To distinguish the claimed invention from those prior art references, the applicant will often wind up drafting claims that offer a monopoly that is narrower than what he is entitled to and what he could have been allowed had he drafted them non-covetously to begin with. A reasonable claim drafting may avoid a situation in which marginal prior art references may inflict substantial damage to the monopoly that the patent will eventually afford. Since an attempt to broaden the scope of our patent may entail dangers, it is worthwhile debating beforehand whether such broadening is sufficiently important that we are prepared to take risks for it, instead of blindly trying to take from the patent all we can.

In this respect (as in most cases), we need to be practical. Even if we resent that if we draft reasonably limited claims, we might be getting less than we might perhaps obtain, the real question is whether, by doing so, we are retaining everything that is truly important to us, setting aside emotional considerations. If, in the claims we drafted, we left out something to which we believe we are entitled, but which we know is utterly irrelevant to our business, we may have done the right thing, provided that narrowing the claims is likely to help us to obtain better protection for the parts of our invention that have real and practical commercial importance. Like at a banquet, it is not wise to eat everything that is put on the table; it is better to pick the juiciest dishes and stop when we are full.

THE "FAST" OR "GOOD" DILEMMA

When the time comes to draft a patent application, inventors are always in a hurry. This is because of all the good reasons and because of all the bad reasons. They are in a hurry because, all of a sudden, they got scared that someone might file a competing application before them. They rush because they fear that the secrecy of the invention has not been properly maintained, and they also hustle everybody involved into moving fast as a matter of principle, because they think that you have to push to get service. When we take our car to the machine shop, we will always tell the mechanic that we need the car back by noon because then, there is a chance that we will get it back on the same day. But if, because of the pressure we applied, the mechanic forgot to check our brakes, we may have gotten ourselves a bad deal.

The same may happen, to some extent, with patents. Drafting a proper patent application involves taking time to study the invention from all angles, and both the patent attorney and the inventor learn from the process—the patent attorney understands the invention, and the inventor understands which details he must supply to help the patent attorney in his effort to protect the invention. During this process, the inventor and the patent attorney study the prior art in depth, exchange views regarding its relevance, and draw conclusions that are important for defining the required coverage and its limitations. This is not a simple and quick process, and sufficient time must be given to all involved not only to read a lot of relevant documents but also to internalize their meanings and their impact on the invention and on the ways in which it should be addressed. It is not possible to speed up this process too much, and the time required for it depends on the complexity of the case and on the background information that has to be studied. In many cases, obviously, the invention is new to the patent attorney, even if he has a good technical knowledge of the field. Even if he happened to handle many similar cases in the past, it should be understood that no two cases are the same, and it would be a grave mistake to apply to a specific case solutions used in the past for a different invention merely on the basis of external similarities.

Nevertheless, in many cases, we don't have the time to let the information settle in our minds sufficiently before we need to prepare and file a patent application, because external factors force us to act without delay. For instance, the need to have a critical business meeting, or the upcoming publication of an article describing the invention, will force us to draft and file a patent application before a given date, even if the learning process has not been completed. In such cases, we know that the results may not be optimal, and it is important to revisit the patent application after a short while to determine whether changes, improvements, or any other activity are required.

Some inventors approach the preparation of the patent application mechanically, like a nuisance that has to be dealt with, similarly to preparing a tax return or a list of items for the insurance company. This type of inventor often sets unrealistic goals for the completion of the work on the patent application because he needs to check the box next to the item on his to-do list. These are inventors who can also be expected to make strategic decisions in the same way—according to unclear rules but always in strict adherence to a rigorous timeline. These inventors should understand that they have to decide whether they want the process to be fast or right, but they can't have both.

WHEN "GOOD ENGINEERING" BECOMES AN "INVENTION"

Every day, engineers around the world make plans. Thousands, and maybe tens of thousands, of engineering plans are created every week.

Electronic engineers plan how to take components off the shelf and combine them into novel products; mechanical engineers plan new ways to improve the performance of the car we drive or design a tiny component of a medical device; material engineers plan how to coat a surface with an appropriate polymer to impart to it improved surface properties; and chemical engineers combine pumps, heat exchangers, and reactors to produce improved products more efficiently and at lower costs. Countless plans are made every day in many fields, and some of them embody important and valuable inventions.

In most cases, the electronic engineer will not design a new component, and the mechanical engineer will not invent a new spring; they will adapt to their specific purposes the engineering knowledge that has been accumulated through the centuries. Similarly, the material engineer will usually not invent new coatings but rather will select the coating material that is suitable for his purposes, pretty much like the chemical engineer, who will not invent a new reactor or heat exchanger but will combine them to obtain the desired process equipment. How, then, is it possible for an invention to hide inside an engineering product that does not involve the creation of a new component? Based on these assumptions, it is clear that there is nothing new in what they did; or is there?

Fig. 11-1: A Colossus Mark 2 computer, one of a series of computers developed for British codebreakers in 1943–1945 to help in the cryptanalysis of the Lorenz cipher

Let's try to explain to ourselves the meaning of "invention" in such a context, and let's do this by using an artistic example. When we look at a statue made from a variety of materials of different colors, we don't only see pieces of metal, stone, or plastic, but we also recognize the artistic genius of its maker. Unfortunately, some "statues" were not created by a real artist, and when we look at them, all we see is a heap of scraps of different colors, which does not exhibit more artistic genius than the newspaper kiosk that stood in that spot before it. But when the very same scraps are handled by a real artist, the result is completely different, and it's easy for us to see the spark of genius that gives the statue its artistic value. But how? The statue is made of the same pieces of metal that were taken from the same scrap pile. The artist did not invent new colors; he only combined them. Nevertheless, we stand before it in awe.

The professional eye sees the result of an engineering development that involves an inventive step pretty much in the same way. The engineer who made the invention took what at the hands of somebody else could have turned out to be an uninspired mixture of standard components that perform their expected tasks and made them into something that achieves unexpected results. The various components still perform their expected engineering role, of course, but the inventive spark of their designer gives them an additional dimension. It may be, as is often the case with inventions in the field of electronics, that the inventive step is not in the selection of the components but rather in the way in which they interact, which may be unusual and can yield unexpected results. The mechanical engineer, on the other hand, may have achieved the strength of a certain component in a way that is known for other applications but which is unconventional in his specific field, thereby reducing the cost of the end product. The examples are many and varied.

Not every engineering design yields an invention; in fact, only very few of them do. It would not be correct to say that every elegant design of a beautiful product will necessarily embody an invention. But it would be appropriate to look for one in the engineering design that causes us, as persons skilled in the field, to be surprised even if only for a moment. We must keep in mind that inventions may hide in many places: in the resulting ease of use, in lower costs, in an improved performance, and elsewhere. A common mistake that should be avoided, therefore, is assuming without scrutiny that an engineering design may not involve an invention.

THE LONELY INVENTOR

Every year in Nuremberg, Germany, the iENA international trade fair[14] takes place, which showcases "ideas, inventions and new products." The exhibition gives independent inventors a chance to present their inventions to the world, but every year, you will hear voices complaining that it is very difficult for an independent inventor to sell his inventions. The level of innovation contributed by independent inventors, they point out, is sometimes greater than that exhibited by the companies, but still, the majority of inventions that find their way into actual products comes from the industry and not from independent inventors. A number of reasons contribute to this situation.

First of all, it is true that many individuals are endowed with amazing inventiveness, which makes them tackle technologically difficult projects for the sake of solving complex problems; but marketing people may find it difficult to come up with a marketing strategy for "a combined light switch and dog whistle," even if the inventive idea behind it is great. Independent inventors too often view technological elegance as a purpose, rather than as a means. In contrast, industry-employed inventors usually apply the amount of technological skill that is required for the purpose of achieving a commercial goal, and no more than needed. This reflects on the user-friendliness of the product and on its price.

Second, most inventions that are developed in industry are born out of a need. In many cases, the questions that inspire an R&D project come from marketing people who sense that the market is in need of a solution. When the idea comes from the R&D people, a serious company will test it extensively with the marketing people before investing too much money in it. A commercial company will not develop a product if they are told by their marketing people that they will not be able to sell it. Unfortunately, before and during the actual development, the independent inventor has very limited ability to get feedback on the marketability of the product he wants to develop.

---

[14] http://www.iena.de/en/home.html

Third, although many independent inventors are experienced, serious, and knowledgeable in their field, not all inventors are like them. **A warning to the investor:** Quite a few self-proclaimed inventors give their peers a bad name. These are people who make inventions that are useless, worthless, and often outright stupid—contraptions that cannot work and which, if by mistake work, lack appeal to the user and are unmarketable. Identifying this type of inventor is difficult because the passion for their invention and their commitment to it are not lesser than what you sense in serious inventors, who have worked in industry R&D for decades and now want to go indie. A warning sign is when they hand you a business card that has beside their name the title "inventor." Only few, well-established inventors, who have successfully brought to the market the fruit of a number of inventions, can flaunt that title without causing eyebrows to raise, and those will usually appreciate how ridiculous it is to use the noun "inventor" as a title.

Fourth, it is obvious that industrial companies have the better chance of being able to market a successful invention. Big companies have R&D divisions that are sometimes spread over different sites, cities, and even countries and, therefore, are not enthusiastic about receiving information from external inventors, who, in the future, may claim that the company has stolen the invention from them, although at the time he contacted the company, a similar development was already being done inside its facilities. Many international corporations, therefore, require an inventor to file a patent application before approaching them and to give up all secrecy and to waive all other rights before they agree to review the proposal.

The problems described above are just a few of the hurdles with which the independent inventor is confronted, but he shouldn't despair; many inventors have fulfilled their dreams, and many others will be able to sell their inventions to the industry. An inventor who believes in the quality and importance of his invention must persevere, but he should take with him on his journey a lot of patience and a thick skin to see him through multiple disappointments.

THE INVENTOR'S OWN UNIQUE INVENTIVE CONTRIBUTION

"An inventor is one who walks the path that others have walked and sees things that others have not seen" is one of the definitions I like best.[15] However, it could be interpreted as meaning that to make an invention, it is sufficient to sit at home, to read about a given subject, and to reach a conclusion that was not reached by those who did the same before us. While that is not impossible and may happen once or twice in a blue moon, it is not the rule.

From time to time, we meet an aspiring inventor who thinks he has done his part in the deal with the world by reading the relevant literature and providing witty comments about it and that a patent should, therefore, be granted to him. Unfortunately (or, rather, fortunately), this is not the case. Patents are not a price for a literature search well done, which may point in the direction of the solution. Even if it should eventually turn out that a solution can be found at the end of a road, the beginning of which is found in the intelligent reading of other people's work, pointing to that beginning is not making an invention. Assume (exaggerating for the sake of illustration) that one should invest efforts in finding a solution to a disease that attacks certain types of cells. An in-depth reading of the extensive literature on the subject will perhaps bring him to the conclusion that an effective treatment requires developing a vaccine for the disease. This conclusion may be correct, but that does not mean that it is enough to obtain a patent on vaccines that treat disease in general. In the vast majority of cases, an intelligent reading of the scientific literature will be only the starting point for the development of an invention on which a patent can be granted. In our example, no patent can be granted on the mere idea that a vaccine should be developed (to replace the standard treatment involving medicating the patient), but he who will pursue this idea and develop an efficient vaccine may be able to obtain strong patent protection.

The inventive process involves different critical stages, and

---

[15] Attributed to Alexander Graham Bell.

having the idea is only the first among them. For the inventive process to be completed, it has to go through additional stages, including reducing the idea to practice. Without a reduction to practice, the inventive process will more often than not be incomplete. There may be many others in the world who have read the same literature that we studied and have reached the same conclusions that we have reached, but they have failed to pursue the idea and to reduce it to practice. This means that our conclusion is no more than the conclusion that an average skilled person would reach by reading publicly available material, which, in turn, means that our mere conclusion does not possess inventive step, which is a basic requirement for patentability. At this point, we need to make our own particular contribution that will embody an inventive step over the state of the art, if we want to be granted a patent.

For completeness' sake, it should be understood that in many fields, there are cases in which an invention can be reduced to practice in our armchair. For instance, in computer science, it is not necessary in many cases to actually build anything different than our PC, which, coupled with appropriate software, becomes a novel machine. Another simple example can be found in the mechanical field. Let's say that a skilled engineer learns from the literature that containers in which certain dangerous chemicals are shipped suffer from corrosion that is due to moisture coming from the outside. Using his knowledge on the structure of the containers, the engineer may design a closure that will not allow moisture in, and he can make this invention in his armchair. Drawing the details of the closure would, in this case, count as reducing the invention to practice, because the remaining steps needed to manufacture the closure would be carried out on the basis of the drawings, without the need for any further inventive process.

Although there will almost always be some distance between conclusion (based on the reading of published material) and invention, we should not exclude the possibility that an Einsteinian genius, who is capable of seeing and solving exceedingly complex systems in his head, will be able to propose practical solutions without doing any other work. But we will do well to doubt anybody who claims to be in this category before we are presented with hard proof of his genius.

CHAPTER 12
Desirable versus Available

In the minds of each one of us, there is a picture describing the perfect invention process. There are those who remember preeminent scientists who made discoveries that underlie our lives while splashing in a hot bath or in the course of a light nap under a sprightly apple tree. The reality, at least in present days, is slightly different. To make important inventions, it is necessary to work hard and also to avoid the many obstacles that lie in wait for us at every corner. A brief discussion of these aspects follows.

THE CHAIN OF INVENTION OF A. G. BELL

In his instructive article, "Discovery and Invention," which was published in June 1914 in *National Geographic* magazine, Alexander Graham Bell notes one important basic truth: inventions are not usually created all at once. They start from simple beginnings. One small discovery, followed by other discoveries that are also small, gradually leads to a major result.

Although Bell then contemplated "major" inventions, such as an airplane that would cross the ocean in one day, the mechanism by which most of the inventions are made is also similar today. The path to the final result goes through small stages, which are interrelated, where each one of them is perhaps a small step, but their connection is greater than their sum. Thus, for instance, the development of a small mobile phone requires the development of miniature electronics, a small and effective antenna, enhanced signal-processing methods, excellent plastics, and so on. Each one of the components of the final result requires, in most cases, inventions that solve technical and engineering problems that stand between the predevelopment know-how and the final result. There are those who believe that it is advisable to wait until the final result is arrived at before endeavoring to protect our invention, inasmuch as so long as the goal has not been achieved, we do not have a working product. This approach is wrong and even ruinous, particularly in cases in which a logical thread connects the development stages.

In a word assembly game, there are letters without which we would not manage to assemble the correct word, and this is also the case with inventions: There are links that if unavailable to us, the road to the final result will be blocked. These links are found along the various development stages, and to attain good and effective protection, we must find them, mark them as critical stages, and block competitors' access to them through patent protection.

Our attentive competitors are also aware of the connecting thread that leads from stage to stage, to the major result, sometimes through a winding path. They diligently track our actions and our products and

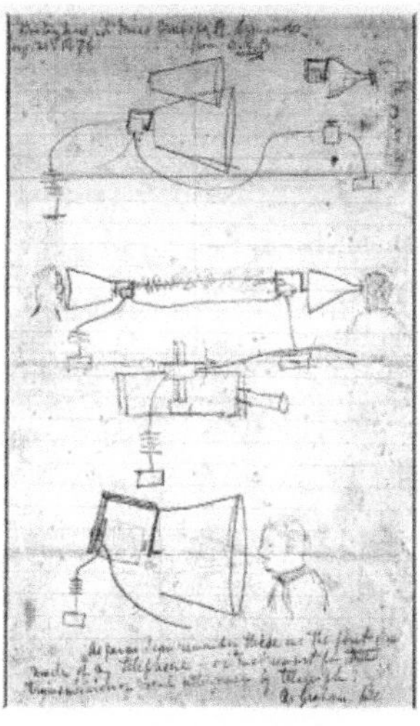

Fig. 12-1: The original sketch of the telephone drawn by A. G. Bell.

attempt to find critical links and to block them from us. Just as an occasional visitor, a competitor who observes the progress of our work may identify future possibilities inherent in the combination of our steps before this awareness arises within us. Bell was, therefore, correct in his advice[16]:

> *"Don't keep forever on the public road. Leave the beaten path occasionally and dive into the woods. You will be certain to find something you have never seen before, and something worth thinking about to occupy your mind. All really big discoveries are the result of thought."*

With our thinking channeled to our preset goal, we might not see the whole value of our inventions, while our competitor, standing at a distance, may sometimes understand their importance more rapidly than we do. Therefore, we must not limit our thoughts and efforts to the immediate satisfaction of an early plan without looking around a bit to see if it may be greater than we originally thought; otherwise, we may wind up with significantly more limited protection than we could have obtained.

THE INVENTOR IN LOVE

An inventor is often naturally in love with his invention. This love, as any love, may cause dangerous blindness and can present the invention in an artificial light. This blindness exists in every realm. In the commercial realm, the inventor sometimes ignores simple facts, such as the lack of marketing potential, and does not differentiate between the scientific quality of the invention, which could be high, and the market needs, which may not require his fine invention at all. In the practical realm, the inventor quite often ignores objective difficulties in realizing his invention, or the unreasonable costs it entails. An inventor who is aware of his inherent limitations would do well to transfer the management of the commercial and practical questions to other hands, so that impartial persons, who are not

---

[16] Bell made this statement in different forms on various occasions, which shows how strongly he felt about it.

directed by emotional considerations, would review them on their merits.

However, ravaging emotions that originate from an inventor's heart may be unconquerable. Someone else's patent, or some previous publication, which is discovered at an advanced stage of our work, could shuffle the cards to the extent of invalidating the entire idea. In a less serious situation, the previous publication could require far-reaching changes in the execution of the invention, which could deviate substantially from the original intention of the inventor, and, thus, this previous publication could take away "the luster" from his work.

Certain inventors do not deal well with situations of this kind. They enter a state of denial, in which they refuse to acknowledge the problem created by the discovery of the previous publication.[17] When a previous patent is discovered with claims covering his invention and that *de facto* block the way to its commercial development, the instinctive response of the inventor is *"Unlike mine!"* Another common response is an effort to find flaws in the description of the patent to show the inferior technical level of its inventor, which does not help in any way to solve the problem. Sentences such as *"he wrote this, but he clearly did not understand . . ."* do not solve anything and only serve the inventor to vent his disappointment and to avoid the need to deal with the problem.

Peculiarly, when the denial sets in, the person with the vastest knowledge, who is naturally positioned to address the previous publication, may also be the person who is not able to do so effectively. A good manager should not rely on the optimistic attitude of the inventor toward a previous publication. An inventor who is immersed in his invention, and is continuously planning its future development, is not equipped with the tools required "to freeze" it in time and to review it with the proper perspective in relation to relevant prior publications. In small companies, in which the invention is the essence, there is also a tendency for those who are not the

[17] **Reminder:** A previous publication is prior art that may have an impact on the novelty or on the inventive step of the invention.

inventor to go into denial together with him, because obviously, the inventor "knows best."

Patent attorneys who do a proper job and tell the inventor the hard truth are often rewarded with enmity. I have seen this happening countless times when I had to tell an inventor that his invention was not new and not patentable. The immediate reaction in many cases was to conclude that, obviously, I did not know what I was talking about, I didn't understand the invention, I had some covert reason why I wanted to humiliate the inventor, and similar pearls of wisdom. You would have thought that they should have thanked me for saving them time and money and for stopping them from going on a wild goose chase, but don't hold your breath—they'll simply go elsewhere and eventually find someone who is willing to exchange some adulation for cash.

Therefore, a manager who seeks to navigate his company in a direction that is not a dead end should require that every previous publication that is *prima facie* perceived as problematic for an invention that it is developing be investigated by a party who is not involved in the invention, with the aim of obtaining a true and emotion-free evaluation.

PATENTS FROM HELL

Patents are not a game and not a hobby but an R&D and marketing tool. However, there is a stage in a person's life when he is exposed to the danger of being carried away into inventive adventures, which could cost him dearly. This stage of life often occurs as part of the forty-plus age crisis, an age when the person has exhausted himself in his professional life and is seeking new intellectual excitement. There is nothing like a "revolutionary" invention to satisfy the sought-after excitement together with the millions that will not be long to follow.

In his work from the 14th century, "The Divine Comedy," the Italian poet Dante Alighieri tells of a person who deviates from his path, loses his way in the forest, and ultimately finds himself at the gate of Hell. And so Dante relates in the first person:

When half way through the journey of our life / I found that I was in a gloomy wood / because the path which led aright was lost / . . . I cannot well say how I entered it / so full of slumber was I at the moment / when I forsook the pathway of the truth.

This description again comes to my mind whenever I am faced with a person who is convinced that, lo and behold, his invention is so good and momentous that, in no time, it will be sold and make him a millionaire. The people who fall victim to this delusion are generally serious, levelheaded people who have high technical ability. These people are imbued with such deep faith in their invention to the extent that they might invest all their money and future in it.

The reality, to our regret, is different. A good invention will result in economic benefit only if it is handled in the right manner and by the right parties—and, even then, not necessarily. An attempt to promote a good invention on his own could lead the inventor to incur expenses unbearable for an individual, and the result could be disastrous. Factories and companies, whether start-ups or well established, budget the patent expenses as part of an orderly and planned budget having clear sources. This is not the case for an individual, who subsists from his salary. While the patent expenses are a standard part of the R&D and of the marketing plans and do not constitute an exceptional expense for a well-planned company, this is not so for a private individual who pursues a personal dream whose dimensions exceed his financial resources.

Just as in a poker game, the game with his last dollar usually ends in loss. An individual who invests his savings cannot abandon a hopeless project, as a commercial company would do, because he has no alternative to recoup his lost money. This is generally "hard" money, which has been accumulated after paying taxes and over a long time, and it is not possible to simply "write off the investment." Therefore, a person who has become entangled in this kind of private investment tends to spend more and more money and to embroil himself in his invention, which as is already obvious, will not rake in millions, just as a junkie will do anything to buy some more drugs.

Fig. 12-2: Dante and his poem. Wall paint by Domenico di Michelino in the Cathedral of Santa Maria del Fiore, Firenze (1465).

Therefore, when meeting a person who is about to embark on such an adventure, we have a humanistic duty to remind him of the inscription on Dante's Gate of Hell:

> ***Through me one goes into the town of woe / through me one goes into eternal pain / through me among the people that are lost / . . . / all hope abandon, ye that enter here!***

Embarking on a costly patent adventure without a clear and sufficient source of sustenance for the project could become a real hell, and no temptation justifies ignoring Dante's warning.

THE RIGHT TIMING

The timing when a patent application is filed can be the critical factor separating success and failure. Here, one can err in at least two ways. The first and very common mistake is filing a patent application only when the product is "mature," or, in other words, subsequent to a completion of the development. There are those who bring this mistake to extremes by remembering the need to obtain patent protection only a few days before their product's launch date.

Filing a late patent application is fraught with many dangers, and the first of them is the loss of priority to a competitor. Under the competitive conditions of the global village, it would be a naïve illusion to think that no one apart from us is developing products such as ours. If a competitor is quicker than we are in protecting his intellectual assets, we could be too late in filing our patent application and, thus, we would lose the priority for our invention. Beyond the aforementioned real danger, the preparation process for filing a patent application is one through which we scrutinize our invention and discover its flaws and pitfalls. Performing this process too late may not reveal all the defects or may reveal them when no time remains to redress them.

The second mistake, which is no less common, is filing a patent application too early—when we have no real invention but only a problem definition and general guidelines for solving it. Many inventors go into a state of anxiety over the concern that their invention will be stolen and hasten to file a patent application, which is not always based on sufficient information, "to protect" it. In this situation, the patent application does not describe a real invention and will not give us any real advantage or protection. Moreover, beyond the unnecessary financial expenditure, filing an "immature" patent application will not prejudice our rights, provided that we understand its limitations and act to redress them. However, the damage is often derived from the unjustified feeling of security that filing a patent application gives us. We quickly forget that the patent application we filed isn't worth much and feel "protected" enough to act freely while publicly disclosing our product, which, meanwhile, is no longer immature and embodies real inventions. In this situation, we might discover that we made our invention public and thereby lost any right to be granted a patent on it, while the patent application that we filed does not protect us at all because it does not describe the invention. This is a disastrous mistake, and it quite often causes very serious problems. To avoid its devastating results, the development should be accompanied by an intelligent "in motion" patent protection plan, or, in other words, a continuous monitoring of the R&D, followed by patent application filings at the appropriate milestones.

Unfortunately, there are many cases in which the developers are too busy with daily life and have no time and attention to pursue an ongoing protection plan. In those cases, we must begin with an early examination of the patent questions and file a patent application as soon as possible but at a point that will provide real protection for the project. Integrating new developments in the patent protection, once the product is ready for marketing, will be much more onerous in the end, but we must remember that patents are here to serve the company and not the other way around.

CHAPTER 13
The Inventor and the Patent Specification

The inventor's dealings with his patent application, at the time of drafting it and during its prosecution with the patent examiners, are not always easy. Various difficulties lie in wait: the difficulty in seeing his invention objectively and the reluctance to deal with the bothersome "details" required for a successful patent application are only two of them. Below is a cursory glimpse into this world.

NOT ON BEAUTY ALONE

It is known that maturity for a preschool age child is judged, *inter alia*, by his ability to delay gratification. It turns out that sometimes inventors who begin to prepare a patent application for their invention behave somewhat like children. Whether this results from the excitement of working on their "baby," due to the special experience of participating in the writing of a patent application, or any other reason, their natural enthusiasm may be deleterious.

These inventors do not see the patent application for what it really is—a dry technical–legal document that is intended to clearly and fully describe an invention and to unequivocally and succinctly claim rights thereon. To them, it is a genuine literary creation the quality of which rests heavily on their shoulders. The weight of the responsibility for the beauty of the document deprives them of sleep. It is difficult to persuade the inventor that no literary competition is involved, that certain sentences, although less beautiful that those that he proposes, are clearer, and that the dry and repetitive language is an inevitable necessity. He will not be persuaded that all the serious aesthetic flaws that he finds in the patent specification are, in fact, virtues and not shortcomings.

The main difficulty is, generally, with the background of the invention. The objective of the background is to clarify to the reader—particularly, the examiner—the problem that the invention seeks to solve in order to properly position the invention in relation to the present state of the art and to enable the reader to understand its substance. In no way is this part of the description intended to show others the knowledge of the inventor and to prove his sublime scientific qualities. To achieve the objective, it is unnecessary to provide a complete and broad review of the entire field. Such descriptions may, under the current doctrine, come back to haunt the applicant as "admitted prior art,"[18] which may be held against the invention. Thus, for instance, if our invention is a new can that, by mechanical action, disperses an air-purifying powder, it is sufficient to briefly review the problem that it is desired to solve in terms of where the odor exists and why it is a bad thing; there is no need to cite dozens of articles on the common causes of odor and on the numerous chemical reactions that result in its neutralization.

An exaggerated description of the prior knowledge could lead to quite a few problems. First, such a description could create a wrong impression that there is nothing special in the invention and, all in all, that it involves a small and insignificant improvement of the many products existing in the field. Positioning our invention in a sea of irrelevant publications that we cite in the background of our application will lead to a trivialization of the invention.

Second, it is very important that the patent examiner examining our application read a description of the field that is sufficient to explain the problem to him and later to allow him to understand the

[18] See also the discussion in Chapter 5.

invention, inasmuch as without minimal familiarity with the field, he will find it difficult to appreciate it. However, an examiner cannot be expected to read dozens of pages, however scholarly they may be, and an exaggerated description of the background will only prompt him to skip right to the end of the section.

Furthermore, there are cases in which we will have to provide the examiner with copies of numerous publications that we cited in the background section. If we referenced irrelevant publications in our application, we will pay for this twice: once due to the need to provide copies and the cost that this entails and a second time due to the complication and prolongation of the examination as a consequence of the examiner's need to read at least some of the publications. If we cited them, the examiner is entitled to assume that they contain pertinent material, even if this is not the case, and we cannot expect him to ignore them because *we* know that there is nothing of importance to our invention in them.

Therefore, the inventor should show restraint with regard to the background material that he wishes to include in the application. An in-depth and thorough scientific discussion of the subject should be left to the article that he will publish (after a patent application is filed). However, prudence is required to avoid making far-reaching statements in any publication attributable to the inventor or to the assignee of his patent, which may be used to trivialize the invention, because statements of fact made by the inventor, even after the filing date of his patent application, carry weight. Made with prudence, scientific articles by an inventor can be useful—or at least, not harmful—and the inventor's need to express his scientific thoughts may be satisfied there. However, the place of these scholarly dissertations is not in the description of a patent application. The inventor must understand that in the patent world, accuracy and clarity come first, and beauty and scientific elegance are of secondary importance.

BLOWING HIS OWN HORN

As stated, the path to obtaining a patent entails an "examination" process, during which the patent examiner raises various arguments against the invention claimed in the patent application. These arguments are of various kinds; some are technical in nature and can be addressed directly, and some are legal and pertain to the manner in which the examiner interprets prior publications and various statements made in them. Our answer to the examiner depends, to a large extent, on our understanding of the way in which he addresses the prior publications that he cited against our invention. Because we must persuade the examiner that his rejections do not prejudice our right to obtain a patent, we have no choice but to discuss them and to bring counter arguments that will persuade him that the cited references do not teach our invention and don't make it obvious (or, in other words, that our invention possesses both novelty and inventive step in spite of the existence of the prior art references that he cited).

Our invention will undergo this kind of process in different countries in which there may be examiners with different and even contrasting opinions who will ask us difficult questions using the same or different prior publications viewed from different perspectives, and we will answer each one at different times. We should beware that in the fervor of the persuasion work, we do not put in writing statements that, even if they are effective at the moment, might cause us difficulties in another time and place. The problem rests in what is known as "prosecution history estoppel"[19]—that is, what can be learned of the positions of the patent applicant, the inventor, and other people connected with the invention from documents that have been submitted to a patent examiner. In advanced countries, it is accepted today that the declarations of the applicant made in one country can be used against him in another country. Thus, when an examiner is told what he wants to hear, to obtain a patent in his country, we may harm our chances elsewhere. Let's look at a simple example. Let us assume that our invention is a potato-peeling device that works by scraping the potato peel with a rubber ball. The examiner in Country A finds an article in which a similar device is

[19] Also known as "file wrapper estoppel."

described, but with a metal ball, which he argues causes our invention to be obvious, because in his mind, replacing the metal ball with a rubber one is a straightforward engineering choice. We decide to focus our arguments not on the structural differences between the prior art and our device, but rather on the peeling effect. To overcome this citation, therefore, we submit arguments to the examiner (and perhaps we also submit to him experimental data supporting our arguments) to the effect that the peel is not properly removed if the ball is made of a material with hardness above a certain critical value, which is much lower than that of the metal. The examiner is persuaded, and a patent is issued covering the design of our device, and because the examiner did not require it, it does not have a limitation that the ball should be made of rubber.[20] After a while, when we have been granted patents throughout the world, one of our competitors emerges in Country B with a device that is identical to ours, but which works with an iron ball. Apparently, he has overcome the hardness problems of the structure material (for instance, by roughening the surface of the ball). When we sue in an effort to stop him, we will discover that he is well aware of our statements made in Country A, excluding the use of iron balls, which enabled us to obtain a patent there, and he is using them to prove that his product cannot, according to our own arguments, be included in the invention protected by our patent. In this manner, we have made it easier to obtain the patent in Country A in which we encountered a problem, but we have weakened the protection that our patent will afford to us throughout the world.

It turns out that the awareness of this problem is extremely low, and applicants and inventors tend to go along the easy route and provide the examiner with what he wants—or what they understand he wants to hear—if the answers are easy and available, without investing sufficient thought in the implications of these statements in future situations. Thus, it happens that instead of working hard to prepare persuasive technical arguments, which would retain maximum protection for our invention, we sometimes make life easy for

---

[20] The examiner should have requested that limitation, but, in this example (as sometimes in life), we got a sloppy examination.

ourselves on our way to a quick grant of a patent and pay for it at a later time with hard currency.

The principle whereby the statements made by an applicant, which are given for the sake of obtaining a patent, are binding on him, is a very important one. It allows us to clarify for ourselves the intention of an applicant whom we do not know, by reviewing the examination documents, and it permits us, therefore, to draw the boundaries of the invention that we must not cross.

SILENCE SUITS THEM

Time and again, we are compelled to remind active inventors what is the role of the patent and, particularly, what it is not. The role of the patent is to effectively protect our inventions to enable us to acquire and retain an effective industrial and commercial advantage—or, in other words, to help us make money—just like so. It is not the role of the patent to disseminate our dogma, our knowledge, and our wisdom everywhere, unless this dissemination serves the primary objective of making money. **If you are shy about making a profit out of your inventions, patents are not for you.**

As stated (see above "Not on Beauty Alone"), time and again, we explain to inventors that no one will judge them for not having included in the patent information that is not relevant to the protection that the patent claims seek to obtain, or if they have not wowed us with scientific explanations of what has been done in the relevant technological field as a whole. This is simply irrelevant, and whatever is unnecessary for a clear and complete description of the invention and is not required to fully support what is claimed in the patent application has no place there.

Superfluous words written in a patent application are divided into three categories: those that we can do without (but are not harmful); those that encumber the document, thereby make reading and understanding it more difficult and result in the unnecessary prolongation of the examination; and those that are harmful in the long term. Let's devote a few words to the last category.

Words that are harmful in the long term are also divided into three categories: the first category includes all the statements that will haunt us in the future and usually at the moment that is the least convenient for us. Among them, for instance, are the various scientific "explanations," which are intended to give a serious scientific feel to the invention. A known rule is that to gain patent protection, there is no need for the inventor to understand why and how the phenomenon occurs, but it is sufficient that he teaches us how to make it happen. However, the inventor of our example cannot be satisfied with this. He must show understanding, and, therefore, he explains that the perfect crystal that he manages to grow is obtained because the forces applied in his centrifuge cause a spiral mixing, which, together with an initial temperature change, achieves the desired result. And when later a competitor manages to grow the crystal without a centrifuge and/or with other temperature changes, our inventor is left with significant and unnecessary difficulty in showing that the competitor's process is equivalent to the one protected by his patent (if at all possible).

The second category is related to the disparity between the claimed invention and what is said in the patent specification. Sometimes, we know how to carry out the invention only under very specific conditions, and we do not know how to achieve the desired result outside these conditions. In this situation, we can claim only a very narrow invention, which is carried out within a limited range of parameters. Years later, we discover that it is actually possible to also work outside the limited boundaries that we knew, and we file a new patent application. At this time, we might discover that in our initial patent application, we exaggerated in our imagination and argued that the invention can be executed under much broader conditions than what we had claimed and gotten covered by our patent. Even if we did not then know precisely how to achieve this, our statements may have caused a loss of novelty for the broader invention so that it would make it difficult for us—and would even be impossible—to protect it with a new patent application.

The third category is the opposite of the second and relates to the restrictions that the inventor expects, without a preliminary review and only by conjecture, will apply to his invention. Thus, the inventor might say, for instance, that "in order to achieve the result, the coil must be made of stainless steel and have a circular cross-section." Such statements often stem from the gut feeling of the inventor that this is the preferable way to execute, but they do not constitute the true boundaries of the invention. We witness quite a few examples where the competitor gains latitude for himself by (in our example) building a nonmetallic spring that has a square cross-section, which in light of the inventor's original description, cannot constitute part of the invention protected by his patent.

Therefore, when we approach the drafting of a patent application, it is very important to differentiate between the essential words, which should be included in the patent application, and those that we may regret having put to paper.

THE INFORMATION REVOLUTION

As is well known, the process of examining a patent application leading up to the grant of a patent includes, as a critical stage, a review of the prior art, which is carried out by the patent examiner. This review is essential so that the examiner may evaluate the novelty and the inventive step of the patent application. Based on the findings of his review, the examiner can determine whether the invention has been previously published in its entirety (meaning that it lacks novelty) or whether the elements comprising it have been published in ways that make the combination thereof obvious, which takes away the inventive step from the invention.

UNITED STATES PATENT OFFICE.

SAMUEL RAUB, JR., OF WILKES-BARRE, PENNSYLVANIA.

OPENING AND CLOSING SAFETY-VALVES OF STEAM-BOILERS.

Specification of Letters Patent No. 75, dated November 9, 1836.

To all whom it may concern:

Be it known that I, SAMUEL RAUB, Jr., of Wilkes-Barre, in the county of Luzerne and State of Pennsylvania, have invented an Improvement in the Mode of Opening and Closing the Safety-Valves of Steam-Boilers, which improvement renders the valve self-acting whenever the water in the boiler descends below the proper water-line; and I do hereby declare that the following is a full and exact description thereof.

I in general construct my safety valve in the ordinary way, using the common conical valve, and seat, and a lever of second kind with its movable weight, and my improvement in extending the lever beyond the fulcrum on the side opposite to that upon which the weight is hung so that it becomes like a scale beam with unequal arms, and receives a counterweight suspended to it by a suitable rod passing through a stuffing box in the top of the boiler, the counter weight being ordinarily submerged in the water contained in the boiler.

It is a well known principle in mechanical philosophy that a body submersed in water loses as much of its effective weight as is equal to the actual weight which it displaces, if therefore there be suspended to the short arm of the lever above described a weight which in air is an exact counterpoise to the weight, by which the valve is loaded on the long arm, the whole pressure would be taken off the valve, but on submersing such counterpoise in water, the valve would be forced down with a power dependent upon the weight of water thereby displaced. Such is the action of my weight within the boiler. When the boiler is sufficiently full of water the weight may be wholly submersed, and the upward pressure of the water will be added to that of the weight by which the valve is loaded be the same more, or less, but when the water sinks below the weight within the boiler its tendency is then to coöperate with the elasticity of the steam and to open the valve, which tendency increases as the water becomes exhausted, and would continue to increase until the weight was entirely uncovered by water, did not the opening of the valve previously take place.

It is manifest that by this contrivance the two weights may be so adjusted to each other as that the valve may be made to open under any required degree of pressure, and that this opening may take place by the elasticity of the steam alone, without the water being too much exhausted as in the ordinary construction, but that when such exhaustion takes place the gravity of the interior weight operates concurrently with the elasticity of the steam. It is also manifest that the operation of the interior weight as described is not the same with those floats which have been applied in different ways either to let off a portion of steam, or act as a tell-tale when the water subsides, or to set in operation a feeding apparatus, but that the only, and direct effect which I wish to produce is the actual opening of the safety valve, and the blowing off of the steam.

The kind of weight which I use will depend upon the construction of the boiler in which it is employed, as for example in boilers the flues of which are but a few inches under water, the weight must be in such a shape as will be adapted thereto. It will be best made of metal, and it may be either solid, or hollow so that its weight, and bulk may bear any desired proportion to each other.

I have thus described what I deem the best arrangement for carrying the principle upon which I proceed into effect, but other arrangements may be resorted to, by which the same end may be attained. There may, for example, be added on the side of the fulcrum opposite to the ordinary valve, a second valve opening inward, and exposing an equal area to the action of the steam, in this case, the pressure of the steam being equal upon both valves they will remain stationary under the elastic pressure of the steam alone, but when the inside weight is not sustained by the pressure of the water, both valves will be opened, and the steam will escape through the double outlet. With the addition of this reversed valve the outside weight may be much diminished, or it may be entirely omitted, the closing of the valve being effected by the pressure of the steam on the reversed valve.

Fig. 13-1: US Patent No. 75

There are advanced options currently available to the patent examiner, which enable him to search the publicly available knowledge quickly and efficiently, including in his search thousands, hundreds of thousands, and millions of documents. In this manner, the examiner can base his evaluation on a very extensive review, which, until a few decades ago, was only a dream. Our heart goes out, for instance, to the examiner who examined and granted US Patent No. 75 in 1836, for "OPENING AND CLOSING SAFETY VALVES OF STEAM-BOILERS." How could the poor examiner have known whether in France or in a remote province of China, they were not building such improved valves as a matter of course? Thus, it is possible that the patent that he granted, according to his limited knowledge, was, in fact, invalid.

Also, after many years, in 1865, the examiner who examined patent no. 50,000, which refers to "Improvements in the manufacture of candles from paraffine," could not have known whether the process described in the patent was truly unique or whether it was common knowledge somewhere in the world.

As opposed to what certain inventors think, the examination of a patent application is not a battle with the examiner, in which the applicant must attempt to deceive him and distract him from relevant prior publications. On the contrary, the strength of the patent that is issued following the examination process depends, to a large extent, on relevant publications having been taken into account during the examination, so that the claims were eventually allowed, taking into account the prior art. It is better to clarify a prior publication and its significance with the examiner at the time of the examination, rather than dealing with it when an interested party first uses it in adversarial proceedings.

UNITED STATES PATENT OFFICE.

CHARLES HAVARD, OF NEW YORK, N. Y.

IMPROVEMENT IN THE MANUFACTURE OF CANDLES FROM PARAFFINE.

Specification forming part of Letters Patent No. **50,000**, dated September 19, 1865.

To all whom it may concern:

Be it known that I, CHARLES HAVARD, of the city, county, and State of New York, have invented a new and improved mode of converting the petroleum-paraffine into a suitable material for making candles, possessing the necessary qualities of such, as whiteness, hardness, and their being freedom from odor, or the casting of such suitable material into solid blocks for the making of candles, or using such blocks as may be applicable for other purposes; and I do declare that the following is a full and exact description thereof.

The nature of my invention is as follows: I put into a wooden or iron tank one thousand pounds (1,000 lbs.) of water, (except well-water,) mix with it one hundred pounds (100 lbs.) unslaked lime, stir the whole well, and when perfectly mixed I let it rest for about two (2) days until the lime has settled to the bottom of the tank. When so I draw off the clear water (which is now lime-water) and use it as hereinafter specified. I take five hundred pounds (500 lbs.) of the last-mentioned lime-water, put it into a barrel, add to this five pounds (5 lbs.) of sulphuric acid, stir it well several times during the day, and repeat the stirring in the same way during three days, after which time this mixture of lime-water and sulphuric acid is ready for further use.

Process No. 1.—Then I take five hundred pounds (500 lbs.) of petroleum-paraffine, heat it in a tank lined with lead, with wet or dry steam, to about eighty (80) degrees Fahrenheit. When so heated I add under constant stirring (which can best be produced by a revolving shaft in and a lid over the tank) fifty pounds (50 lbs.) of above-named lime and sulphuric-acid water, raise the steam until the whole is boiling, and keep it boiling for fifteen (15) minutes. Then I turn off the steam and let the whole rest until perfectly clear. When so I let this mixture run into square tin pans of the size and capacity of four pounds (4 lbs.) each, (made so that the cake or piece, when hard, will not be thicker than (½) half an inch,) leave it to cool and harden. When hard I take it out of the pans, place each cake or piece into a strong woolen bag of the same size and shape, and place this again into a strong linen bag of same size and shape. When done I place it under hydraulic pressure of about three hundred (300) tons, and press it until no more oil or liquid can be extracted. When thus pressed I take the compound out of the bags and take of it—

Process No. 2—Three hundred pounds, (300 lbs.,) place it into a tank lined with lead and heated by dry steam, turn on the steam until this compound is melted. When so I add under constant stirring four (4) gallons of white naphtha of a gravity of seventy to seventy-five degrees, raise the steam so that this whole mixture will be heated to about eighty (80) degrees Fahrenheit. When so heated I turn off the steam and let the whole rest for about fifteen (15) minutes. Then I let it run into square tin pans, and proceed with the same pressing operation as in the Process No. 1, using, instead of three hundred (300) tons pressure, now eight hundred (800) tons pressure, and press it until no more liquid can be extracted. Then I take it all out of the bags—

Process No. 3—Melt all of it, and repeat all and everything named in Process No. 2. When the pressing is finished I take all out of the bags—

Process No. 4—Place it into a tank lined with lead, and raise the heat of the compound by dry steam to about sixty (60) degrees Fahrenheit, and keep it at that degree of heat. Then I add under constant stirring five per cent (5%) of powdered animal-charcoal, continue the stirring until all is well combined. Then I add four per cent. (4%) of common chalk, whitening, or pipe-clay, resume the stirring until this is again well mixed. Then I add, resuming the stirring, ten per centum (10%) of caustic soda-lye of a gravity of two per cent. (2%) by Baume's hydrometer, let the whole mix well, and boil for five (5) minutes. Then I turn off the steam and let all stand until the animal-charcoal, chalk, whitening, or pipe-clay has settled to the bottom of the tank. When clear, this composition will be of a beautiful white, and can, by addition of suitable colors, be colored to any tint desired.

Process No. 5.—Then I let it run into a clean tank lined with lead and heated by dry steam, add under constant stirring twenty per cent. (20%) of stearic acid, or increase the quantum of stearine as the candle shall be made more hard. I then raise the heat of this mixture to two hundred (200) degrees Fahrenheit. When

Fig. 13-2:
US Patent
No. 50,000

It seems that the world is marching toward coming full circle in this regard, where the multitude of information that the information revolution has made available to us threatens to make it unusable. In a situation in which the number of documents that emerge in a search carried out by the examiner is greater than he can study and analyze thoroughly, there is no value in the availability of the information. The courts in the United States addressed this problem when they ruled that it is improper that a patent applicant bury the invention in a heap of irrelevant documents that turn potentially relevant information into "a needle in a haystack." However, this ruling may only help with problems that are caused deliberately by the applicant, and it does not solve anything when the problem is innate in the system and the multitude of publications is the inevitable result of the attempt of the examiner to do a thorough job.

And what will be the long-term result? Perhaps we will revert to the times when the examiner granted a patent based on knowledge and review that were limited in advance and thereby "the presumption of validity" of a patent will be lowered—that is, our degree of confidence in the true validity of the patent that was granted will be degraded. The true value of the patent will then, in most cases, become known only in adversarial proceedings in which there will be an interested party who will invest the time and money required to rummage through the massive pile of important publications and analyze them. And, in the meantime, what can be done? The patent applicants must undertake a larger share of the work to help examiners reach those same important prior art publications that they want him to examine in depth and avoid inundating the examiner with irrelevant publications.

AN INVENTOR IN THE TIME TUNNEL

The preparation of a patent application that adequately protects an invention is work that sometimes requires considerable effort from the inventor. Even disregarding the financial aspect, there is no option but to invest the time and thought necessary to create a description of the invention that is complete, comprehensive, and accurate. If we do not do so, the degree of protection that our patent application will afford us may be less than we deserve.

It is not always possible to file a patent application that includes all the details that we would have wanted it to include, due to a lack of information and the time that it could take until the data become available or due to an imminent event that requires us to file "what there is," for instance, before a publication that is going to take place in the next few days. However, these must remain within the realm of exceptional constraints and not become a standard procedure. There is no excuse for filing a patent application that is not adequately detailed, just to make life easier for us, inasmuch as any omission in its preparation could come back and haunt us someday.

Too many inventors are tempted to take advantage of easy solutions and to file patent applications with inferior or even questionable value so as not to invest the work required for their preparation. One of the chosen routes for this purpose (though not the only one) is filing a provisional patent application in the United States.[21] Substantively, there is no difference between a provisional application that has not been written properly and an application filed anywhere else, or through any other route, which has not been written properly. The only difference is, perhaps, that inexperienced inventors have often been led to believe that "it is okay" to file as a provisional application something that would have been deemed inadequate if filed by any other route. However, inventors should be aware that a patent application with insufficient description is not adequate anywhere, irrespective of the route that we have chosen to take or the name that we have attached to it, and it cannot form the basis for real priority rights.

But worst of all is the feeling that now, when we have filed our superficial and incomplete application, our time is ours. Now, we may relax, speak with investors, and wait for the expiration of the priority year. The inventor who filed an application whose description is incomplete is, in most cases, not in a hurry to take any actions required to obviate the deficiency. Consequently, we often witness situations in which an inventor who has filed such an application (for instance, a provisional), the priority year of which is about to expire in a few weeks and sometimes even days, has not done anything to improve it and to obtain the information required to bring it to a condition that would justify the effort of filing it as a regular application wherever in the world he needs protection for his activity. Taking this path sometimes leads to the filing of an international patent application that was prepared hastily, based on an initial

[21] See Chapter 6.

application that is lacking. When adding up all the deficiencies, nothing good can result.

The method of filing "initial" patent applications is similar to the method of addiction to hard drugs. First, a soft and inexpensive drug can be purchased, which gives us a good feeling that is not based on reality (I'm not speaking from personal experience, but I was told that this is how it works). After a while, there comes the time (the end of the priority year) when we are drawn into the harder and much more expensive drugs (patent applications abroad), but then we have reached a point where we can no longer stop. Time has gone by, and tomorrow is already here. In comparison, the process of preparing a serious and complete patent application requires considerable clear vision that sees through the initial euphoria and comes down to reality, in which the fixed time ranges and the work facing us are taken into account. In this manner, we can enter the time tunnel that connects the filing of our initial patent application and its filing worldwide, knowing the stations along the way and the cargo that we must accumulate before we reach the last station. In this manner, and only in this manner, will we reach our destination in the best condition possible and will not be forced to embark on the long journey toward obtaining patent protection in the world with a patent application of doubtful value.

CAN IT BE DONE LATER?

From time to time, we find ourselves in a situation in which it is necessary to protect an invention at a very initial stage, when many of its aspects have not yet been elucidated. The need may stem from many reasons, such as the fear that the mere work on the continued development of the invention will reveal it for all to see or the worry that some competitor might precede us slightly in filing a patent application while we expand our knowledge and review all aspects of the invention.

The difficulty in this situation is that while we believe that our work will lead us to a certain result, it might actually lead in a different direction or in more than one direction. At the stage we are in, it cannot be known for certain what the result will be, and therein lies the difficulty in the description of the invention, its boundaries, and its results. Then, the question arises of whether it is correct or advisable to file a patent application that includes a majority of the possibilities (even if they contradict each other) so as "to be covered," which allows us after conducting the actual research to choose from all the possibilities that we listed those that were correct while abandoning those in which we erred. This is a clever idea but an incorrect one.

A patent, it should be understood, is not a reward for the ability to list the greatest number of possibilities. A patent application is conceptually a device that is similar to what is known in mathematical language as a "transform." As a transform enables us to enter manageable data and obtain a meaningful result by processing these data in a manner that gives them the meaning that we are seeking, so a patent application is a device in which, on the one end, we enter knowledge and, from the other end, we extract legal rights. Just as if we enter into the transform random data, which do not represent any physical phenomenon, the result that we will obtain will be meaningless, if we enter into a patent application a jumble of words that do not represent specific knowledge on a patent-worthy invention, we cannot expect that it will reward us with meaningful rights.

A patent application freezes the situation at the moment when it is filed. Therefore, we will gain from it, at the end of the day, only the rights that this device can "squeeze" from the knowledge that was entered there. If we do not enter knowledge there, we are not entitled to any rights. To make lists of all the possibilities is not deemed to be "entering knowledge." On the contrary, the knowledge that we must disclose must enable the patent reader to select the correct answer out of the entire field of possibilities. The "list idea" is similar to a person who mixes wine with water, orange juice, and mouthwash and subsequently seeks to persuade us to drink and to sense only the taste of the wine. The concept of "written description requirement," embraced by the US courts, seeks to deal with such situations, inasmuch as it requires that the fact that the inventor was in possession of the invention at the time of filing his patent application must arise clearly and unambiguously from the patent specification as filed. Failing to fulfill this condition may result in an effective loss of priority rights.

Naturally, this does not mean that this "trick" cannot succeed, sometimes, to some extent, if, for instance, the irrelevant options are removed from the claims. A combination of ambiguous writing and a superficial review by a patent examiner could result in a patent being issued to someone who, when filing the patent application from which priority is claimed, was not the owner of the invention that is claimed there, because the invention had not yet been made at that time and the applicant arrived at it only later. However, it should be remembered that obtaining a patent is only the first step in the life of our intellectual property. Any use of the patent against a third party means that it will be examined carefully by various entities who might find good reasons for its invalidity. These reasons, in the described situation, shall be visible for all to see in the original filing documents of the patent application. There, one may learn of the lack of knowledge of the patent owner at the time of filing the patent application, and then it will not help us that we managed to deceive the patent examiner. In many cases, we will have lost twice: once because we worked hard and did not receive the rights we hoped for, and a second time because a little patience could have led us to filing a patent application based on real knowledge of the invention, which would have given us a valid and strong patent.

CHAPTER 14
The Inventor and His Rights

The inventor of a patentable invention has rights. Depending on the circumstances, these rights vary and may include full rights to the invention and to its fruits or only the right to have his name mentioned as an inventor. However, the inventor also has duties, and this is illustrated by the following examples.

A SPECIAL BRAND OF THEFT

The following conversation between a patent attorney and his prospective client is not rare:

"And one more thing," says the man: *"the inventor is my son."*

"And how old is your son?" he is asked.

"He is fourteen."

"I'm sure he's precocious, but isn't it a bit strange that at his age he made an invention in a field that is very technical?" the man is asked.

"Well, then the inventor is my wife," he concedes. *"Or would it be better to say that my cousin made the invention?"* he asks finally.

At this stage, the situation is already clear. The man sitting across from us is the inventor, but apparently the invention is connected with his work for his employer and, therefore, it will be deemed a "service invention."[22] He obviously arrived at the invention while under employ, and it is within his duties, in respect of which he is paid his salary. Therefore, the invention he made is the property of his employer, and if the man identifies himself as the inventor, he will be forced to transfer it to him. At this moment, an impressively great idea is born in his creative mind: he will transfer the glory of the invention to someone else—a relative or another reliable person—and so he will be able to file a patent application that would not be identifiable as belonging to his employer. A simple and brilliant idea, he believes.

But the world does not work this way. Theft from an employer is theft, even if the employer is not aware that an invention was stolen from him, because he was not at all aware of its existence. In this situation, any respectable patent attorney will stop his client and refuse to cooperate with him in the planning and commission of the theft. He will do so not only to avoid becoming an accomplice in a theft but also to safeguard his client, who is on the verge of becoming a thief. It turns out that there are cases in which the inventor will not understand in advance the gravity of the planned act and will treat it lightly, due to a small difficulty he is experiencing in differentiating between "mine" and "his." The justifications for his act can be numerous, beginning with the (well-known) fact that his employer is a miser and that keeping him from making more money will do his character a lot of good, and ending with the deep self-persuasion that without the private initiative of the inventor, in any case, the employer would never have arrived at the invention. In most cases, an orderly explanation and an exhaustive discussion with an objective person will lead a respectable inventor to acknowledge his mistake.

But what happens when the patent attorney is not aware of the situation and does not have any particular reason to suspect that the person introduced to him as the inventor has no rights to the invention? Then, the patent application will be filed specifying the name of the fictitious inventor, an act that may not be rectifiable. We will not discuss here the implications of a theft from an employer, which are clear and serious even when the object of the theft is not an

---

[22] See Chapter 3.

invention. However, by submitting an inaccurate detail, the applicant inflicted a serious defect on his application. First of all, there is a question of the status of the patent application. According to general principles of law, a patent application on an invention may be filed by the owner of the invention, who has the right to do so because he invented it, or because the ownership of it has been duly transferred to him. If a fictitious inventor files the application in his own name, he does not meet any of the criteria. If the application is filed in the name of the true inventor, after the ownership is transferred to him by assignment from the fictitious inventor, the defect is not cured either, because the alleged inventor did not have the right to assign an invention he doesn't own. This situation may have serious implications for the validity of the patent application and of a patent that is issued thereon, and the level of severity may vary from country to country. Here are examples of who can apply for a patent in four countries:

In the United States of America:
According to the law, the inventor, or a person to whom the inventor has assigned or is under an obligation to assign the invention, may apply for a patent, with certain exceptions.

In the United Kingdom:
Section 7 of the Patents Act (1977):
(1) Any person may make an application for a patent either alone or jointly with another.
(2) A patent for an invention may be granted – (a) primarily to the inventor or joint inventors; (b) in preference to the foregoing, to any person or persons who, by virtue of any enactment or rule of law, or any foreign law or treaty or international convention, or by virtue of an enforceable term of any agreement entered into with the inventor before the making of the invention, was or were at the time of the making of the invention entitled to the whole of the property in it (other than equitable interests) in the United Kingdom; (c) in any event, to the successor or successors in title of any person or persons mentioned in paragraph (a) or (b) above or any person so mentioned and the successor

or successors in title of another person so mentioned; and to no other person.

In India:

6. Persons entitled to apply for patents—

(1) Subject to the provisions contained in section 134, an application for a patent for an invention may be made by any of the following persons, that is to say,— (a) by any person claiming to be the true and first inventor of the invention; (b) by any person being the assignee of the person claiming to be the true and first inventor in respect of the right to make such an application; (c) by the legal representative of any deceased person who immediately before his death was entitled to make such an application.

(2) An application under sub-section (1) may be made by any of the persons referred to therein either alone or jointly with any other person.

In China:

The inventor or the owner of the invention.

As we see from the above examples, the principle that only who actually has rights to the invention can file a patent application is pretty universal. While in different jurisdictions (such as at the EPO), no great importance is attached to the correctness of the inventors' names, the willful failure to name an inventor or naming an incorrect inventor are cause for revocation of the validity of a US patent. In other countries (and, to a certain extent, also in the United States), a bona fide mistake in naming an inventor is rectifiable (just as other mistakes made without malicious intent); however, inaccuracy in specifying details, with fraudulent intent, could have far-reaching implications for the rights being derived from the patent.

The next question that the inventor usually asks is, "But who will know?" In the course of patent litigation, perhaps more than in any other case, technical and factual questions are thoroughly examined, and named inventors should expect to be forced to take the witness stand and to reply to piercing questions on various details of their invention and the manner in which they arrived at them. If our hair contains knots, sooner or later they will reach the comb. A fictitious inventor may find it hard to answer some of the questions that will expose that his contribution to the invention was only lending his name to an improper cause.

WHOM DO I OWE?

The development of inventions is, in most cases, a matter that requires financial resources. Many industries invest to this end from their budgets, and sometimes, private inventors also do so. Opportunities also exist to receive financial subsidies from various entities. There are government foundations and grants, binational foundations, consortiums, and whatnot. All these may enable someone who is not deterred from filling out abstruse forms to receive funds needed for initial stages of development in return for submitting a few periodic reports. This may look to many as not a bad deal. However, strings may be attached to the enticing deal that have to be taken into account.

There are various kinds of liabilities that arise in the wake of our consent to receive "easy money" from a supporting entity. One kind pertains to the restrictions imposed on exploiting the inventions—for instance, restrictions with regard to the ability of the supported entity to trade in the technology itself and to transfer it to another country. It is clear that the development of a technology that is wholly intended for overseas, under such restrictions, could prove to be a futile exercise.

Another kind of restriction, which occurs in consortium research, is the duty to allow free access to our technology to all members of the consortium free of charge. When all of our significant competitors are members of this type of consortium, we must take into account that real exclusivity will not accrue to us from this exercise. This being the case, the support from which we benefited in the immediate term may, in the long term, constitute a major obstacle to our business development.

Certain agencies, which grant enticing research grants, regularly enter into research contracts with entities at home or abroad. The contracts that the research entity is required to sign are often thick, and I have heard people say that the effort required to understand the content and the meaning of these contracts could be greater than that required to conduct the research itself; so, contracts are sometimes signed without full review on the assumption (usually wrong) that "it will be all right." This is a well-known behavior among those who open a bank account and waive reading the documents in advance on the assumption that they must be "okay" because of the respectability of the entity that issued them. However, the term "okay," in this context, has varying meanings. For instance, it really is okay as far as a government entity that gave us generous financial support is concerned to require that it and all the state entities be able to exploit the research results free of charge. It is also perfectly okay to require that the entire production be carried out in the same country, even if the developing entity really conducts its business in another country.

Receiving "free" financial support is certainly something that cannot be given up easily. However, as human beings, we tend to forget that there may be crippling conditions attached to the easy money, and sometimes, we are amazed to discover that after the research was successful and yielded meaningful business results, we are not free to do with it as we wish. But, at this stage, it is too late. After we have fallen into the golden trap, there is no way out of it. Therefore, as in many other cases, think before you act: before reaching out for the sparkling bundle of dollars (or euros, doubloons, etc.), we must ascertain what payment we will have to make for it one day. If the required payment is unbearable, we must gather up the courage and let it go.

THE ILLUSION FACTORY

Who has not dreamt of becoming a millionaire? And who does not know nowadays that the shortcut to the first millions passes through his ability to innovate? The numerous success stories sometimes blind even the eyes of the most cautious people. It should be added to this that the press, which enjoys igniting our imagination with the amazing success stories that happen by chance from time to time, does not fulfill its role of balancing the picture by bringing to us the hundreds of stories of the failures that occur for each success.

Just as someone who sells us a lottery ticket is not quick to mention the miniscule prospect of winning next to the alluring prize, wherever a dream can be sold, we will find those who promote it, and the innocent public time and again closes its eyes to the dangers. Who would not invest a hundred dollars that may bring him fifty million within days? And what does it matter that the prospect of winning these millions is one in trillions of trillions against us? Fifty million is still a lot of money. What is it that you are not getting here?

This method also works on inventors. It works to such an extent that the USPTO periodically issues warnings such as the following:

> *Every year thousands of Independent Inventors, like yourself, are targeted by unscrupulous invention promotion, marketing and licensing firms. These firms take advantage of an inventor's enthusiasm for their product. They not only solicit inventors with exaggerated promises to obtain valuable patents but they make false claims about the potential market success of those inventions. These firms provide you with basic market research at a large fee and ultimately obtaining an overly narrow or useless patent that is worthless in the marketplace. Remember, if it sounds too good to be true, it probably is.*

All you have to do to see them is to Google "USPTO warning fraud." The entities that earn a living from fraud in this area are companies known as "invention promotion companies," whose real aim is to promote only their own pockets. These companies offer services to inventors to promote the sale of their inventions to the industry. These services are sometimes offered "for free," at least in the initial stages. However, after an "initial review" (which has been conducted, as stated, for free), the company's representative discovers that your invention is amazing and has excellent prospects of being sold to a major and rich industry. At this stage, the free chapter of the story is over, and the further services are rendered for payment, which may reach thousands and even tens of thousands of dollars, before you realize that the person standing in front of you is nothing but a swindler who will not garner any benefit for you.

In dealing with such swindlers (which are extremely common, as stated), it is difficult to distinguish them from respectable companies that engage in trading technology and that really do their utmost to promote the sale of your invention. These companies, unlike the fraudulent companies, have some ability (each one according to its own level). However, the swindlers quickly learn the work practices of the legitimate companies, making it difficult to identify them immediately.

So, despite this, how will we know? Even if we will not know for certain, we can at least know when and with whom we should be cautious. First, we should beware of anyone who asks for prepayment from the inventor to handle the commercialization of his invention. Serious companies usually expect to make a profit directly or indirectly from the deal they will broker, not from the inventor, although it is quite possible that a respectable company will ask for some (modest) amount from an inventor as participation in its expenses, particularly if it is unsure of the commercialization prospects of the invention.

Second, you should not do business with a company whose identity and the identity of the people working for it are not clear. Such can be found on many websites, as well as in advertisements in various newspapers. Serious companies introduce themselves outright and identify their principals and employees. Third, before you entrust this type of company with your invention, you should consult with a patent attorney to know whether it is at all patentable. The swindler who seeks to lighten your wallet will be all too willing to shower compliments on your invention, your wisdom, and your brilliance; in any case, he knows that he will have the last laugh. A preliminary professional review can save you a lot of anguish by clarifying for you in advance the real value (or lack of value) of your invention.

And above all, as hard as it is to acknowledge, we must remember that the chances of an invention becoming the hen that lays golden eggs are, statistically, small. And if after having considered all this, you still believe that you have an important and valuable invention, definitely yes: go for it!

Part III: The Patent and We

"If your facts are wrong but your logic is perfect, then your conclusions are inevitably false. Therefore, by making mistakes in your logic, you have at least a random chance of coming to a correct conclusion."

[*Arthur Bloch* – Murphy's Law Complete, *p. 229*]

This part deals with our reactions as patent consumers, which are typically dictated by a lack of knowledge, lack of understanding, or lack of will to understand, or by a mixture of two or more of these.

CHAPTER 15
All the Mistakes (and One for the Road)

It is amazing to discover how we sometimes err in the most important things because we act according to an incorrect gut feeling or because of false and misleading information that we heard by chance. But the greatest danger comes from clueless people who believe that they are acting with great wisdom in an area in which they have no training, only because they have excessive and unfounded self-confidence. These situations are fertile ground for choosing wrong paths that lead to fatal mistakes. Below, we will look at a few typical examples.

THE HIGH-TECH MACHO

The macho phenomenon is not unknown in high-tech, especially with entrepreneurs who have had some degree of success in their previous endeavors. Our macho is a person who is full of faith in his superior intelligence, particularly in areas in which he has no clue or experience. His strength stems from his ability to glean fragments of rumors and disjoined statements and to transform them into a plan of action. He does not spare his words and is ready to share his theory with everyone. Thus, for instance, he "does not believe in patents," and he has "never heard of anyone profiting from patents." Just as a sweaty Rambo, who destroys monstrous tanks with a homemade bazooka, so the macho knows well how to fight the giant international companies that are expected to block his path with their own patents: He will "talk business with them," inasmuch as in the business world (so he explains to us), no importance is attached to property rights but only to understandings between the seasoned businesspeople (he being one of them, of course). And if a patent blocks his path, then just as Rambo removes obstacles by pressing the trigger without hesitation, he "will pay a few bucks and take a license on the patent." Because he can overcome any obstacle, it does not occur to him at all that a competitor may even exist who will not want his "few bucks" but, instead, will want to use patents to block his activity. Failure is not part of his vocabulary, as befitting a cartoon hero of computer games.

Our macho is, nevertheless, willing to lower himself to a certain extent and to file several patent applications (while overcoming, with undisguised effort, his natural recoiling from the subject) and for one good reason: there are potential investors (unsuspecting simpletons, as far as he is concerned) who believe in the value of the patent. Therefore, our hero is willing to prepare several patent applications to satisfy the demands of the investor (which are childish, in his opinion). However, after fulfilling his obligation by filing them, he does not devote adequate effort to exploit the potential of his patent applications, which, in his view, constitute only a nuisance.

An attempt to trace the origin of the hi-tech macho, who appeared on the landscape with no clear connective Darwinian link, reveals that, in most cases, he previously worked in a system and in a position in which there is no direct correlation between the business results actually achieved and the advancement and remuneration. In his previous position, our macho "learned" that, to him, there is no system of reward and punishment. Just as with the same cinematic hero, who cannot be stopped by the bullets that whistle around him, so our hero witnessed the failures and stupidity occurring by his hand and under his direction and always found a way to argue that the failure was, in fact, a success.

True hi-tech people are not of the macho variety. On the contrary, they are clever, calculated, and highly intelligent people. The level of their self-criticism is high, so they plan their steps ahead of time and correct their mistakes while in motion. A true high-tech person knows his strength in his field of expertise and his weaknesses in other fields. Therefore, he knows how to exploit the special knowledge of others in specialized areas and does not purport to understand them better than they do. Our macho, on the other hand, came to high-tech by mistake. He has no place there, inasmuch as his strength rather lies in his arrogance and in his lack of understanding. A true hi-tech person who finds himself in a system managed by this type of macho would do well to identify him promptly and quickly distance himself from him.

SONG OF THE SIRENS

On the path to protecting our R&D results, one concern haunts us and does not relent: Is it possible that, while we were working, some publication preceded us by a patent, by an article or otherwise, making the protection of our work difficult or even impossible? This concern is like the sword of Damocles hanging by a thread over our necks, and the potential publication is our greatest demon, which could foil our plans with a stroke of the pen. But, for the most part, we do not recognize ourselves in that demon and do not realize that the hand wielding the pen is none other than our own.

The protection of industrial R&D is characterized, generally, by its continuity. When the initial idea develops into preliminary results that allow, and even require, patent protection, most of the practical questions have not yet been examined. At this initial stage, we do now know what only practical experience will teach us, and the knowledge in our possession is only sufficient for preparing what is usually referred to as a "basic patent application." Here usually lies the first root of the problem: the confusion between the solid information, on which a patent application can be based, and our dreams of what the future has in store for us. Working with feet on the ground and realizing the implications of the limited data in our possession should restrain us from laying out all our dreams in such a basic patent application. This patent application will be published, in most cases, after a year and a half, and all our future development plans and dreams will be published along with it.

Some of the problems can perhaps be rectified, at least to an extent, if our R&D program proceeds well and if we protect its results prior to publication of the patent application. However, one problem that we created cannot be rectified: our patent application contains too much information on our future plans (a bonanza for our competitors), and it might constitute damaging "prior art" against our own future patent applications. When our development work is completed and a more advanced patent application is filed, we may discover that we have, by our own hands, closed the door to obtaining broad protection for the applicative results of our work. On the other hand, since when we laid out our plans, and we did not have real results, we cannot expect that the first, basic patent application will be able to provide us strong protection for important commercial aspects for which we had no real basis in our original filing. The better our vision of the future, ironically, the worse we may have harmed ourselves.

Exercising the necessary restraint in choosing what we say in the situation described above is not a simple task and requires considerable effort and a detailed analysis of the meaning of every statement. It is very easy to be tempted to exaggerate with descriptions full of imagination and to include our entire vision in our initial patent application. Greek mythology tells of the need to tie the sailors to the mast so that they will not be tempted by the song of the sirens that will lead them to their demise. When we embark on a protection plan for our R&D, we had better "tie ourselves to the mast" and not allow ourselves to be carried away and to exaggerate in our descriptions, because otherwise, we may not arrive at the place of our desired haven.

Fig. 15-1: Odysseus and the Sirens – A 5th-century drawing.

THE PATH OF THE JUST [MESILAT YESHARIM]

Some patent applicants decide not to invest in reviewing what is known as the "state of art," and instead, they immediately start drafting a patent application without any real preliminary review. These applicants believe that a preliminary review, even if precursory, does not justify its cost. Others believe in a state of "blessed ignorance" that will, so they hope, immunize them from the effects of the prior art because not being aware of novelty-destroying publications that may be out there allows them to hope that a patent examiner will also not learn about them and, thus, will more easily grant them a patent. This human tendency has already been cautioned against by my ancestor, Rabbi Moshe Chaim Luzzatto (the Ramhal), in *Mesilat Yesharim* (The Path of the Just), while addressing "The Trait of Watchfulness":

> *One who walks this world without considering whether his way of life is good or bad is like a blind man walking along the seashore, who is in very great danger and whose chances of being lost are far greater than those of his being saved. For there is no difference between natural blindness and self-inflicted blindness, the shutting of one's eyes as an act of will and desire.*

It is true that any preliminary review, thorough as it may be, will not ensure that all the prior art will come to our attention and that hiding somewhere, perhaps even within information that has already passed in front of our eyes, there may be a "fatal" publication, which would make our invention not new and not patentable. However, this limitation does not have to lead us to the opposite extreme—that is, to the same self-inflicted blindness against which the Ramhal cautions. A serious review, even if incomplete, provides us with valuable knowledge that allows us a better feel for our invention and permits us to position it in its proper place in its field. A preliminary patent search, even if limited and such that does not purport to reveal all the relevant publications, is valuable for enriching the professional knowledge of both the inventor and those who help him to attain patent protection. In short, the result of a search is, usually, a better patent application.

And of all the inventors, those who especially go astray are the ones who believe that their expertise in the field is so great that if ***they*** have not heard of such an invention, no other search or check is worth pursuing. However, the pace of the technological progress is so fast nowadays that, with perhaps few exceptions, no single person can be up to date with the entire field in which he works. Moreover, the details relevant to the questions surrounding an invention that we want to protect with a patent greatly exceed the general question of "whether such an invention exists." What we need to examine are detailed questions, which are sometimes somewhat boring, whose meaning can only be properly evaluated if the inventors devote sufficient effort to understanding what has been done by others. Disrespecting lesser experts is a mistake that may cost an inventor dearly.

In the patent system, every bit of prior publication can easily lower us from the heights of the professional Olympus to a low point where our invention has no patentable part left. There are few systems in which the passage of time can lead to such extreme changes as in the patent system and, therefore, it is advisable to invest a little in acquiring a reasonable measure of humility and read other people's stuff as well before it is too late.

ASLEEP AT THE SWITCH

There are those who believe that there is no rush to protect an invention with a patent when it is possible to keep it secret within the company and to postpone dealing with patent protection to another time. However, a failure to promptly seek patent protection means, in certain cases, waiving the rights to an invention.

In most countries of the world, the rights to an invention are established on a first-to-file basis. Someone who makes an invention and hides it will not have acquired any proprietary rights for himself. On the contrary, the patent system is designed to encourage the disclosure of the invention, and the patent protection, which confers exclusivity for 20 years to the patent holders, is granted with the aim of enabling this disclosure. By the same logic, someone who does not disclose his invention "merits punishment," and his punishment is that if someone files a patent application before him, even if he arrived at the invention long after him, that someone will be granted rights thereon.

It is not uncommon for a company to discover that an invention that it has developed and for which it did not file a patent application suddenly belongs to a competitor, who filed an application and even obtained a patent for the invention. Then, all the explanations and the excuses for the omission will be of no avail, inasmuch as the patent is a fait accompli. This situation emerges often in relation to process inventions. Certain managers believe that there is no point in filing a patent application for an innovative process that is implemented within the company, because they heard somewhere that "it is difficult to protect a process." They may discover that it is indeed difficult, but worthwhile, for a competitor to use his patent to make their lives difficult.

Filing a patent application of this kind should be done as part of a policy of risk management. Not every patent is sought to attack the competitors, and many patents are used for the sake of preserving freedom of operation and for preventing a risk of blockage from a competitor. Scholarly analyses that address a certain invention and take into account the ability to keep the know-how in confidence and the costs that are consequently saved are irrelevant to real life, inasmuch as they do not take into account the element of risk of losing the rights to practice the invention in important jurisdictions.

DEPOSITING IN A BLACK HOLE

In an attempt to easily bypass the necessity to file a patent application within a reasonable time, a new-old affliction has come to the neighborhood, and it has felled casualties among naïve people. This affliction is called by various names, such as "depositing an invention," "a sealed envelope," "placing into a vault," and other such creative names. Naïve people are convinced that it is enough to deposit an abstract of their invention into the vault of a certain person, who surely presents a respectable and confidence-inspiring façade, for their rights to be protected. And the price? Affordable—usually a few tens of dollars.

These obsessive depositors, it should be noted, are often people who believe (not always justifiably) that their invention is worth hundreds of millions of dollars at least and that there is none more important. However, the savings in choosing the deposit "option" captivate them. It would have been interesting to explore whether those same people would have hastened to establish their rights, for instance, for an apartment that they purchased at a cost of "only" several hundred thousand dollars by depositing an appropriate letter in the same vault—something that would have spared them the effort and the expense entailed in registering their ownership at the relevant authority.

It is also interesting to see how these good and naïve people, before they deposit their important property with "the owner of the vault," do not devote a minute to thought. Had they done this, they perhaps would have wondered why the entire world has been making, at least in the last hundred and fifty years, monumental efforts to develop complex international systems, enact laws, establish costly entities, and formulate complex international conventions. If this is so simple, why complicate it? It is enough to deposit an envelope containing the magic words with a person who appears sufficiently respectable so that the date of the deposit will be proven beyond any doubt, and we can forget all the annoying problems surrounding the patent systems.

Nevertheless, the deposit practice is not entirely detached from the conceptual world of patents. It stems from the former very distinct law of the United States, whereby the ownership of an invention was established by determining the date of invention—the so-called "first to invent" system. The law has (mercifully) been changed so that the United States now recognizes the right to an invention on the basis of a "first to file" system like everybody else. In the past, when it had to be determined who invented first, importance was given to any evidence of the date of the invention and any stage of the inventive process. This is no longer the case, however.[23]

For completeness' sake, we should note that some countries do grant a limited right to a business entity that, at the time that a patent application was filed by a third party, was making actual preparations for exploiting the invention or was already exploiting it. The rights, however, would not go beyond the status of the development at the time of filing and would not extend to other countries. I would not envy anybody who had to rely on such provisions.

Therefore, an inventor who plans to deposit/forfeit his invention with some depository institution would do well to assess his actions and their implications thoroughly before doing so. Although the price may be cheap on the date of the deposit, it might be exceedingly onerous down the road.

DO NOT JUMP TO CONCLUSIONS

There is much blessing in the search engines that are accessible to everyone on the Internet, such as the patent database of the EPO and of the USPTO, as well as, of course, sources such as Google Patents. These databases allow an inventor to consult with a patent attorney after having reviewed at least some relevant publications. Because the inventor had the opportunity to ponder various questions arising from the prior art that was found in his search, the discussion begins from a much better starting point than in the past, when this option was not so freely available.

However, one danger lies in the ease with which prior publications can be accessed today and in that many inventors also draw firm conclusions from the patents that were found, and these conclusions are, in many cases, wrong. Nevertheless, inventors have been known to make important decisions on the direction of the development and even regarding the business progress, based on mistaken conclusions that they reached by improperly reading prior

[23] Patents granted under the old law, however, may still be the subject of "interference proceedings" in which a determination of who was the first to invent would still be required.

patents.

This is the place to mention that with patents, not all that glitters is gold, and not every wall is insurmountable. For instance, we remember well the dispirited inventor who was just about to halt the development and abandon his project because he found a patent that mentioned his intended result. This inventor did not understand that vague statements regarding a desired result are insufficient to negate the novelty of an actual solution to the problem, if the person who expresses a wish to find the solution does not at all know how to solve the problem in a practical manner and does not provide any hint regarding how to go about it. Such statements cannot prejudice the right of someone who found a practical solution to the problem and reduced it to practice. However, patent specifications, by their very nature, are full of these kinds of vague statements, and a person who reads them with simplistic eyes could see in them an obstacle to obtaining a patent on a substantive development, which does not exist in reality.

Another problem, which is also common, is the problem of "the pseudo obstacle." Every now and then, we encounter patents that, *prima facie*, claim broad inventions together with small improvements. While the small improvement does not bother us, inasmuch as the improvement that we are attempting to develop is entirely different, the fact that the patent also claims (or to be precise, it seems as though it claims) the underlying invention appears to be blocking our path. Sometimes a fata morgana is involved and not a genuine claim. Let us take, for instance, a patent on an electric car window, which claims an improvement in its mechanical operation. This kind of patent claim may certainly begin with the words "electric car window, including glass . . ." and continue with a complicated and convoluted description of the cog-wheel system and the electrical connections and all this to arrive at accurately claiming a cotter pin found deep inside the mechanism. The unprofessional reader may be given the impression that this patent blocks the manufacture of electric car windows in general. However, does this prevent any person from manufacturing and marketing an electric window that is not equipped with the novel cotter pin? Naturally, the answer is no. A proper reading of the patent claims requires us to, first of all, separate the known from the new and to thereby isolate the invention on which the patent grants the monopoly. All that was known prior to filing the patent application cannot be part of the monopoly granted by the patent, and adding a cotter pin (in our example), even if it achieves advantages that justify granting a patent, cannot make the entire window, without the pin, part of the invention protected by the patent.

Therefore, while it is okay to take advantage of the easy accessibility to information to gather it, to study it, and to ask ourselves questions, the reader should not jump to conclusions based on an ordinary reading of these documents. Patents have to be read as a whole document, and arriving at conclusions on the basis of a sentence or a paragraph can be disastrous. Patents are also not free of typos, and to correct these frequent typos, a Certificate of Correction can be requested. However, the correction is not performed in the document itself but in a separate one, so the dilettante reader may not be aware that some significant mistake has been corrected and could base his strategy and steps on inaccurate assumptions. This brings to mind P. G. Wodehouse's poem on the typo, the first stanza of which is reported below[24]:

As o'er my latest book I pored,
Enjoying it immensely
I suddenly exclaimed 'Good Lord!'
And gripped the volume tensely.
'Golly!' I cried. I writhed in pain. 'They've done it on me once again!'
And furrows creased my brow.
I'd written (which I thought quite good)
'Ruth, ripening into womanhood,
Was now a girl who knocked men flat
And frequently got whistled at,'
And some vile, careless, casual gook
Had spoiled the best thing in the book

[24] The complete poem, which is well worth reading, can be found on the Web, for instance, at http://allpoetry.com/Printer's-Error-.

By printing 'not' (yes 'not', great Scott!)
When I had written 'now'.

ONLY [NOT] HERE

Many pitfalls lie in wait for those who do not understand the territorial nature of the exclusivity granted by the patent. The logic behind beginning the patent protection process in our own country, and not in a foreign country, is based on cost considerations and on convenience and flexibility down the road and sometimes also on a necessity to abide by the law and not to file a patent application abroad that could be important to the security of the state,[25] before having afforded the competent entities the opportunity to examine it in accordance with the law. However, time and again, it has become clear to us that not everyone is aware of the simple rules behind this part of the patent system. The following is a pertinent example.

A certain company manufactures all its products in Israel and exports them to Europe and to the Far East. It filed the patent applications on its inventions in the United States.

"Why in the United States?" we ask in wonder.

"Because this is the most important market in the world," comes the answer.

"But you are not selling in the United States at the moment, so why not ask for patents in Europe and in the Far East?"

"Because," they explain to us, with a smile of forgiveness toward our naiveté upon their lips, *"we hope to sell in the United States, and everyone knows that the United States is the most important market."*

"And what about Israel?" we question. *"You manufacture in Israel."*

"Israel is not important," comes the decisive answer. *"Israel is not a market for our products; everyone knows this."*

This situation reminds me of the story of the chief in black Africa

---

[25] Many countries have severe provisions relating to the first filing of a patent application by a citizen of that country (e.g., the United Kingdom) and even if not by a citizen, limitations regarding inventions made in that country (e.g., the United States of America). Permission to first file abroad—often termed a "foreign filing license"—can usually be obtained by following the procedure prescribed by the relevant country.

who purchases a luxury car by personal import. He attaches no importance to the slight problem that he has no gasoline nor roads, or that he has never left the forest surrounding his village. He was assured that the car he bought was strong and powerful and, therefore, a good purchase.

Perhaps we should begin by saying that a business that manufactures in a given country, or even only engages in R&D there, and does not apply for patent protection for its inventions in that country may be courting trouble. By doing so, it is extending an open invitation to potential infringers in that country to freely manufacture there all the products of the originator. Moreover, if the company has a serious competitor, it will not be long before the day when this competitor (who, unlike the manager of our example, does understand what a patent is) will institute a policy of patent protection in the country the originator is neglecting, covering every little thing that it can imagine may be associated with future products or related to those with which it competes. Experience teaches that it is only a matter of time until a "bull's-eye" is hit and one of its patents becomes a serious obstacle to the activity of the originator.

Moreover, a patent is a territorial right; in other words, we need it where we do business. A US patent, as nice as it is, will not help us at all in the war with a competitor that copies our products in Europe. Therefore, the patent plan must always be in tune with the marketing plan of the product. These plans may differ from product to product; therefore, a basic law is "beware of formulaic decisions." If someone tells you that it is always advisable to adopt a certain strategy for each product and in each case, he obviously does not know what he is talking about.

Finally, there are certainly cases for which it is advisable to first file patent applications in a country other than our country of origin. However, this can be done in close proximity to, or concurrently with, filing a basic patent application in your country. Because the effort involved in filing a domestic patent application, if an application for filing in another country has already been prepared, is minimal, there is no justification or logic to avoiding it. To someone who asks not to file patent applications in his own country because he is a man of the world and "his country is too small for him," and only filing patent applications in a foreign country will grant him the self-importance that he believes he deserves, to him, we would say only that he certainly deserves the bitter consequences expected from his decision.

THE WRONG MAN FOR THE JOB

"Don't express your ideas too clearly. Most people think little of what they understand and venerate what they do not."
(***Baltasar Gracian***)

"In a hierarchical organization, each employee strives to reach his/her level of maximum incompetence."
(***Laurence J. Peter***)

Different organizations, such as research institutes, where many good inventions are made, sooner or later come to the recognition that their important knowledge should be managed. But how do they choose who is the person to manage it? Why, this is business, so obviously a business manager is required. But inventions involve science and technology; so, surely, it is necessary for the person to also be a scientist. However, if the person understands business and science but is not knowledgeable enough to secure proper patent coverage, all his other qualifications will be of no use to him. This is a dilemma.

This dilemma has a relatively simple solution, and many institutes have found it, sometimes after having been once bitten and still not shy. You must come to the recognition that a person who understands patents at the required level will not, in most cases, be a business person. It should also be acknowledged that no matter how qualified the scientist is, he cannot be an expert in every field. What remains, this being the case, is to place in this sensitive position a good manager. It should be kept in mind that, in many institutes, the knowledge conveyed to the manager is a highly important asset. With inventions, the distance between commercial success and utter failure could be extremely short.

From the aspect of patent protection, a good manager seeking to manage highly valuable knowledge must have certain qualities. First, he must relinquish the attitude of the common manager as an omniscient and omnipotent person. The wrong kind of manager does not ask direct questions, which could expose his lack of familiarity with the subject. Instead, he mutters a series of fuzzy statements with the aim of receiving responses from his listeners, from which he can learn whether what he thinks he understands is at all relevant. If his perplexed listeners choose not to correct him, his erroneous assumption becomes a truth cast in stone. If his interlocutor dares to correct him in an overly direct manner, for the removal of doubt with regard to the true state of affairs, his relationship with the manager may no longer be the same, and his opinion will not be asked again.

A good manager is not afraid to admit to a lack of knowledge in fields with which he is not supposed to be familiar. He knows how to ask a professional's advice and to act upon it. Eventually, he will educate himself through experience and will come to understand and to ask rational, focused questions. And along the way, he will not make fatal mistakes.

Mistakes made by bad managers, who are concerned, above all, with the need to hide their ignorance and lack of understanding of critical issues, are not generally rectifiable. This should be said in a loud and clear voice, inasmuch as irreparable damage is often done, and those who appointed the manager who messed things up are unable to discover the damage in real time. A long time may pass until the cumulative damage is discovered and its extent appreciated. In patents, the processes are long, and many years may pass until it becomes clear to whoever has appointed the ineffectual manager what magnitude of disaster he has unnecessarily brought down upon his organization. But precisely for this reason, before entrusting your intellectual assets with another person, you owe to yourself a thorough and ongoing examination of the qualifications and the conduct of that person. But how should this be done? Of course, there is no miracle formula; however, several signs should cause concern and require a more in-depth examination. Here are some:

- If it turns out that the decision making on patent questions is based on fixed parameters, there is cause for concern. Banality in patents is a bad quality.

- If ways that are not known to average civilized people have been miraculously found to save on expenses that were, until that time, deemed to be unavoidable, do not hasten to rejoice. In patents, there are no free meals.

- If the manager does not require qualified legal advice concerning patent matters and is capable of making decisions without professional assistance, get an objective evaluation from an outsider.

- Operating a system whereby patents are a major component requires vast and up-to-date professional knowledge. The successful manager draws this knowledge from professionals. The others—and there are still quite a few like those abroad—it is best to identify and neutralize in the early stages before their arrogance places the intellectual assets of their employers in a hopeless situation.

HOW COME I'M INFRINGING IF I HAVE A PATENT?

One of the common mistakes we hear about is the belief that obtaining a patent can "immunize" us against infringing the patents of another. Every now and then, we meet managers who believe that they may manufacture a product, regardless of the existence of third-party patent rights, because they have obtained a patent "on it" ("it" often being an undefined entity that has "something to do" with our product). This is the place to clarify: although we have managed to obtain a patent that relates to some part of a product, this does not derogate, and cannot derogate, from the earlier rights of others.

This situation can be clarified by a simple example. Let us assume that a company has developed an electric shaving machine with an innovative motor, which makes it possible to use a razor with two parallel blades for a much smoother shave than that achieved currently by way of manual shaving. The company files a patent application on its shaving machine and obtains a patent thereon. The significance of obtaining the patent is that from that moment, this company has the exclusive right to manufacture and to market the shaving machine. However, if the double blade is protected by a patent of another company, it will not be possible to manufacture and market the complete machine, because the manufacture and marketing of the double blade would constitute an infringement of a patent owned by this other company. To be able to sell the shaving machine, it will be necessary to purchase the double blade from the holder of the patent protecting it or to reach a license arrangement or another commercial arrangement with it.

In other words, even if the patent granted on the shaving machine as a whole also includes, among the machine parts claimed in the patent, a double-edged blade, this does not constitute an authorization to this patent holder to manufacture and to sell the complete machine and to include in it a blade that infringes somebody else's patent.

When examining a patent application, the patent authorities do not evaluate questions of patent infringement. These authorities (through the patent examiner) only evaluate the questions pertaining to the patentability of the invention that is the object of the application (the shaving machine, in our example), and they are not concerned with commercial questions pertaining to the relations between various patent holders who have a connection to the relevant product. The role of the patent authority,[26] which examines the application, is only to evaluate whether the invention claimed in the patent application meets the legal requirements in terms of novelty, inventive step, and the other eligibility requirements for a patent. The evaluation work of the rights of others and their importance to the proposed product remains in the hands of the manufacturer, and it is

[26] **Reminder:** The generic term "patent authority" is used here to refer to the central patent office of a country, not to be confused with a patent law firm, which is also sometimes referred to as a "patent office."

his sole responsibility.

Any manufacturer would, therefore, do well if, before commencing preparations for production, it will not only ascertain what rights its company has acquired but also what are the rights of others and will not treat its success in obtaining a patent for itself as an authorization to do with the product as it wishes, regardless of relevant third-party patent rights.

CHAPTER 16
How to Act When . . .

When we file a patent application, we may encounter various situations to which we will have to respond. The instinctive response is not always the correct one. This chapter may help us decide how to act when . . .

OUR PATENT APPLICATION IS ABOUT TO BE PUBLISHED

When coming to file a patent application, we must take into account the date when its contents will become public. Patent applications are published in most countries 18 months after the filing of the initial application. On this date, our patent application is published in its entirety. At the time of its publication, our patent application becomes part of the general knowledge and constitutes a "prior publication" (i.e., part of the "prior art") to any subsequently filed patent application.

There are two facets to the publication of the patent application: In some countries, a provisional protection is granted from the day of the publication of the application. Furthermore, the publication of our application prevents the grant of patents to similar inventions to competitors in countries in which we have no protection. Another positive result, which is immeasurable, is that a competitor who learns of the existence of our patent application early enough may refrain from investing money in developments that may infringe our future patent; thus, we will achieve a competitive advantage even before the patent is granted. If, on the other hand, he is made aware of our patent application only after having invested a lot of money in developing a potentially infringing product, he may have no choice but to stay the course and may have to fight our patent in an effort to maintain his own freedom of operation.

Of course, the disclosure of the contents of the patent application at a relatively early stage may be problematic, but very few valuable inventions are not filed in important countries, such as the United States, European countries, China, and Japan, or as international applications, where publication after 18 months is the standard.

The publication of patent applications has another important role: to allow newcomers to evaluate in the most updated manner the state of knowledge in the field and to enable them to invest their effort and their money in productive directions and to avoid as much as possible situations that necessitate conflict with third-party patent rights.

When coming to plan improvements and the related broadening of the protection for our invention, we must take into consideration the timing of the publication of our patent application. And when filing parallel patent applications in other countries, we must not forget that the hourglass is working against us and that we must prepare in a timely manner to perform all the required activities.

WE DISCOVERED A RELEVANT PRIOR PUBLICATION

When coming to judge the strength of a patent, we initially examine the novelty and the inventive step of the invention it covers. Any serious patent authority reviews these aspects of the invention, using publications that are placed before the examiner. In some countries—for instance, in the United States—the law requires the patent applicant to bring to the attention of the examiner any publication of which he is aware and that may be pertinent to the question of the novelty and inventive step of the pending claims. However, in other important countries, there is no similar requirement, and the examiners rely only on publications that were found independently by them.

It, therefore, happens that we may have discovered a prior publication that we fear could harm our prospects of obtaining a European, Japanese, or other patent, but the examiners in those countries did not find it in their searches. Now, the question arises regarding whether we should bring this prior publication to the attention of the examiners, even where we have no legal obligation to do so, and thereby risk reducing the scope of protection of the future patent, perhaps even making it hard for us to get the patent. Although there may be cases in which we will decide that it is inappropriate to bring this publication to the attention of an examiner, for pertinent reasons, the answer will usually be that it is advisable that the examiner also examine our patent application in light of this publication. There will be cases, however, in which we will decide that the advantage of cleaning the record by having the examiner include a certain reference in his examination is not worth the complication that may ensue from disclosing it where we were under no obligation to do so.

There are two basic scenarios: in the first one, the publication does not harm our invention—at least in our opinion—but the reasons for this are not self-evident, and they require a detailed and extended explanation. In the second case, the publication clearly negates the novelty or the inventive step of at least some of the claims of our patent application.

In the first situation, it would be a mistake not to take advantage of the option available to us to have our patent application examined in light of this publication. An examination that took the prior publication into account would highly strengthen the patent that will be issued and would, in effect, close the door to various uses that could be made of it by anybody seeking to invalidate our patent.[27] By

---

[27] Examination proceedings are *ex parte*—that is, they are a discourse between the applicant and the examiner, with no external intervention. In contrast, opposition, some reexamination procedures, and court litigation are *inter partes* procedures in which one or more interested parties also take part, who are able to provide arguments and information purporting to invalidate the patent.

contrast, if this publication is discovered when our patent is involved in proceedings that may lead to its invalidation, our position would be much more difficult than in the course of the examination.

In the second situation, by contrast, we could obtain a patent of a scope that is inconsistent with the prior art. This patent would be vulnerable and ineffective and would be easy for our competitors to fight it or simply to ignore it. It is preferable for us, generally, to obtain a more limited patent, which is not open to attack, provided, of course, that the resulting patent has real value. To do so, we do not necessarily need to disclose the damaging reference to the examiner,[28] and it is sufficient that we limit the scope of our claims so it is commensurate with what can be reasonably obtained in light of the prior art.

However, beyond all these practical considerations, there is also one fundamental consideration that we must not forget: someone who seeks to be granted a patent must come with clean hands, and concealing an important prior publication from the examiner may not be the smart decision.

WE ARE SEEKING TO FIRST-FILE A PATENT APPLICATION ABROAD

Some applicants from different countries file their first patent application abroad and not in their own country—often in the United States.[29] There is sometimes a good reason for a first filing in the United States, but a significant problem, of which many applicants are not aware, is the risk of breaking the law.

The patent laws of several countries—notably, the United States of America, and the United Kingdom—include an express prohibition on filing a patent application outside the country of origin of the applicant or inventor without first obtaining formal authorization to do so. Particular emphasis is placed on inventions relating to weaponry, ammunition, or which are otherwise of military value or pertain to national defense. Unless a foreign filing license (i.e., a

[28] In countries where there is no obligation to do so.

[29] Typically, for a business reason, not a legal one.

permit to file abroad) has been obtained,[30] you may be in serious violation of the law, which, in some countries, may be punishable by imprisonment or fine. These obligations apply to everyone involved in the patent application filing process. Thus, for instance, if an inventor helps his company to file it abroad by signing formal documents, he and his managers are collectively violating the provisions of the law.

The risk, therefore, is not small. And, in general, who wants to knowingly harm national security? However, it can also be harmed unknowingly by a failure to comply with the provisions of the law. There are inventions that, it is clear to us beyond any reasonable doubt, cannot have any relevance to national security—for instance, a game for the cognitive development of preschool children. Nevertheless, in some countries, you would still need a foreign filing license.

The straightforward way of dealing with this problem is to either file the patent application in your country of origin and to wait for the foreign filing license to arrive, or to wait out a prescribed period of time after filing before you are automatically allowed to file abroad. These activities will normally take much less than 12 months, during which the invention is protected under the Paris Convention, and in many cases, there is no drawback to waiting a few months before filing a patent application abroad. There may be cases, however, in which an early filing is needed for business reasons, and then petitioning for an early grant of a foreign filing license may be required.

WE SEEK TO EXERCISE "COMMON SENSE"

Too often, we encounter someone who seeks to wield logic against the patent system and, incidentally, he decides that this or that fact "simply cannot be true," inasmuch as it is inconsistent with what he sees as common sense. While the patent system has vast and

---

[30] A foreign filing license is usually obtained either by filing a petition, or if a patent application has been previously filed in the country of origin on the same invention and, according to the local regulations, a foreign filing license is granted, typically, automatically after a given period of time.

impressive internal logic, it is not necessarily the same logic that can be exercised in other areas of life. Exercising inappropriate logic could lead to disastrous results. The following are representative examples of exercising bad logic:

- *I do not need to worry about the patent that I found, because a competitor of mine also manufactures the product protected by the patent and nothing happens to him.*

This statement, which is heard quite frequently, ignores two basic facts. The first is that if the infringing competitor has not yet run into problems, this does not indicate that he never will. There is also a possibility that this competitor has made use of the patent with permission, either by purchasing it or by entering into a license agreement with its holder. There is always a need to worry about a patent that we may be infringing, even if unintentionally, and we should not stop worrying until after the facts have been fully elucidated.

- *There are several similar patents; therefore, probably none of them are "worth anything," and I am free to do as I wish.*

This is a particularly pernicious variation of the first logic. This conclusion disregards the reality that similarity is not sameness. There may be several similar patents, each one of which covers a different aspect or a different manner of execution, and all of them can coexist side by side. Before drawing such a conclusion, you should consult a professional in the patent field and understand the differences between the protections afforded by the various patents—differences that may sometimes be minute in words but huge in effect. If there are several similar patents, it does not necessarily mean that they are all worthless. It may be that an examiner erred and issued to an applicant a patent that is invalid given the existence of a prior patent. But this does not deny the first patent holder his right to the invention protected by his patent.

And then some people cannot see the difference between a

granted patent and a published patent application because the documents look alike. We can write anything we want in a patent application, but it doesn't mean that we will be granted a patent on any stupid idea. Therefore, the existence of many patent applications claiming the same thing doesn't mean anything at all.

- *I must not disclose my invention in the patent. Therefore, I will describe everything in the patent application, apart from the important bits.*

This conclusion is particularly interesting inasmuch as it explicitly contradicts not only the patent laws of most countries, which prescribe that full disclosure of the invention is a fundamental condition for the validity of the patent, but also operates contrary to the logic of the patent system as a whole, which is designed to reward inventors for publicly disclosing their invention. It seems that this approach is based on a "the law was not meant to also apply to me" reasoning.

- *If my patent application is sufficiently incoherent, so that no one can understand what is written there, it will cover everything, because I can always claim that everything is written there.*

I really like this one. It never stops amazing me when I hear it. This is a highly favored logic, based on the assumption that the entire world—except, of course, that same applicant—suffers from advanced mental retardation. It is another piece of logic produced by the common "cunning person," which ignores the need to rely on reasonable interpretations of the contents of the patent application in the eyes of the adjudicating authority and the various professionals who are supposed to interpret it. But how, this applicant asks, can it be proven that what I am claiming that the application says is not written there, when the reader is unable to understand its contents and cannot negate my claim? Our answer to this applicant is: "Think about it at home. Eventually you will understand."

But perhaps all this is inevitable, if we reconcile ourselves with the existence of a less-known Murphy's Law: "Technology is dominated by two types of people: Those who understand what they do not manage and those who manage what they do not understand."

WE HAVE INVENTED A NOVEL MEDICAL TREATMENT

The patent laws of most important countries define patentable subject matter and explicitly address the subjects that are not patentable. Among those, there are all the methods related to the treatment of the human body.[31] This restriction is based on the will to maintain free access to therapeutic solutions.

There is much logic in this approach, but as with any sweeping determination, it does not take into account all the possible situations. For instance, we understand why it makes sense not to grant a patent on an orthopedic surgery method, during which various incisions and in vivo procedures are performed to implant artificial bone. This is a therapeutic technique that, even if it is particularly clever, should be available to the general public, so that any physician in any hospital in the world may be able to perform it and to bring relief to his patient. Moreover, this does not involve an industrial method, and sometimes it does not even involve the product of the expensive R&D of a commercial company but only a great idea of a gifted surgeon. However, it is not certain that these considerations are correct, for instance, in the case of hair transplant surgery. This type of cosmetic surgery is, by its very nature, a commercial activity, and there is no fundamental reason why someone who worked diligently on developing a method that gives better results than its predecessors should not profit from the fruit of his development. The first weakness of the system that prohibits giving a monopoly to "a method for treating the human body" in a sweeping manner is that it does not differentiate between treatments that are lifesaving or that are important purely in terms of health from those that belong to an affluent society, such as cosmetic surgeries. Plastic surgeons, for instance, may derive nice profits while exploiting surgical methods

[31] In the United States of America, it is possible to patent medical methods, but these patents are not practically enforceable in most cases.

that were developed by another person, and there is no justification for exempting them from paying royalties to the person who enabled them to enjoy a nice income.

Moreover, this system has an internal contradiction. The entire world understands that patents should be granted on medications, and even countries that had opposed this for many years eventually had to recognize the need to give patents that grant a monopoly on pharmaceutical preparations. Without this recognition, the pharmaceutical industry would not be able to continue to spend hundreds of millions of dollars to develop new medications. Let us take, for instance, a politician who comes to perform a face lift to improve his prospects in the upcoming elections. This politician will pay a nice sum, from which royalties will derive to the manufacturer of the anesthetics, to the manufacturer of the pain medications, to the manufacturer of the scalpels and the operating room equipment, and perhaps even to the manufacturer of the modern lamp that illuminates the surgeon's work; but not one cent will reach the pocket of the inventor of the surgery that will allow our politician, ultimately, to place a fresh face on his propaganda posters.

In spite of all this, sometimes, we can find ways to protect a medical procedure through the equipment and the materials needed to perform it and, therefore, before giving up the idea, the invention should be analyzed in detail.

WE FEEL THAT EVERYONE KNOWS WHAT WE KNOW

The information revolution has already arrived to every computer. Anyone who can afford to pay a modest subscription fee to an Internet provider can today wander the information superhighway and access an enormous amount of information. Furthermore, the information revolution brings with it a further result: the information sources are made uniform, and the availability of the information depends less on the searcher's knowledge and skill than in the past. These facts have a tremendous impact on the patent system.

The most significant result of the information revolution is reflected in the shortening of time available to the inventor to protect his invention. Everyone is connected to the same information sources and responds to the needs coming from the market. Everyone learns the technological background and seeks solutions to the same problems in the same sources in real time, inasmuch as information coming to the databases of "the information superhighway" is available to everyone simultaneously.

Consequently, we witness a growing phenomenon of the same inventions being made independently and concurrently by different people, where the filing of the patent application of one precedes that of the other by weeks and sometimes only by a few days.

Therefore, the availability of the information constitutes a double-edged sword. On the one hand, we obtain the information that is crucial to our work almost instantaneously. But, on the other hand, our competitors also do so, with efficiency no lesser than ours, and thereby force on us a new dimension in the battle for obtaining rights on our work—the time dimension. At least one practical conclusion should be drawn from this situation: we must not delay the filing of a patent application (which is always true), particularly when the motivation underlying the invention can be found in databases that are visible to everyone.

CHAPTER 17
Some Important Concepts

Among the less popular patent topics are hidden those that are important to know and understand if we wish to use patents to their fullest.

KEEPING OPEN SKIES

Most hi-tech entrepreneurs understand the basic need to protect their inventions. However, few understand the need to devote serious effort to preventing competitors from obtaining patents that could harm their everyday activities. This is similar to an air force that carries out successful sorties deep in enemy territory but fails to secure the skies above its own land. A patent is a weapon in the battlefield of business competition. According to this metaphor, every hi-tech company must also make arrangements to keep "open skies" in its region. A patent could also be used by a competitor to force us to seek more expensive routes to the market, to waste our time and our resources in searching for alternatives, and, in the extreme situation, to also block us completely.

The examination that is carried out by the patent authority,[32] as good as it shall be, cannot entirely prevent the grant of patents on

[32] **Reminder**: The generic term "patent authority" is used here to refer to the central patent office of a country, not to be confused with a patent law firm, which is also sometimes referred to as a "patent office."

inventions that are unpatentable. The means available to the examiner are not perfect, and information that is relevant to the patentability of an examined invention does not always reach him.

The opposition (or similar) procedure[33] allows all interested parties to bring before the patent authority information and reasons why a patent application that was examined and found to be patentable by an examiner should be rejected in full or in part. Within the framework of an opposition or other invalidation procedure, you may bring to the attention of the judicial body that hears the argument (typically, a board of examiners or a judge) details that were unknown to the original examiner, which shows the invention in a different light. This option is sometimes available to the public for a limited period of time,[34] and different ways to oppose patents are available in different countries. In some countries, you must wait for the patent to be issued before you can "oppose" it, while in others, you must oppose it while the application has not yet matured into a patent. The procedures are tortuous and evolve with time, so there would be little benefit to the reader to list them here. However, the reader should obtain country-specific, up-to-date advice from his patent attorney whenever the need arises. The purpose of this chapter is to make sure that the reader understands that the need *may* arise and, consequently, to prompt him to seek advice from his attorney whenever the business situation seems to call for it.

For this option to work, every company that wishes to maintain its freedom of operation must track the activity of competitors in the relevant country and timely oppose unjustified applications of competitors for patents. The responsibility for asserting the freedom of operation falls on every company in its own field, if it wishes to maintain its vital interests.

---

[33] See also Chapter 10.

[34] For instance, in post-grant procedures, such as in Europe, oppositions must be filed within nine months from the grant of a patent, while in pre-grant systems, such as in Israel, the opposition period is three months from the publication of the allowance of the application.

PROCESS PATENTS

We often hear people say that a patent that protects a manufacturing process of a known product is a "weak" patent whose benefit is questionable. But is this popular belief justified?

Indeed, there are cases in which a real difficulty arises in enforcing a process patent, because the process is carried out in a distant country, if it cannot be seen from the final product that it was indeed manufactured using the patented process. Obtaining evidence of infringement may also be more difficult than with other types of inventions. However, these cases are not the rule.

The patent laws of advanced countries recognize the need to protect the property embodied in a process and, therefore, prescribe that the protection conferred by a process patent shall also apply to the direct product of the process. These laws confer broad protection, inasmuch as a product manufactured in a foreign country using a process that is protected by a patent in the country into which the product is introduced shall constitute an infringement of the process patent. The holders of the patent that protects the process shall, therefore, be entitled to use it to prevent the marketing of the product in a country in which the process patent is valid. To be able to rely on the patent that protects the process, it must be demonstrated that it is likely that the suspected infringing product was manufactured using the patented process. In many cases, the process leaves traces that constitute almost a "fingerprint" on the infringing product, which permit us to determine that indeed, the product was manufactured using the patented process. These fingerprints can be of various types, beginning with traces of materials used in the specific process and ending with the outer or microscopic appearance of an object, which indicates the use of a specific production method or apparatus.

For instance, in a process for coating an object, there may be a process patent that allows for achieving a coating level (uniformity and thickness) exceeding that known in the market. In this situation, the product per se may be proof of infringement: if it is of the quality obtained using the patented process, and if no other processes are known that achieve the same quality, then it is reasonable to assume that it was manufactured according to the process of the patent and, therefore, infringes it. In this case, it is clear how the process patent protects the obtained product.

Of course, not every case will be as easy as in this example. Other cases may be extremely difficult and require considerable effort to prove that the patent has been infringed. But it is clear that potential or anticipated difficulties do not justify failing to attempt to protect our process and waiving our rights in it.

NO "QUICK FIX"

Patents and patent applications are not a hard asset. Patent applications are, in fact, only a "conditional asset," inasmuch as the very fact that someone has decided to apply for a patent does not ensure that he will be granted the patent for which he is applying. It is important to understand that a portfolio of patents is an entity in a constant state of creation. As opposed to a tangible asset, it is impossible to record the evaluated company's portfolio value (after a careful examination) in the books, according to depreciation, discount, inflation values, and various other economic calculations, because if we have neglected the handling of a patent application or of a patent in a certain country, its value has not depreciated but, rather, has zeroed instantly.

An investor who gives considerable weight to the quality of the patents of a company in which he is investing might discover after a year or two that the value of its patents is no longer what it was. Suddenly, the portfolio that had seemed so promising and compelling at the time of the investment is no longer so. How did that happen?

There can be a number of reasons for a decline in the significance and value of a company's patent portfolio. Many entrepreneurs work under the "quick fix" system—that is, they file a large number of patent applications in the early days of the company, and when the long-awaited financial investment arrives, the patents drop in their awareness and on their list of priorities. However, a company developing technology is like a person suffering from mild diabetes, who, for his entire life, must maintain a diet and proper insulin levels in the body. Just as he cannot cure the disease by injecting himself over a short period with large doses of insulin, while adhering to an extremely strict diet, so a company that needs to protect its continuously developing intellectual property cannot file multiple patent applications in its early days and then lose interest in them.

As stated, a portfolio of patents is a dynamic asset, and it should be examined in relation to the entire world, not only in relation to ourselves. The actions of our competitors could make patent applications that we relied on irrelevant, and a patent application to which we paid less attention may turn out to be the most important of all. Moreover, the company may have valuable technological knowledge that could be squandered if the level of commitment of its managers to protect it diminishes when it is overshadowed by other demanding daily needs. Conversely, some companies invest great amounts in handling patent applications and renewing patents that have long ago ceased to be relevant to their activity.

However, it is also possible to mishandle an important patent application. For instance, because we postponed or procrastinated in the handling of a patent application in a certain country, we may find that when the time comes that we need the patent to maintain our market, it is not close to being issued. Because it is usually not possible to apply to the courts in the various countries before the patent is issued, it may happen that despite all our investment, we have no tool that allows us to fight the competition. In many cases, this problem is related to the incongruity between the patent system and the marketing system. The marketing considerations must be taken into account in the planning of the patent activity. In general, it is important to plan our patent activities proactively and not to limit ourselves to handling our patent applications only when a need arises to meet a demand of some patent authority.

To derive maximum benefit from the financial and other efforts invested in patents, one must act as a diligent gardener who fells treetops, plants saplings, and sows seeds—all in the right season and in the right dose. Only in this manner will a healthy and spectacular vegetable garden be obtained. Otherwise, he may wake up one morning to discover that his beautiful garden has become a field of thorns.

PATENTS: NOT ONLY FOR HI-TECH

The hi-tech rush of the last two decades has brought many more to a healthy awareness of the importance of patents in the everyday life of a company that develops technology. As a result of the high-tech revolution, a large number of people have become exposed to the patenting process and to the advantages that could accrue to their company from holding good patents.

The world economy has, to some extent, gone back to the basics, and the hi-tech market has become more difficult, more competitive, and more ruthless. The days are long gone when entrepreneurs received a nice investment for a project that was presented on paper only. Today, substantive content for the company must be shown, and the value of the technology is an integral and major part of this content. Here, too, just as in any other field in the life of companies, this has become much more difficult. While in the not-so-distant past, the investors did not overly scrutinize the real value of the company's patent applications, today, a patent application that is not serious and does not properly reflect the value of the technology will not bring much value to its owner.

Now, the time has come to recall that a patent is not a device that is exclusive to hi-tech companies and that inventions that require patent protection are not only those inventions that purport to change the Internet. To be effective, a patent must follow the development of the industrial and commercial activity of the company and should be used to further its marketing objectives. Therefore, whether or not the needs of the company are met largely depends on the understanding that its managers have of the innovation embodied in its products. This innovation can have a fairly modest scientific nature, and nevertheless, it may have high economic significance. For instance, a slight change in a seemingly minor detail of a product may lead to significant savings in its production. This may be reflected both in the price of the product and in its profitability for the company. If the change embodies novelty and inventive step, then it should be protected by a patent even if we do not see great scientific progress in it. A similar consideration should be applied to a change that will make the product better or more attractive to the consumer, inasmuch as the consumer's image of the product is a decisive factor on the road to its success. The role of the patent in this case is to maintain the exclusivity to the advantage within the company that developed it.

When we work with both our feet on the ground, we realize the need to plan ahead with our real everyday products and to compete with them in the world markets. The patent is our good friend on this daily journey.

CHAPTER 18
A Little about the World around Us

To become familiar with the patent system and to understand it in greater depth, it is important not to close our eyes to what is happening around us in other countries. Important events pertaining to this field sometimes occur on the basis of considerations that are irrelevant to the country in which the reader lives. The following is a nonrepresentative selection to arouse curiosity.

NIH (NOT INVENTED HERE)

One of the most important objectives of the patent system is to bring to the attention of the public new developments from which we can proceed to advance technology one step further. The protection afforded by a patent is what enables inventors to disclose their inventions and, thereby, a free flow of information is made possible because patent-protected knowledge cannot be exploited without payment and without the approval of the owner.

Every year, a myriad of patents are published in diverse fields, and from them, we can extract both important information and useful ideas. Those who know how to properly take advantage of the system regard it as a great source of information and attempt to see how, in their field, they can derive benefit from this knowledge. This approach is contrary to the unfortunate trend in many companies and entities, which is known by the nickname NIH (Not Invented Here). According to this approach, inventions made outside the system are regarded with contempt or with hostility (or with a mixture of both). Entities that adopt this kind of approach sometimes turn a blind eye and a deaf ear to any idea coming from the outside.

More than likely, there are at least two people in the United States who feel that the system has missed out: George M. Scott and Kornel J. Feher. In US Patent No. 4,706,091, which was published in 1987, Mr. Scott explained that:

"Based on past hijacking situations of commercial airliners, the crew members are invariably instructed to break off any communication with the ground tracking stations . . . Accordingly, authorities on the ground frequently have a limited knowledge of the facts and circumstances surrounding the hijacking. A complete knowledge of the activities and intentions of the hijackers would of course greatly aid authorities in the proper treatment of a given situation . . . This would be particularly true in situations where the conversations between the cockpit crew and the hijackers were relayed to the proper authorities without knowledge of such relay by the hijackers."

Mr. Scott's patent goes on to describe a fairly simple system for achieving this goal. As far as we know, this method was not implemented commercially on airplanes flying in US skies, and during the hijacking on September 11, 2001, the authorities did not have adequate information on what was happening.

No less frustrated than Mr. Scott should feel Mr. Feher, who, a year later, in US Patent 4,816,828, discussed at length the problem that, years later, led to the terrorist attack on the twin towers. And so Mr. Feher explains:

"A factor of increasing importance in complicating air carrier safety is an ever increasing threat of sabotage, hijacking or terrorism . . . In the case of terrorism, there is no adequate system for monitoring the events surrounding an aircraft hijacking by terrorists or other hijackers, while an aircraft is in flight . . . The lack of this information prevents government authorities and the police forces from adequately responding during a hijacking."

Mr. Feher goes on to describe a system that includes simple surveillance cameras, such as are installed in many supermarkets, which transmit images to a ground tracking station of what is happening on the aircraft. Use of one, or both, of the systems described in those two patents could reveal what is happening during a hijacking through periodic surveillance or pursuant to some signs that indicate a problem during flight. We may assume that the existence of such a system on the airplanes that were hijacked in the United States might have at least enabled a lessening of the severity of the resulting injury and loss of life.

It is true that sometimes an independent inventor, who does not come from a relevant organization, is not aware of all the problems and obstacles, and the solutions that he proposes may not be optimal or even feasible. It is clear, however, that already, many years ago, the aforementioned inventors understood that a problem of lack of information during a hijacking exists and that the solution lies in transmitting information, audio and video, automatically to a ground tracking station that would be able to learn about the problem and respond accordingly.

Let us assume for a moment that perhaps the solutions that Misters Scott and Feher proposed were not optimal. The question is still posed why nobody provided a more feasible and effective solution, which would achieve the goal. Unfortunately, the correct answer to this question may be NIH.

HERO OR VILLAIN?

Every now and then, some angry journalist[35] feels that the time has come to publish an article discussing the question of whether a patent is "intellectual property or a technological barrier" (and because he is, for reasons unknown to us, angry, the answer to him is certainly that patents are a negative factor). The confusion of terms does not end with the posing of the aforementioned question but usually finds expression throughout the article. It should be noted that this is not the only case of using terms that could confuse the reader and distance him from the patent reality.

---

[35] It is usually difficult to find out why he is angry and what he is really angry about.

The depth of the problem can be appreciated through the following quotation from one such article[36]: "*Company A was awarded a patent that provides it with the exclusive right to use technology for 'storing television programs while the viewer sees other programs.' The primary injured party from the patent is the competitor of Company A, Company B.*"

Just a moment! **The primary injured party?** What are we actually talking about? Company A made an invention and filed a patent application to prevent a competitor, Company B (and others), from exploiting its invention. The patent authority[37] examined the application, found it patentable, and granted a patent on it, thereby protecting the rights of Company A on its invention. From this moment, Company B is precluded from infringing the rights of Company A. So was it injured? Yes, it was injured just as the poor bank robber who cannot carry out his plans because of the security system of the bank, or just as the hapless burglar who has difficulty breaking into my apartment because I, with unforgivable arbitrariness, have timely arranged to install grilles in my home. Of course a patent constitutes a barrier against the competitors. This is precisely its role!

One argument constitutes the spearhead of those who seek to benefit from the labor of another in the software and Internet field: "A patent constitutes a technological barrier that prevents the development of the industry."[38] A nice-sounding argument, but it is lacking substance. The proponents of this argument apparently hope that with the rapid pace at which the Internet market develops, the public will be swept away toward the sounds of the argument without examining it thoroughly. Surely, barriers are bad things, and we should rise up against them. If patents that constitute a "technological barrier" are granted, then the patent authority is working against the public, its actions are illegitimate, and it should be denounced.

---

[36] The details of the companies involved are withheld.

[37] **Reminder**: The generic term "patent authority" is used here to refer to the central patent office of a country, not to be confused with a patent law firm, which is also sometimes referred to as a "patent office."

[38] This idea is expressed in many versions. See, for instance "D Nicol and J Nielsen, **The Australian Medical Biotechnology Industry and Access to Intellectual Property: Issues for Patent Law Development** (2001) 23 *Sydney Law Review* 347, 348., in which the authors argue that "the regimes protecting IPRs [intellectual property rights] may prove to be a significant barrier for the development of the Australian industry."

This strategy has found quite a few supporters, particularly among those who do not understand what a patent is. The truth is that the rules of the game in the software and Internet field are no different from those in any other field.[39] The inventor who arrives first at a basic invention in any other technological field will receive a patent that will allow him, and him alone, to exploit the invention. Let us assume, for example, that a company has found how to package white cheese so that it is preserved for a long time without refrigeration and has obtained a patent on its packaging method. This means that throughout the life of the patent (20 years from the day of filing the application), no other company will be able to package white cheese in the patented packaging. The immediate result will, of course, be a commercial advantage to the inventor, inasmuch as the consumer will surely prefer to purchase cheese that is preserved better, even if the refrigeration conditions are inferior. Does this patent pose a technological barrier to competitors? Of course it does, but it is a welcome technological barrier.

Precluding the option of copying the packaging of the originator company will constitute motivation, at least for some of the companies, to develop independent solutions that do not fall within the scope of the patent and, thus, perhaps an even better method will be developed, which will serve the consumers better. This is what happened throughout history when a company found itself facing the need to narrow a commercial disparity that the competitor created, by investing in a new development. By contrast, if we had allowed the competing companies to simply copy the packaging of the first company, even the innocent among us could not have expected them to invest any money to develop alternative solutions.

It, therefore, follows that the patent precisely fulfills its role to advance technology in the public interest by placing barriers that require the industry to develop, to advance, and to invest in new products. What all those lamenting the profusion of patents seek is legitimization to act as loafers who suffer from chronic mental palsy, which could lead to stagnation in technological development. This

---

[39] However, see Chapter 21 for a reality check.

proclivity is contrary to the public interest. Therefore, we should hope that the patent authorities of the world will grant lawful patents without paying attention to the crocodile tears of the opportunistic public, which invests in whining instead of in technology.

PYRRHIC VICTORY

Intellectual property always plays a significant role in the discussions of the World Trade Organization (WTO). So it was in the discussion known by the nickname "Uruguay Round," which encountered difficulties in preventing copyright infringement in some member countries of the organization. This discussion round, which began in 1986 and ended in 1994, gave rise to the General Agreement on Trade and Tariffs (GATT) and its annex TRIPS, which deals with Trade-Related Aspects of Intellectual Property Rights. All this, as stated, was to regulate multilateral issues pertaining to trade between countries.

In the discussion round of 2002, representatives of the WTO countries convened in Doha, Qatar for a heated discussion of all matters related to patent rights. This trend followed the populistic wave, according to which drug patents are the root of all evil, and were it not for them, there would be a cure for the ailments of the entire world. This is the place to recall that patent rights were created to encourage R&D, including for finding medications with which it would be possible to heal the ill, a fact that the medications-for-everyone knights often "forget." In this context, there was an effort in the WTO discussions to obtain a "note" from the organization, with which countries that view themselves as sufficiently poor would be able to disregard patent rights. These questions arose particularly in the context of the AIDS epidemic in Africa.

The wrath of those seeking to obtain a release from the rights of the pharmaceutical companies came out in particular in a study that was published in mid-October 2001 in the *Journal of the American Medical Association.* This study, a work by Dr. Amir Attaran, Director of International Health Studies at Harvard University, and Lee Gillespie-White, Director of the International Intellectual Property Institute, severely threatened to confuse the attendees of the Doha meeting with facts. The study revealed that pharmaceutical companies rarely bothered to protect their rights with patents in Africa. The 15 known anti-AIDS medications could have earned a nice portfolio of 795 potential patents altogether in 53 African countries. However, the study estimates that only 22 percent of all the possible patents in Africa were actually issued. Therefore, the study authors reached the conclusion, whose logic is not difficult to understand even for someone who is not a researcher himself, that patents are not the cause of lack of treatment against AIDS in the African population, and the reasons should be sought in the poverty prevailing in those countries.

The United States, Africa, and Japan suggested and assessed various proposals to alleviate the distress of African nations, but all the proposals seemed inadequate to those fighting against the pharmaceutical companies, probably because they were not sufficient to destroy the patent system. In their efforts to hurl various accusations at the pharmaceutical companies, these groups sometimes have a slip of the tongue. For instance, an argument was heard that the pharmaceutical companies do not invest in research to discover medications against tropical diseases and prefer to invest in problems of obesity and impotence, for which there is a lucrative market. Well then, we have news for these activists: if you succeed in your mission to destroy the patent protection for lifesaving medications, such as anti-AIDS drugs, the pharmaceutical companies will not be able to develop them either. Then, all that you will be able to purchase are drugs against obesity and for preventing hair loss, because the pharmaceutical companies will not have the money to develop medications that do not yield profits.

In general, there is no dispute that a supreme effort must be made to help disadvantaged populations to purchase medications and fight diseases. The league of nations should address this and mobilize various aid agencies to this end. But the WTO is not a global charity organization.

In 280 BC, Pyrrhus, king of Epirus, defeated the Romans in Heraclea and incidentally "succeeded" in destroying a great part of his own army. These kinds of victories, in which the victor is the greatest loser, have since been known under the generic name "pyrrhic victory." Since then, nearly 2,300 years have elapsed, but apparently we still have not learned, and we are still busy winning pyrrhic victories, whereby companies are required to agree to a drastic lowering of prices of medications that they produce. What is truly worrisome is the shortsightedness of those working to attain these pseudo victories. The situation is similar to an incident that occurs on a toll road, where the collector (the government) approaches the innocent driver (a pharmaceutical company) when he is about to pay the transit tax and orders him at gunpoint to empty all of his pockets. This trick succeeds, it should be said, because the pockets of the victim are full. The robber then stands on the main road and waits for the return of the passerby. After some time, the same victim returns and passes the place where the robber has settled himself, and he is all dressed in rags, and there is no money in his pocket to pay the tax. It turns out that the money that was stolen from the pocket of the victim was intended to develop his business, but because it was taken from him, his business withered to such an extent that he has no money left to pay the toll.

When we take the money of the pharmaceutical company, we take, in effect, the future of our children and their ability to obtain drugs to heal their ailments. It doesn't really matter if you like the pharmaceutical industry or dislike it. That won't change the reality. Pharmaceutical companies are not nonprofit entities: they develop to make a profit, and if we take their profits away, there will be no development. Perhaps they will decide that it would be preferable to invest the money in real estate and not in new drugs, because the real-estate roads are safer and are less congested with robbers.

Part IV: Patents and Business

"Young men are fitter to invent than to judge, fitter for execution than for counsel, and fitter for new projects than for settled business"

[Francis Bacon (1625) – "Of Youth and Age"]

This section sheds some light on business considerations surrounding the patent, which are often unrelated to technological considerations.

CHAPTER 19
The Investor and the Patent

Entrepreneurs and investors alike have an interest in the company's patents, but each addresses them from a different perspective. It is important that there be a coordination of expectations between the parties with respect to the significance and value of the patents to the life of the company. To have proper workplace relations, the patent tool should not be misused. The following is a little food for thought.

THE PATENT AS A TOOL FOR RAISING CAPITAL

Who among those developers who work with patents has not prayed for the moment when his work will attain practical recognition by the significant act: a capital investment in his invention? However, only some of those developers thoroughly understand the need for a solid protection of the invention, which will prevent the potential investor from feeling that he has invested money in a dubious venture.

In general, any person or entity that invests in a technological development today is highly sensitive in relation to the proprietary rights that he is acquiring. To guarantee his investment, he must ensure that the technology in which he is investing is free of the danger of infringing patents of other companies, inasmuch as the fear of infringing a patent could prevent the exploitation of the technology.

The cautious investor must also ensure that his investment will yield technology that is protected, or protectable, at least at a minimal level, with original patents. This is so as to ensure a degree of exclusivity that will allow a return of the investment and a reasonable profit.

Accordingly, as part of his due diligence process, the potential investor will examine the patent "status" of the candidate company and of its potential competitors. If the patent status has not been examined in advance, and the necessary steps have not been taken to ensure the proper position of the technology in terms of patents, the invention that the company is developing may not meet the minimum criteria of the investor, and the investment may not happen.

Generally, when the time for the investment has arrived, the developer will not have the time necessary to address all the problems pertaining to the IP issues, and so it sometimes happens that available capital is allocated to safer channels, or at least such where the IP issues have been addressed at a higher level.

To avoid this situation, it is advisable that the developer ask himself at an early date all the questions to which he will have to reply in the course of the due diligence process that the investor will perform, and pay heed to the problems stemming from those questions, so as to find solutions and bypass obstacles during his R&D work. It should be remembered that solving important questions pertaining to patent protection often constitutes a critical condition for an investment.

STOPPING THE CLOCK

One of the cornerstones of the patent system is the priority right granted to a patent applicant.[40] This right, which is available to him for 12 months from the day when the application was first filed, allows an applicant to publish his invention, and the publication will not prevent the filing of parallel patent applications in other countries, provided

[40] See Appendix B, Article 4 of the Paris Convention.

that this filing is done "during the priority period"—that is, during the same 12 months. The priority right also guarantees that each patent application that is filed in respect of the same invention by another, during said period, will be rejected due to the priority of the first filer.

Therefore, filing a patent application constitutes a "stopping of the clock" with respect to the rights of the applicant and fixes them at the same time when the application was filed. Consequently, we can stop worrying about the effect of any patent application filed subsequent to this time, inasmuch as it cannot bear upon the applicant's rights. And what about patent applications that were filed before our application? Those patent applications naturally create priority rights for their owners according to the very same principle, and we must take them into account in all matters, but we cannot know of the existence of some of them when filing our application.

Patent applications are usually not published for at least 18 months from the day they are filed. Therefore, there is a period of uncertainty of a year and a half for which we have no information and during which patent applications that threaten our rights may have been filed. However, approaching the time of the 12 months of the day of filing our application, when we must decide on filing patent applications in other countries, the period of uncertainty has been reduced to only six months. With each passing month, our patent application continues to "improve" pretty much like the wine in our cellar, whose quality improves with time. The haze surrounding the period of uncertainty dissipates as more and more patent applications are published, and the picture becomes clearer as we learn more about the rights of others. The potential investor (and the applicant himself) has a greater sense of security as time passes from the filing of the application and, thus, his willingness to invest increases gradually. Due to the "stopping of the clock" resulting from the priority right, the value of our patent application increases as the chance of discovering a competing and earlier patent application decreases.

All the foregoing depends, of course, on us retaining the priority right. If, on the passage of the 12 months, we have not exercised it, this right is lost forever and for all the countries in which a parallel application was not filed. In this situation, a constant period of uncertainty is created. Only when we file parallel patent applications abroad will we again stop the clock, but this stopping will be at least a year late in relation to what we were granted by the priority right that was not exercised. This delay of a year, in many cases, could cost us all our rights.

Therefore, not only retaining the priority right is extremely important, but it is advisable in general to ascertain from time to time, throughout the priority period, how the chances of our patent application have improved or whether an earlier and competing application has emerged and our wine has turned sour.

A PATENT AT ANY PRICE

"Sir, there is no invention here. Everything is old, known, and obvious. Don't waste your money," explains the patent attorney.

"Yes, but I need a patent for this," insists the man.

"But you cannot obtain a patent," explains the patent attorney patiently, *"because in order to be granted a patent, your invention must be new and has to possess inventive step, which is not the case here."*

"Then let's file something just for the investors . . ."

This is not an uncommon conversation, which occurs when an initial review of an invention, on which the entrepreneur has built a house of cards, reveals that it is not new and that there is no chance that a valid patent will be issued on it. At this stage, the entrepreneur enters a state of denial and considers himself obligated to file a patent application at any price. He does not understand why the patent attorney refuses to cooperate with him, because he is the one paying for the work. In some cases, the entrepreneur takes his invention (ostensibly) elsewhere, and, having gained experience from the first time, he finds a way to persuade another patent attorney to file a patent application for it. At this stage, the entrepreneur believes that he acted wisely to achieve what he wants. But is this really so?

Much has been said of there being no obligation that a patent application be filed only on a "major" invention, and, in many cases, there is justification and commercial sense to filing a patent application on a "small" invention. There is also no obligation, or possibility, to ensure ahead of time that the patent application will indeed be allowed and, in the end, will yield a patent. Many patent applications are filed by their owners in the hope of attaining exclusive rights but are ultimately rejected because they are found to be unpatentable due to a lack of novelty or inventive step. There is also nothing wrong with this. Moreover, there may be, in many cases, scathing professional arguments and fundamental disagreements among different professionals regarding the patentability of the same invention, and in case of doubt, when the invention is important, it is always advisable to attempt to obtain a patent on it and to put its eligibility to a practical test. In many cases, we will do so even if we believe that the chances are not particularly good, if nevertheless there is a conceivable chance that, eventually, a patent will be granted on some aspects of the invention. All these are possible situations, and they are not problematic. As long as there is even the tiniest of doubts with regard to the patentability of an invention, and if the circumstances so justify, it is advisable to put it to the test.

What is not acceptable is to attempt to obtain a patent on an invention that is not patentable, where its absolute ineligibility is clear and obvious. Not done. Not cricket. **Let's forget about political correctness for a second, and be blunt: that is fraud!**

If the entrepreneur insists on obtaining a clearly invalid patent, he will not only abuse the patent system but will also, in most cases, mislead his investors and cause them to believe that there is some likelihood of obtaining exclusivity on the invention. Therefore, filing a patent application "only for the investors" is not a legitimate act. Under these conditions, the investors will ultimately feel deceived, inasmuch as someday it will become apparent to them that the entrepreneur did not disclose the factual situation to them.

We should distinguish between the situation described above and the situation in which a company decides to file a patent application on an invention that, in the opinion of experts, has almost absolutely no chance of success, to avoid the possibility that a competing company will succeed, against all odds, to obtain a patent thereon and will thereby hinder its activity. This situation may occur when a slight doubt remains with regard to the patentability of the invention. It is impossible to completely rule out this likelihood and then, in quite a few cases, a patent application will be filed as a defensive action. However, the filing company is aware that there is a high likelihood that its money will not yield results, and it reconciles itself with filing the patent application even if with a negligible chance of success. This is a completely different situation than that in which an investor considers the filing of a patent application a declaration by the entrepreneur that he is working, with some reasonable chance, to obtain exclusivity on the invention.

Therefore, we should regard with suspicion an entrepreneur who insists on filing a patent application at any price. This may be a welcome consequence of persistence, but it is also possible that all the entrepreneur is seeking to achieve is to check the box next to the requirements of the investor.

THE ONE WHO CANNOT EXPLAIN

Further to "walking the line" as discussed above, it is surprising to discover how shrewd businesspeople might fall into the trap of an "inventor" who is shrewder than they are, who commercializes an invention that never existed. The phenomenon may be attributed to the respect of the common man toward scientists in general and inventors in particular. And perhaps the source of interest is rooted in the desire and the prospect of becoming rich and achieving great success through the invention of another. Either way, sophisticated swindlers frequently manage to extract considerable amounts of money from naïve people.

To avoid insofar as possible falling into such a trap, it is customary to carry out what is known as "due diligence." However, this review does not always delve into the technological roots of the invention and sometimes even has difficulty inspecting the authenticity and the implications of the results presented by the developer. Thus, we witness cases in which the object of the project is inspected thoroughly from every angle, except from the substantive aspect—the quality and operation of the invention. Because the differences between the status quo and the invention can be fairly minor, but still significant, a thorough inspection becomes critical. The ability to produce a deliverable using a biotechnological process in a much shorter time than usual, for instance, may have profound economic significance, such as the ability to compress an image above the standard without losing quality. If the demonstrated advantage does not exist, or is minimal, the expediency of the project as a whole is in question. Even worse, there are inventions that are sold at the conceptual level, without the proof of concept having actually been provided, with the inventor not having solutions to all the practical problems entailed with its performance.

The process of preparing a patent application can help in discovering these flaws, if it is carried out properly. In the course of the process, the inventor is questioned to fulfill the requirements of the law that require a minimal level of knowledge of the modes of carrying out the invention. The inventor is required to present very specific information and cannot satisfy the needs of the patent attorney with vague answers. To ensure that answers are provided in full, it should be insisted that the inventor provide his answers in writing. When pointed questions are posed, the vulnerabilities are revealed.

A clear indication that something is wrong can be found in the answers of the inventor to the questions of the patent attorney. When a direct and simple question is posed (such as how to build a certain part of the device), we are entitled to expect a direct and concise answer. But, sometimes, the answer received consists of a litany intended to clarify for us that our question is incorrect; that everyone understands the answer, and, therefore, there is no need to answer it; and that we should not have posed the question in the first place. Experience shows that this behavior indicates that we are faced with an inventor who has not completed his invention and perhaps even surmises that it cannot be completed. Therefore, he attempts to frighten us lest we expose our ignorance, in the hope that at the end of the day, we will abandon our question. We must not be deterred and must continue to persist in investigating the key questions that we have set for ourselves. Above all, if the inventor does not provide the exact details necessary for preparing a good patent application, we will be left with information whose dubious value will reflect the value of the project.

We should keep in mind that because an inventor is clever does not guarantee that he is not a wolf in sheep's clothing, which should be investigated without compromise, particularly if it becomes clear that he does not know how to explain his invention in clear, simple, and practical terms.

ARE YOU SERIOUS?

For someone who does not deal with patents on a daily basis, the existence of a patent application constitutes somewhat of a confirmation of the seriousness of the invention it describes. The patent application is generally printed professionally and appears on official-looking paper. Prima facie, this is a document of import.

Any person can file a patent application, on any invention and topic whatsoever, and it will be printed when the time comes, even if it is not worthy of serious consideration, because in most countries, this printing precedes the examination of the application.

There are cases when filing a patent application serves, apparently, as a kind of therapy for the applicant to deal with his personal nightmares or perhaps with his dreams. Because there is no way to prevent a person from submitting a stupid invention, we must exercise common sense when reading patent applications and not automatically treat them with respect.

There are quite a few examples of this. For instance, international patent application publication number WO 93/14973 shows us a "spaceship shaped like a flying saucer." The design of the patent application, which is somewhat fictional, will not persuade even someone who is not an engineer to think that the beautiful saucer will rise up and fly off into the distance.

But the aforementioned patent application, which originates in the African continent, is not the only one that deals with our galactic problems. A German patent application (DE 3403865) was filed, which shows us a system that enables humanity to erect the first six supporting points outside our galaxy (whatever this may be) while using "only" six galactic spaceships. And what can be fairer than that? The mission is not too difficult, inasmuch as the inventor explains to us that at a flight speed of 299,792.35 kilometers per hour, it is possible to erect the system during the lifetime of a solitary astronaut. There is only one minor problem, and it is that to satisfy the mission, humanity will have to extend the average life expectancy to 200 years. Relatively, this certainly appears not to be a major problem. The inventor assures us that this project will unite the nations of the world, will bring perpetual peace to humanity, and will overcome worldwide unemployment and famine. Definitely worth it!

As we advance toward conquering outer space, we must not forget to look inwards. In France, they have already taken care to plan (meanwhile on paper) a "transmitter/receiver of gravitational waves" (French patent application FR2661295), which will enable us to produce telepathy at very long range. The planned device will enable humans to communicate over long distances while being in spaceships and perhaps could help the German galactic plan. However, beware! The Russians already have a method for analyzing extrasensory phenomena, including telepathy (patent application RU 2127546) and someone transmitting over long distances is subject, if so, to eavesdropping. But do not worry: in Japan, a patent application (JP 7306259) has already been filed which provides a "telepathy defense system for communicating with living entities." Do not despair!

In folk literature, it is customary to show the inventor archetype as an eccentric, strange, and borderline balanced person. There is nothing farther from this: a real inventor is a technological person who is levelheaded, balanced, and serious. This does not mean that there are no more crazy people in the world; but they are weirdoes, not inventors. When coming to invest in them, please do not be confused.

BEWARE! INTERNATIONAL PATENT

If you do not deal with patents often, it may be easy to misrepresent the true value of the assets presented to you. An inaccurate presentation of the patent protection status of the technology could be used to generate interest by a potential investor and could lead to unwarranted investments.

Memorize this: **there is no such thing as an international patent**. International patent applications exist[41]; they are also called "PCT" patent applications ("PCT" stands for "Patent Cooperation Treaty") and published as WO (the two-letter symbol of the "World Intellectual Property Organization"). An international patent application may, in due course, enter the national phase in various countries that may or may not issue a patent that stems from that application, depending on its patentability. The above, however, does not stop people from claiming that they own an "international patent."

It should be noted, for the sake of fairness, that often the deception is not deliberate and stems from the inaccurate use of professional terms by the entrepreneur, either as a result of ignorance or due to an innate aversion to precision. In many cases, the deception is, therefore, caused unintentionally. However, the ultimate result of a basic misunderstanding with regard to the value of the proposed technology could be very damaging, regardless of the circumstances of its creation.

It is not particularly difficult to find examples of such. If we casually browse the Internet, we can reach, for instance, one of the many sites that offer inventions for sale. If you Google "international patent," you'll see what I mean.

Because, as explained above, a PCT application can never become a patent itself, it is only an initial stage on the long road to obtaining patents in the countries that are members of the PCT. While an international patent application (and national patent applications in the various countries) confers rights on the applicant, these are "preliminary rights," which do not guarantee that a patent will ultimately be granted in any country. The patent rights of the applicant will be established according to the results of a careful and specific examination of his patent application, and it may be found that the invention described in the patent application is not new, that it lacks

---

[41] See also Chapter 7.

inventive step, or that it is not patentable for any other reason. Moreover, the patent that is ultimately granted may be more limited than it appears from the published PCT application. This does not mean that an international patent application has no value. On the contrary, it may be extremely valuable; however, its value is derived from the quality of the invention described in the patent application and not from the mere existence of the application.

This is similar to a patent holder who argues that his technology is "proven" because professional examiners have examined it and granted him a patent. But this argument is also misleading. Patent examiners do not conduct direct laboratory tests on the invention. They rely on the results that are presented to them by the patent applicant (unless these results are prima facie absurd) and ascertain the patentability of the invention according to criteria that differ from those of interest to the investor. Therefore, the grant of a patent on a given invention does not guarantee to an investor that the technology is given to effective commercial implementation, nor does it express any commercial opinion on it.

It is recommended to suspect anyone who bases his commercial arguments on the status of his patent application. Although obtaining a patent is an important and even crucial stage in many cases, on the road to the commercial exploitation of the technology, it is by no means a guarantee—or even an indication—of potential economic success.

PATENTS AS ENTERPRISE ASSETS

It is no secret that patents are important in determining the value of a company that holds them. A patent is an intellectual asset that has three principal facets: first, it constitutes a direct and immediate tool for competition in the relevant market. Second, it is deemed a basis for expectations with respect to the company's potential for future technological advances, and third, it reflects the uniqueness of the technology that is developed by the company, more so if the company's patents are not one-offs but rather a series of related patents that constitute exclusive accumulated knowledge.

Examining the significance of the company's patent policy to its activities is not an easy task. Clearly, not every patent adds to the value of the company. If, for instance, we are dealing with a company that develops food products, the added value of a patent found in its portfolio, which relates to high-quality shoe polish, will probably be very low. By contrast, there may be in its portfolio high-quality patents that enable the development of new food products, or with improved features (such as shelf-life duration), which may be critical to its present and future enterprise value.

In the not-too-distant past, many believed that the number of patents was the decisive factor in evaluating the worth of a company and that we should, therefore, file a large number of patent applications, without any regard to their quality and their significance to the company, to increase its value. There were quite a few cases of entrepreneurs managing to inflate the value of their company in the spirit of days gone by. By returning to the old economy, in which a company depends, to a great extent, on long-term technology, we must seek more sophisticated ways to raise the value of our enterprise.

Researchers of economic phenomena have understood for some time that patents may be used as an effective measure to evaluate enterprise value. Already in 1965, Scherer[42] understood the relationship between the value of an industrial company and its patents. Since then, numerous studies have been done that analyze the significance of the patent portfolio of the company. In 2002, a particularly interesting article was published in this regard.[43] The article analyzes the relationship between the number of times in which a patent was cited and the value of the company that holds the patent. The analysis is based on the assumption that valuable technology will produce patents on which the researchers will rely, and they will, therefore, be cited by them. The study found that the average number of citations of a patent is six. The most notable result observed is that companies whose patents are cited above average show a significant rise in their market value. Companies whose patents were cited more

[42] (F.M. Scherer, 'Firm Size, Market Structure, Opportunity and the Output of Patented Inventions," *American Economic Review* 55: 1097–1123)

[43] B. H. Hall et al., "Market Value and Patent Citations," eml.berkeley.edu/~bhhall/papers.

than 20 times (each) enjoy a market value that is 54% higher than what would have been expected on the basis of the capital invested in research and their patent portfolio. The study also explored the significance of self-citation (i.e., patents that cite other patents held by the same company). An interesting result is that a self-citation was also found to have significant value, although its validity differs from that of third-party citations. However mid-sized companies (those having an annual sales turnover of at least $500 million) cannot afford not to have significant self-citation in their portfolios, and the absence of such citation has an adverse effect on their enterprise values. An absence of sufficient self-citation could constitute evidence of a lack of significant development activity of the company.

Therefore, a manager who seeks to retain and increase the market value of his company can no longer afford to ignore what the patent portfolio of his company says about the economic significance of the technology that it holds.

CHAPTER 20
Patents for Business

One of the questions that are often raised is "How does the patent help me in my business?" The answer is not short and simple, inasmuch as a wise use of the patent as a business instrument may help us on many levels.

THE NDA AND THE PATENT APPLICATION

Many entrepreneurs are aware of the importance of maintaining the confidentiality of their inventions before filing a patent application so as not to jeopardize the chances of obtaining the patent if the invention is prematurely divulged. These entrepreneurs know, for the most part, that it is possible to reduce, to some extent, the risks of conducting commercial negotiations before filing a patent application, by having the other party sign a nondisclosure agreement (NDA), which will restrict the use of the information conveyed to him.

However, few entrepreneurs are aware of the advisability of signing an NDA after also filing the patent application. This need arises for two primary reasons: first, it is necessary to protect developments made after the patent application was filed, which constitute part of the product that the entrepreneur is seeking to commercialize. These developments, even if they are sometimes only "minor improvements," may be of commercial value. In the absence of an NDA, the entrepreneur will have to be constantly careful not to discuss these improvements and will have to regularly assess and remember what parts of his products he is not allowed to talk about. This causes difficulties when conducting negotiations, and the NDA may alleviate them. The second reason is that a patent application cannot protect commercial information; for instance, it is not possible to protect the names of suppliers or potential customers in a patent.

Nevertheless, the NDA may be an obstacle to conducting effective commercial negotiations because large corporations are often not willing to sign them, or getting them signed may require long negotiations. Consequently, in many cases, the entrepreneur wishes to refrain from requiring the signature of an NDA prior to a meeting, but then he must watch his mouth. He must refrain from revealing information on inventions, or an improvement of inventions, which were not included in the patent application that he filed, and he must refrain from conveying commercial or other information that cannot be protected by his patent application. Above all, filing a patent application that relates to a particular invention does not confer any protection on inventions that were not described and not claimed in it, even if they are improvements of the same invention that is the subject of the patent application.

Finally, it should be kept in mind that an NDA has implications above and beyond maintaining patent rights. Therefore, it is recommended to use an NDA that is tailored to the needs of the entrepreneur, which has been reviewed by an attorney who is involved in the commercial questions relevant to the project, and not to make do with using a standard form pulled out of the Internet.

EYES WIDE SHUT

We have operated for a while undisturbed by a potentially infringed patent, but this does not mean that we are off the hook. Patent holders do not always hasten to exercise their rights against patent infringers, and the reasons for this are many and varied. For instance, a patent holder may not be aware for a long time that his patent is being infringed, or, for some reason, the timing when the infringement becomes clear to him "will not be right" for him to engage in legal proceedings. This patent holder could "wake up" at a later stage, after the infringers have already made major investments, and file a patent infringement lawsuit against them. The burden of ensuring that they are not infringing the patents of others is on the potential infringer, and there is no way around it.

It should be borne in mind that a patent is equally valid throughout its life. It does not confer fewer rights toward the end of its term than at its beginning. The patent term is a fixed period (as stated, in most cases, 20 years), after which it expires. There are many cases in which the patent-protected technology becomes commercial on a significant scale only many years after the grant of the patent. This is not an uncommon situation in biotechnology and pharmaceuticals, for instance, which are fields in which, sometimes, the economic importance of a patent actually increases toward its expiration.

The patent holder is not required to enforce his rights immediately. As long as the patent is valid, it is his right to do so. It is true that, in many countries, a delay in exercising a patent has a price, which is sometimes reflected in a difficulty or inability to obtain interlocutory relief, such as interlocutory injunctions; however, these are procedural questions that do not pertain to the essence of the patent per se or to its scope.

One of the principles of the patent system is the public nature of the information with regard to a patent. A basic condition to granting any patent is that its contents will be published so that whoever wishes to develop a related technology can know of its existence, learn from it, and avoid infringing it. Take, for instance, Company A, the owner of an important, basic patent in the field of the Internet (this is a real-life example, but the actual name of the company has been omitted). Only in the last years of the life of the patent did the company start suing many alleged infringers that had used the technology protected by its patent for several years. The patent of Company A was open to everyone, and anybody could have studied it and assessed its significance. It may be assumed that quite a few companies were familiar with it before embarking on developing potentially infringing products. However, it seems that a flock syndrome was at work here, where "everyone was doing it." This being the case, it seems that many companies blindly followed other companies that chose to close their eyes wide open to the patent of Company A. It is the duty of commercial entities to analyze the patent field surrounding a product they wish to develop independently, and not march in single file, in the dark, and blindly after others.

THE DAY AFTER

The expiration of a patent generally heralds a marked drop in the prices of the product of the patent because, upon expiration of the patent, anyone who so wishes can lawfully produce and market the product. Many products are vulnerable to stiff competition from countries in which the production is particularly inexpensive, such as the People's Republic of China. The manufacturers in these countries cannot market patent-protected products in Western countries, even if there is no parallel patent that prevents production in their country, because importation into a country in which the patent is valid constitutes an infringement of the patent. But when the patent expires, in many cases, the original manufacturer cannot compete with the low prices of his competitors from the east, and his sales fall. It is true that this phenomenon is particularly acute in the pharmaceutical market, due to the major investments in research, development, and licensing, which are reflected in the final price of the product; however, there is no doubt that the prices of many other patent-protected products fall significantly when a generic version appears on the market.

How do we deal with this hard reality? It must be admitted that, in many cases, there is no cure for it, but if the patent holder enjoyed exclusivity for 20 years and has recouped his full investment (and afterwards profited nicely), he may have gotten a fair deal, and the loss of exclusivity does not harm him above a reasonable degree. However, sometimes, the patent holder fails to recoup his investments and to make an adequate profit, such as in the case of certain drugs for which the effective exclusivity period is relatively short, due to the need for lengthy licensing proceedings before the patented product can be marketed.

However, if we look at the overall market—the market of products intended to improve our standard of living—the expiration of the patent after 20 years constitutes an important driving force for someone who prepares himself in advance for the day after. In this field, there is one important way to defend oneself against competition following the expiration of the patent: to develop improved products, which will make the old product less attractive to consumers. If we succeed at this, when our competitor from the east comes with an old and inexpensive product, there will be at least a segment of the population that is willing to pay more for our improved and new product, which we have, of course, arranged to protect with a patent ahead of time. Unfortunately, experience shows that relatively few companies prepare properly for the day after and, instead, begin seeking answers to competition only when the competing product has already appeared on the market.

Do not forget that everyone can play "the improvements game." A shrewd competitor, who is aware that a patent on an important product is about to expire within three to four years, will invest thought and effort to arrive at an improvement that will make the product more attractive in either performance or price. He may do so if he, too, has other competitors in addition to the originator, who will compete with him on the generic product. If this shrewd competitor manages to file a patent application at a relatively early stage, he may find himself with exclusivity on an improved version when the original patent expires. For the sake of illustration, imagine what would have happened had a company obtained a patent that prevents all its competitors from using i3-i7 processors in their computers. Nobody would agree to continue purchasing new computers with old Pentium processors when a manufacturer with exclusivity sells computers with much more powerful ones.

When, if so, is the right time to begin thinking about a product improving on a successful commercial product? The answer is immediately and all the time. Immediately because there is no telling how much time will be required to arrive at the improved product, and all the time because the technology evolves every day and opens up new possibilities for manufacturing better and less expensive products. What we thought yesterday would be our spearhead the day after could prove to be irrelevant tomorrow.

THE DEATH BUSINESS

Everywhere and at every opportunity in this book, one important truth is emphasized: a patent is an aid for making a profit from investments in R&D. It is a business instrument, and it must fulfill a business need. This being the case, we must understand the role of the patent so as not to err and deny ourselves the proper use of it when our business so requires. The following examples may stimulate our imaginations and take us "out of the box."

Who said, for instance, that death is not a business? It turns out that an extensive industry thrives around our departure from this world. It begins with the simple things and ends with veritable hi-tech. To begin with, as long as we are able to decide for ourselves, we should arrange to make the appropriate preparations for the afterlife. Therefore, to help us in selecting the burial and memorial objects, display systems were invented that will facilitate our selection of the accessories that will accompany us after our deaths (US Patent Nos. 8,091,713 for "DISPLAY FOR A CASKET SELECTION ROOM" and 7,107,222 for "DEATH CARE MERCHANDISING SYSTEM").

The death industry does not stop only with human beings, however. Special pet cemeteries have been established in the United States, along with memorials for our four-legged friends. For those of us who form a close relationship with our pets, here is an indispensable facility: a special case for easy burial of pets who died far away from home (US Patent No. 8,453,303 for "HEART PET BURIAL VAULT").

And if we have already facilitated our task of selection and purchase of our burial paraphernalia, it is certainly advisable to know to what extent this is relevant for us. Many science-fiction stories have already been written about mortals who learn of the precise time of

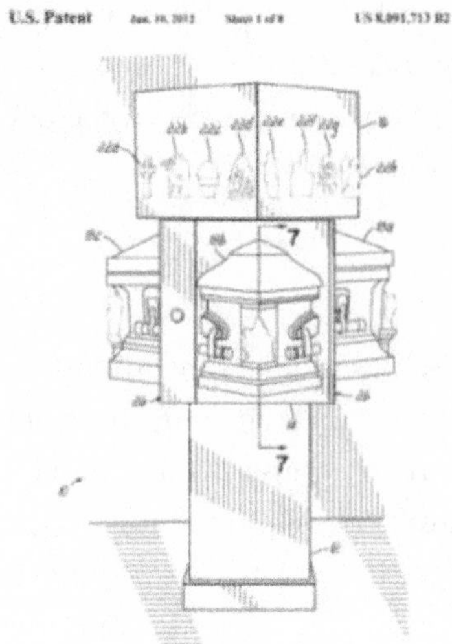

FIG. 1

Fig. 20-1: Representative figure of US Patent No. 8,091,713

their death. This is no longer science fiction: to this end, a "SYSTEM FOR PREDICTING FUTURE HEALTH" (US Patent No. 6,059,724) has been developed, which is based on an analysis of biomarkers of our bodies according to statistical methods. The manifestation of specific markers in our bodies will allow the system to predict the state of our future health. While this system does not purport to predict the precise day of our death, it will provide us with important information of our chances of contracting a variety of serious diseases, which, for some reason, is deemed by the designers to be a measure that improves our quality of life. After we receive this important information, we will be able to estimate the time we have left until the day of our death.

More precisely, however, US Patent No. 7,330,818 provides us with a "HEALTH AND LIFE EXPECTANCY MANAGEMENT SYSTEM," which we can carry with us to be constantly reminded of when we are expected to die, and what can be more soothing than this? Of course, if we suffer from some cardiac problems (which is very common in the adult population), our situation is even better, because US Patent No. 4,957,115 has provided us already many years ago with a "DEVICE FOR DETERMINING THE PROBABILITY OF DEATH OF CARDIAC PATIENTS." This is a clever device that is able to give us, in percentages, the probability of our death, through analysis of an electrical signal that is sent to us and that goes back from our hearts to the device.

There will probably be those whose strength will not withstand the constant ticking of the life-expectancy timepiece. To them, we can offer "EUTHANASIA COMPOSITIONS," which are described in US Patent No. 5,290,775. This composition, so we are assured, provides effective euthanasia "without unwanted side effects," and we will surely be reassured to know that the device is based on substances that do not require FDA[44] approval, so that there is no fear that they might cause health damage. But this is not easily done at all, because researchers have already foreseen the future and developed a method for "DETECTING NEAR-TERM SUICIDAL RISK UTILIZING VOCAL JITTER" (US Patent No. 7,565,285), with which it is possible to evaluate our predisposition to take leave of this world before our time. When it becomes clear that we have such predispositions, the matter will be taken out of our hands; European Patent Application No. EP 232,947 provides us with a "SUICIDE ATTEMPT WARNING METHOD AND SYSTEM." When we are attached to this system, we will have no choice but to look patiently at the digits of our life expectancy timepiece and to wait until they change and draw nearer to the deadline.

QUO VADIS?

Religion is also a business—a big business, generally speaking—and it is, therefore, also a target for various patent applicants.

The well-known Christian legend tells of Saint Peter, who, with great wisdom, fled Rome, where the Christians were persecuted by the Romans. On the way (on Via Appia), Jesus appeared before him, and Saint Peter asked him in amazement: "Quo vadis, Domine?" ("Whither goest thou, Lord?"). According to the legend, Jesus replied to him that he was going to be crucified again. Saint Peter interpreted Jesus's answer as an instruction to return to Rome, where he was indeed crucified by the Romans.

---

[44] US Food and Drug Administration.

In modern times, instead of "to be crucified again," Jesus's correct answer could have been "to the cover page of US Patent No. 5,456,625." This patent, titled "DOLLS FORMED IN THE LIKENESS OF THE LORD JESUS, WITH A MOVEABLE HEAD AND EXTREMITIES," is one of the more interesting inventions, inasmuch as it includes conductive nails that cause the cross to be illuminated when the doll is crucified with them. This is not the only patent on the subject. At the end of December 1999, precisely to seal the millennium, another US patent was issued (No. 6,007,404) titled "JESUS DOLL FOR TEACHING CHILDREN."

As stated, religion is a big business, particularly for religions in which religious symbols, such as images of Jesus and the saints in Christianity, are common. Therefore, we will not find these kinds of patents related to Jewish symbols, because the Jewish religion does not allow the creation of images for worship. On the other hand, a large quantity of Japanese patents was found that are related to ritual objects of the Buddhist religion. However, the largest economic entity of the Christian world—the Vatican—does not take part in any of it. No patent was found that is owned by or originates from the Vatican. Nevertheless, the Holy See does not ignore the importance of intellectual property, and it arranges, at least in some cases, to protect its trademarks through nonprofit entities. For instance, the trademark "CARITAS INTERNATIONAL" (International Christian Love) is registered in the United States in the name of a nonprofit entity whose address is in Vatican City, in respect of an assortment of charitable services.

The question posed is whether any religious faith can constitute a basis for a patentable invention. Prima facie, this amounts to a cynical exploitation of the weaknesses of others for the sake of profit making. However, isn't this definition correct in many other fields? When we invent a new face cream, which is an industrial product whose fundamental patentability is clear and not in any doubt, we are exploiting the faith of women that if they spread it on their faces, it will help maintain their beauty, their youth, and who knows what else. Sometimes, this is true, and sometimes, it amounts to pure voodoo. Still, these products are sold in vast quantities throughout the world.

Another example is found in the slimming instruments that sprout like mushrooms after the rain. With their mechanical springs and knobs, they are certainly an object worthy of patent protection. However, their benefit depends entirely on the user's strength of faith in their efficacy and in his perseverance. Therefore, if we look at the business side, we will discover that the ritual objects have characteristics that do not differ from other industrial products that are associated with laic rituals.

The concept of "utility," which is a cornerstone and condition to the patentability of an invention, is interpreted primarily on the basis of the point of view of the industry and not necessarily of the individual. This approach is appropriate and logical in most cases, if it is not brought to the absurd, while taking advantage of the gullibility of the consumers. And with respect to the other cases, the correct answer to the question "Quo vadis?" will probably be "Laughing all the way to the bank."

ATMOSPHERIC PATENTS

As at the writing of these lines, the NASDAQ is no longer what it used to be, and hi-tech is in pullback. And together with them, the age has thankfully ended in which every dot-com entrepreneur lacking technology and originality sought to register "something"—any patent application whatsoever—just to satisfy the investors, just so that the mandatory patent line will appear on the list of things that a company should have, not because he thought that he really needed a patent. By the time that his atmospheric company has to rely on its intellectual property, a year or two will pass, and by then, it will have already been sold to a nice American uncle with an uncontrollable impulse to part with the hundreds of millions of dollars that weigh heavily on him. In this situation, it is also not so important what is written in the patent application: the most important thing is that there is a paper that evidences that the entrepreneur was obedient and fulfilled this onerous task. Or so they thought back then . . .

But all that is behind us, and investors have mostly come to their senses, which means that we must again address the intellectual property of the company with our feet on the ground to build value for our enterprise and to maintain its technological advantages and our freedom to operate in our markets. Now (thank goodness), we have to again address our intellectual property and particularly our patents according to their importance and actual value and with the appropriate seriousness. This relationship between the technology that we are developing and our efforts to maintain it as our exclusive property—a non-severable relationship that was nonetheless lost to us for a moment in the maelstrom of the high-tech rush—has reemerged as something that requires judgment, understanding, and the investment of deep thought.

A company's patent portfolio is an important measure of the value of the technology it owns.[45] The interrelationship between the products manufactured or designed and the ability of the company to maintain exclusivity in a particular market for an expected period of time are parameters on which a merger or acquisition or an investment by a serious entity may rise or fall. These parameters permit us to evaluate the true value of the enterprise and not only its ability to manufacture stock exchange-related dreams. Since once bitten twice shy, we see now hyper-wariness among potential investors, who want to be convinced that they are no longer investing in a company only because an entrepreneur has a particularly long or outlandish ponytail and is careful to wear his shirt outside his trousers, to display some unspecified creativity. "This age is over," they say to us. "Now show us the real stuff."

The day after the bursting of the hi-tech bubble was quite similar to the day after an atomic bomb, but also here, just as in any science-fiction movie with a happy ending, a better and more stable world was built on the ruins. The patent system can greatly assist companies and entrepreneurs to remain with their feet firmly on the ground and to examine the technologies that they seek to develop through an impartial professional lens. It is true that this requires a much greater effort than writing "mood patents," and it is true that, to this end, we must invest in understanding the technology and in evaluating it

---

[45] See also Chapter 19.

against the outside world before we plan our patent. But this is one of the important roles of the patenting process, and saving on the understanding and planning stage is tantamount to spoiling the ship for a hap'orth of tar.

CHAPTER 21
The Competitors and Us

In many cases, the impression is that a company manager or entrepreneur, when preparing to address patent questions, does not take into account that he is not operating in a void. The reality is that our planning must take into account what our competitors do or might do and what effect the competitors have on us. Let's look at some examples.

SEE NO EVIL, HEAR NO EVIL

> *"I don't need a patent. In any case, I will not sue a major competitor that will infringe it, because I don't have money to fatten attorneys."*

This sentence, or something analogous, is thrown from time to time into the air, and we have difficulty understanding if this is a joke or if perhaps the man believes what he is saying. And indeed, we have met people who possess "wisdom" that is hidden from everyone else: the solution to the problem is to ignore it.

We can liken the patents in the possession of a small company to a nuclear weapons arsenal. A sane country does not manufacture nuclear warheads to attack the United States, Russia, or even smaller powers. The chance that a small country would detonate its nuclear weapon is minimal, except in a state of clear and immediate existential danger. According to the logic discussed above, it is not worthwhile to spend a great deal of money on manufacturing atomic bombs that in any case are not intended for use. However, nuclear power has various objectives, beyond actually detonating a bomb. First of all, if you can manufacture a nuclear arsenal, you are a country to be reckoned with. This is also the situation in the world of hi-tech: if you own good and strong patents, you are a player that cannot be ignored, and your patents are an admission ticket to the big guys' league. Furthermore, nuclear bomb production capacity shows technological capability. This is also the case in relation to patents: if the company is capable of producing good patents, this demonstrates its technological power—that is, its value.

But above all, there is the deterrent power. No one can guarantee that a small and weak country will not feel threatened, justly or unjustly, to an existential degree that will require it to exercise its nuclear power earlier than expected. The situation is even less clear in the patent world. A small company with a good and strong patent can also be a threat to an international giant. So long as the giant is afraid that the small company might actually use its patent, it cannot ignore its existence. A patent is a power equalization tool and is one that can balance between the limited powers of a small company and that of a larger competitor through the courts, which have a duty to protect the rights of the patent holder. This is not a game in which the small company stands alone against a large competitor. It has a formidable ally: the justice and legal system.

Nevertheless, a patent can fulfill this important deterrent role only if two conditions are satisfied: it must be good and strong, and its owner must not be perceived as one who is reluctant to assert his rights.

SYNERGISM BETWEEN PATENTS

Professionals always like to speak about "strategic planning." It always sounds good, regardless of whether it has real meaning or not, and that's why it is often a dislikable affectation to bring it up. In the patent world, however, "strategic planning" is a basic necessity. Investing work and thought into planning is always worthwhile in the long term.

An announcement given several years ago by Dr. Jackson, President of NPS Pharmaceuticals, when the company announced that it had been granted 14 patents for its major technology in the field of biotechnology, captures the essence of strategic planning: *"Every individual patent is valuable, but together they constitute a cohesive proprietary position covering all stages of drug discovery in this area, including potential drugs . . . This intellectual property platform has been diligently created over almost 10 years . . . and this work is now delineated and secured by these patents."*

Those who oppose investing effort in planning offer some interesting (though mistaken) explanations. For instance, they say, "It cannot be known what the research will yield, and, therefore, it is impossible to plan accurately," or "The market conditions at the end of the development are unknown, and, therefore, in any case, there is no point in planning." Others believe that "The effort required for strategic planning is greater than the potential benefit, and it diverts the developers from the immediate needs," and "Strategic planning leads to sure expenses but to unknown benefits."

It is true that strategic planning in the patent system incorporates an element of significant uncertainty and considerable effort, but the correct conclusion is not that everything should be left to the hand of fate. The objectives and courses of action should be examined regularly and updated according to the circumstances to converge toward the most suitable outcome for the company.

Planning is not guesswork. Proper work must take into account all the possible outcomes of the development work, even such that are not planned at that moment; steps must be taken toward creating protection through patents that will take possible scenarios into account. It is necessary to reanalyze the situation from time to time, according to the work progress, taking into account our competitors and their intellectual property and trying to precede them before they block us.

Importantly, we must understand and plan how one patent, when it is issued, will affect others in the same field. A patent does not exist, generally, in a vacuum. It is surrounded by the patents of competitors and by others we own. It is comparable to a secluded island in the sea, which is intended to block an enemy fleet's access to our shores. A well-planned patent portfolio will create a chain of islands that will prevent our competitors' ships from reaching our shores. Moreover, even if these islands are not contiguous, they may constitute an effective barrier if the distance between them was planned so that no ship would be able to pass between them undetected. In this manner, synergism is created between patents that constitute an effective barrier without covering the entire area.

PATENTS ON "BUSINESS METHODS"

The attitude of patent authorities around the world toward various topics is dynamic in nature and varies in light of different circumstances. For the most part, the approach of a patent authority[46] of a country is influenced by the position of the courts that examine some issues in depth, or by the enactment of binding laws, and by the promulgation of regulations that carry out these laws. There are also quite a few topics that are influenced by a need that arises with the emergence of a new technology, or of distress among "the clients" of the patent authority—that is, the patent applicants. It should be borne in mind that the patent authority serves the public as a whole and, therefore, it is very important that it is attentive to the needs of the public and that it takes its opinions and needs into consideration within the boundaries of the law. However, politics also plays a role in this field, and laws are sometimes legislated under the pressure of interest groups.

Patents on methods of doing business are a class of patents that pertain to all areas of our lives. In principle, they teach us to carry out a series of acts, in a certain way and order, to achieve a desired result. Each one of the steps alone does not have to be new, but the

[46] **Reminder**: The generic term "patent authority" is used here to refer to the central patent office of a country, not to be confused with a patent law firm, which is also sometimes referred to as a "patent office."

particular way in which they are combined, and their sequence, is what leads to a new and useful result. From this perspective, there is no difference between this kind of process and any industrial process that uses machines and tools that process materials in a specific order and eventually make a finished industrial product. However, in most cases, complicated tools are not necessary to carry out a business method, and in many cases, all that is needed is a computer with Internet access to carry out the process.

You would think that because methods of doing business are easy to copy, there is an excellent reason to grant them enhanced patent protection; after all, the goal of the patent system is to protect the inventor against the copying of his invention. Gotcha! That would make sense, so, of course, it is off the table.

The grant of patents in this field has incited actual hysteria on the Internet and in newspapers, and pages are filled almost daily with self-righteous nonsense regarding the need to keep everything on the Internet free.

At this point in time, it is next to impossible to foresee where the patent system will go with business method patents because legislation and court rulings pop up like mushrooms after the rain. However, it would be fair to say that the major patent authorities, including the EPO and the USPTO, have taken a dislike to this class of patents. Laws have been designed to make the life of owners of business method patents a living hell. If your patent is suspected of having anything to do with business, you are in bad shape; the witch hunt is broad and very likely will get to you.

There is no doubt that the pendulum will eventually swing back to a less nonsensical position, and we will again judge inventions according to their contribution to human knowledge and welfare. But until then, we can expect difficulties in this field and sometimes even unjust prejudice to the rights of an inventor of this class of inventions. So, if you can invent something that cannot be suspected of involving a business method, go ahead and do that and leave that business method idea alone—at least until they blow the "all clear."

GOLIATH SETTLES

"What, do you want me to sue Microsoft?" the managers ask sardonically. The answer is twofold: first of all, a giant company is not immune to a justified lawsuit, and if there is no other option, the patent holder may be forced to resort to an infringement lawsuit. But many lawsuits, including some involving giant companies, are settled at a relatively early stage.

Not every large company (and perhaps not even the overwhelming majority of the large companies) discounts the proprietary rights of others. On the contrary, the tendency of large companies is to avoid deliberate infringement of third-party patent rights. It is true that if we place an absolute barrier against the activity of a company through a patent, we might force it to fight the patent and perhaps even to infringe it. But so long as a reasonable commercial settlement can be reached, which allows continued activity with payment of reasonable royalties, many companies will not choose to commit a deliberate infringement of a good and strong patent.

Did we say a good and strong patent? That is a patent that, in the eyes of the potential infringer, could constitute a substantial problem. Such a patent should withstand legal tests and emerge from them sufficiently strong to block the path of the company. Just as beauty, the strength of a patent is often also "in the eyes of the beholder," and two companies may regard the same patent differently because their activities and products differ. However, a patent that is prima facie invalid will not help us in our dealings with another company, large or small.

What should be learned from this is that not in every battle between David and Goliath is it necessary to slay the giant. It is also possible to bring Goliath to the negotiating table and to ultimately reach a settlement with him that will serve both parties.

CROSS-LICENSING

Sometimes, a company that is sued for patent infringement turns around and bites back by filing an infringement counterclaim. The result, in some cases, will be a cross-license agreement between the two companies, according to which each company is allowed to use the other party's patents.

It is a mistake to regard a patent as a tool that is only meant to block the activity of the competitor; patents have many other facets and play a role in the balance of fear. In a commercial war between competing companies, just as in a war between superpowers, it is extremely important to equip ourselves with all the weapons that may give us an advantage over the competitor. Moreover, it is also important to be prepared to use our weapon, if necessary. However, the sides to this war will not lightly use a "day of judgment" weapon, knowing that the other side also has a similar one. The inevitable result of this situation is an arrangement with which both companies can live.

The pacifists say: *"That being the case, we do not need patents. Let us settle all our affairs in a commercial agreement between the companies."* These kinds of statements belong to the group of sayings that the well-known British writer P. G. Wodehouse once said are "like Shakespeare: sound well, but don't mean anything." Human nature does not allow us to reach an agreement on important matters (and, sometimes, even not on matters of petty importance) before being convinced that we have no other option. The threat of suing for infringement of the patent is an inevitable ritual, just as a teachers' strike at the opening of the academic year or a war between two dogs for the attention of a female. Only after we sustain a few bites and feel the adversary's arm will we be convinced of the need to reach an agreement with him. It is true that if we follow the path of the pacifists and do not develop an arsenal of patents, the problem will solve itself immediately: our adversary will have patents that paralyze us, and we will have nothing with which to fight back. After our rapid commercial demise, certainly quiet and peace will prevail in the sector, but this is not usually the desirable solution.

What should we, therefore, do on the practical level? When planning our patent portfolio, we should not limit ourselves to those aspects that are of immediate importance to us and to our products. We must be thoroughly familiar with our adversaries and must make sure that we have some patents our arsenal, which may serve us to create a balance with the competition. These patents will stem, of course, from R&D that we did for ourselves, but looking through the eyes of our competitors, those inventions may acquire a different significance. Strategic planning, remember?

Because any patentable invention at which we arrive is an asset in which we have invested money and effort, common sense requires us to exploit it to the maximum extent—if not to protect our products directly, at least to maintain our position vis-à-vis the competition. Any knowledge that we developed and did not cover with a patent is a weapon that we knowingly let fall from our hands. Therefore, before relinquishing it, it is highly advisable that we verify that indeed there is no chance that we will need it in the future.

MILITARY PATENTS

Military patents are a matter that entrepreneurs are not normally exposed to, particularly because they involve systems that are not sold on the free market. Furthermore, the top priority of a developer of military systems is the quality of the system engineering, which must perform its work under extreme conditions. Price considerations are usually only secondary. The issue of ballistic missiles makes the headlines from time to time, when security incidents occur somewhere. Beyond the obvious strategic importance of the issue, there is no doubt that there may also be a lot of money in anti-missile defense systems. Therefore, large companies operating in the field have spared no efforts over the past decade to position their products in this attractive market. Clearly, every country would want to provide its citizens with an anti-missile umbrella and thereby contribute to their sense of security, whether real or perceived.

Among the players in the field, we find companies from several developed countries, notably the United States, France, Germany, and the United Kingdom.

One wonders, therefore, how does any country grant a patent on a strategic or tactical defense system, the whole purpose of which is to protect its citizens? The taxpayer would have expected the country to provide for a solution from its own resources. Surely, to this end, we contribute generously to the local treasury. But it should be borne in mind that this is a big business, which no country having appropriate technological capability is willing to relinquish.

An interesting similarity can be seen here between the development of the systems in question and the development of novel medications. In both cases, we would have liked the country to provide us with solutions, inasmuch as if it does not provide for defense nor for health, to what end does it collect taxes? To promote the enormous investments required for finding effective solutions, the prospects for a profit commensurate with the investment must be clear and real. A patent is a device by which the developer may reap that profit. Governments can and should help, but the thought that politicians will disburse from their government's meager coffers a fortune for the sake of an objective whose achievement, in the case of success, will be credited to a future government is, how should we say, naïve.

DIRECT AND INDIRECT COMPETITORS

Earlier in this chapter, we already touched on the subject of agreements arrived at before or during a patent infringement lawsuit. These kinds of agreements are part of the routine life of technological companies. The course of events is clear: a company that holds a patent discovers that it is infringed by another company and files an infringement lawsuit against that company. Promptly on filing the lawsuit, or after some bloodletting by both parties, negotiations begin in an effort to settle the dispute. The parameters that enable agreement are also clear: the price has to be such that the defendant company would be able to endure it business-wise and sufficient so that it is worthwhile for the plaintiff to settle. It is also generally necessary that the agreement be such that it does not cause the defendant (and sometimes even the plaintiff) to "lose face." Moreover, the parties, or one of them, would be averse to encouraging other potential litigants to sue it, if the money involved in the settlement is substantial, and, therefore, more often than not, the settlement terms are kept secret. These are the cases that we read about in the press releases of the various companies. However, sometimes, the process begins before the filing of a lawsuit, with initial contact by the patent holder, and in this case, the public is not aware of the existence of a patent license agreement.

In few cases, such an agreement can be reached between direct competitors, where both compete for the same product market segment. However, there are cases in which natural competitors have no other option but to cooperate in the marketing of a product because both of them hold patent rights that pertain to the same product and a failure to agree would result in a clear loss for both of them. These kinds of intersecting rights can be territorial (i.e., when one has a patent in one key market and the other has a patent in another key market) or can pertain to different parts of the product (for instance, when one has rights to a chemical substance and the other has a patent on its use). In many other cases, this involves a company that is the patent holder but is not the manufacturer of the product, which is dealing with a manufacturing company. For instance, a company that develops machines for manufacturing beverage cans is not willing to allow a beverage manufacturing company to use its machine free of charge, but it would certainly be willing to reach an arrangement whereby the infringer will purchase the future machines from it at full price.

The key to all these is the very existence of the patent. Without having a patent in our hands that may be of importance to another company, we have no foundation on which to conduct negotiations. A technology that is developed by a company, as a byproduct or accidentally, may be valuable to other companies. Strange as it may seem, many companies do not even take this into account in their overall considerations of patent protection. Those companies employ shortsighted policies, "are content with their lot," and protect only those aspects that are important to them for personal use. This leads to an unfortunate waste of assets, inasmuch as broader protection can often be obtained with very little effort.

These companies frequently ask why they should protect aspects of the invention that are relevant to other industries but are remote from the company's field of activity. The answer is this: precisely because they are in a different field! Technology that under no circumstances we would want to see in the hands of the competition, we would be glad to market to a company that does not compete with us. If we were too lazy to broaden our protection, all in all, we lost prospective profits, and to other companies we gave as a gift assets that we could have sold for money. Therefore, if we are not philanthropists, we have wasted resources and assets.

Part V: World Patent Policies

"My home policy: I wage war; my foreign policy: I wage war. All the time I wage war."

[George Clemenceau, speech to the French Chamber of Deputies, March 8, 1918]

This part addresses the policies of bodies that shape the patent systems of the world.

CHAPTER 22
The Impact of Patent Policies on Our Lives

Regular people are not aware of the many ways in which the patent system impacts our everyday lives. A representative and non-exhaustive selection follows.

WHOSE GENOME IS THIS?

The patent system sometimes touches the most personal and basic concerns of each and every one of us. A good example is the field of genetic engineering and patents granted in that area, which have been at the center of worldwide public debates for years.

With the outbreak of one of the controversies in this field in the Western world in 2000, the then-president of the United States, Bill Clinton, and the British Prime Minister, Tony Blair, released a joint statement in March of that year, saying "human genome data should be made freely available to scientists everywhere." Some biotechnology companies' stocks fell sharply, and the statement led to a heightened preoccupation with the subject in the media around the profound questions related to patents on human genes. It is hard to free oneself from the feeling that this statement did not come from a deep understanding of the issues—particularly due to its timing—at the center of a sensitive public debate. It resembled more the other scientific adventures of Bill Clinton, which began with the bacteria from Mars (which apparently never existed).

The argument continued for many years thereafter and is still ongoing, although the pendulum has moved toward those who deny the patentability of genes, with the US Supreme Court ruling, nicknamed ***Myriad***,[47] in which the validity of gene patents in the United States was challenged, specifically addressing claims in issued patents to Myriad Genetics that cover isolated DNA sequences, methods to diagnose propensity to cancer by looking for mutated DNA sequences, and methods to identify drugs using isolated DNA sequences.

The case was originally heard in the Southern District Court of New York, which ruled that all the challenged claims were not patentable. Myriad then appealed to the United States Court of Appeals for the Federal Circuit. The Federal Circuit overturned the previous decision in part, ruling that isolated DNA, which does not exist alone in nature, *can* be patented and that the drug-screening claims were valid, and confirmed in part, finding the diagnostic claims unpatentable. The plaintiffs appealed to the Supreme Court, which remanded the case to the Federal Circuit, which did not change its opinion. On September 25, 2012, the American Civil Liberties Union and the Public Patent Foundation filed a petition for certiorari with the Supreme Court on the second Federal Circuit Decision. On June 13, 2013, in a unanimous decision, the Supreme Court invalidated Myriad's claims to isolated genes. The Court held that merely isolating genes that are found in nature does not make them patentable. Although the ruling of the Supreme Court is what counts, the continued differences of opinions and the nuancing of the issue illustrate how complex these questions are.

Following the lead of the US Supreme Court, in a decision issued on October 7, 2015, the High Court of Australia ruled unanimously in ***D'Arcy v. Myriad Genetics Inc.*** that three related patent claims held

---

[47] **ASSOCIATION FOR MOLECULAR PATHOLOGY et al. v. MYRIAD GENETICS, INC., et al.**, No. 12–398. Decided June 13, 2013.

by Myriad Genetics, Inc. under Australian Patent 686,004 were invalid.

The question of patenting inventions related to the human genome is not simple, and it is no wonder that it incites worldwide public debate. These are subjects that pertain to our very existence, which it is customary to exclude from the intellectual property sphere and not to grant patents on them or to restrict the scope of the monopoly granted by the patent. A good example of this is the methods of treatment of the human body. Most patent laws in the world explicitly prohibit granting patents, for instance, on methods of performing surgeries or on other therapeutic methods.[48]

TECHNOLOGY VERSUS ART

Not every invention is patentable, and some inventions may not belong to one of the categories for which patent protection should be granted (i.e., patentable subject matter). An example are inventions that relate to the methods of treatment of the human body that were mentioned before in this chapter, such as methods of performing surgeries, where it is accepted by most of the world that granting exclusivity on them would be unethical. A less successful example is denying patentability to inventions that pertain to computer software. However, trouble is more than brewing in this area, with the US Supreme Court leading in creating uncertainty and challenges. In ***Alice Corporation PTY. Ltd. v. CLS Bank International, et al.***, handed down on June 19, 2014, the US Supreme Court held the Alice claims invalid under 35 USC § 101, using a two-step test for determining patent statutory subject matter according to which one first determines whether the claim recites non-statutory subject matter, such as an abstract idea. If it does, then one "determines whether it contains an 'inventive concept' sufficient to 'transform' the claimed abstract idea into a patent-eligible application."

In applying the second step to the method claims in Alice, the court stated: "Viewed as a whole, these method claims simply recite the concept of intermediated settlement as performed by a generic

---

[48] See also Chapter 16.

computer. They do not, for example, purport to improve the functioning of the computer itself or effect an improvement in any other technology or technical field. An instruction to apply the abstract idea of intermediated settlement using some unspecified, generic computer is not '*enough*' to transform the abstract idea into a patent-eligible invention."

While this ruling created many challenges for patent applicants, you will not find a US patent attorney who will claim that he knows exactly how to overcome the issues it created, but you will be offered diverse options that, hopefully, will help to mitigate the problem. The net result: more headache and work for patent practitioners and, of course, more of that and added costs for patent applicants.

Not in all fields we have Supreme Court rulings similar to *Myriad* or *Alice*, and the rulings of the Supreme Court of one country are not binding on other countries (although we are aware of copycat tendencies in some jurisdictions). The correct and healthy approach, therefore, is that each invention that meets the criteria of the law must be awarded patent protection. However, beyond the letter of the law, society must insist on minimal behavioral norms to protect itself.

Art is an expression of the originality of man, his internal quality, and his personal ability to express that which is within him. Seemingly, art has nothing to do with inventions. However, in fact, technology had already some time ago initiated a not-so-quiet war for the destruction of man's artistic ability. In the United States, a patent was issued (No. 6,037,064), which claims a "Revolutionary method in the art of painting and decorative art the three-dimensional art object created thereby." This patent describes, step by step, how to create the claimed image by preparing different layers in a kind of "reverse autopsy." Another older US patent (No. 4,885,193) surpassed itself, claiming simply and modestly a "new art form." Removing art from the realm of the private expression of the artist and transforming it into something "industrial" is per se a spine-tingling phenomenon. However, these examples refer to "new arts" and do not endanger our delicate cultural fabric, even if the opinions will surely differ with respect to their appeal and their contribution to humanity.

There are much more dangerous inventions than those. An

obvious representative of these inventions is the disaster called karaoke. This is the same perversion that allows perpetrators to take advantage of electronics to eliminate the importance of the human voice. These satanic devices enable any person to sing to the sound of the song's melody without requiring actual musical ability. The relationship between the singer and the result has, therefore, been severed, and we obtain a fake product whose source quality we are unable to judge. Additional confusion is provided to us by US Patent No. 5,889,223, titled "KARAOKE APPARATUS CONVERTING GENDER OF SINGING VOICE TO MATCH OCTAVE OF SONG," which relates to a means by which the singer's voice changes automatically from male to female and vice versa, depending on the desired gender in a given song. Our influence as human beings, therefore, is becoming negligible, and the drive to attain artistic achievements in our own right is under attack.

From this perspective, we can understand what was once said about the fine singer who failed to attain success: "She has two basic flaws that do not allow her to succeed on a large scale as a singer," it was said. "She has a nice voice, and she can sing."

AN INTIMATE MOMENT WITH THE FLY

The morning cup of coffee is a very personal moment when man reconnects with his surrounding world. Therefore, when a fat and sluggish fly decided on one of these mornings to land on my mug and to stubbornly stick to it, that did not herald the coming of spring but rather was an unwarranted intrusion into the intimacy of the moment. In these moments, the question arises of "how the modern world has not yet managed to rid itself of the plague of flies." The fly is a tangible enemy of man, of his beasts, and of his agricultural crops. Among the well-known haters of the fly, we can include Mark Twain, who pondered whether the fly could be the work of the Creator, and Martin Luther King, who believed that flies were sent to him by the Devil to interfere with his reading.

The fly is everyone's problem, and no one, to date, has provided a concrete and comprehensive solution to it. If we look at patents on the subject, we can discover a US patent (No. 6,022,705) to Cornell University, which exploits advanced biological knowledge of the sodium channels of the common housefly and of the relevant gene to develop specific fly exterminators, which would eradicate the housefly without harming other beneficial insects. Sadly, since the grant of this patent some 15 years ago, very little activity has been found in the patent field in this respect. This could be, according to one conspiracy theory, that we actually want to keep the flies for some underhand reason. For instance, a recent international patent application (WO2015/134033) relates to "the use of insect protein hydrolysates to replace other protein constituents in animal and human foodstuffs" and uses, among others, the larvae of Musca domestica (i.e., the housefly) as a protein source. Yikes! They plan to feed flies to us.

Around the same time when the aforementioned ingenious US patent was issued, two much more pragmatic Chinese patents were published: one (No. 2361085) relates to a "FLY CATCHING BOTTLE," and the second (No.2361596) brings us a "FLY KILLING DUSTBIN." If we assume for a moment that advanced biological methods can eradicate the fly problem, the question is posed regarding whether there is justification for granting a patent on a much more primitive solution, which requires catching one fly at a time inside a bottle. The answer is, of course, yes. If we recall the three principal criteria of patentability—novelty, inventive step (non-obviousness), and utility—we must ask ourselves, assuming that the first two conditions are met, whether the invention lacks utility only because there is an invention that is ostensibly more useful, inasmuch as it addresses the problem on a much larger scale. In the example at hand, does the chance of eradicating the housefly by reaching its sodium channels, using a pesticide for mass extermination, make an invention such as the Chinese dustbin, or the bottle in which the flies are killed individually, less "useful" to the poor Chinese peasant?

The concept of "utility" must be examined in direct relation to the problem. That same Chinese peasant, who lives in a fly-ridden hut, will find peace from his suffering if we issue to him a bottle that kills his personal flies, even if not involving a systemic solution that liberates China as a whole from that plague. Therefore, under some circumstances, the fly bottle is very useful, and it is worthy of patent protection even if much more sophisticated solutions exist. The moral of the fly story is, as far as we are concerned, that we must not discount a simple invention that actually solves a problem, only because something much more ingenious has been proposed elsewhere.

In the case at hand, the fly has a faithful friend that protects its interests, in the form of the various environmental authorities, which, every now and then, find flaws in various pesticides that are designed to fight the fly and the damage it causes. The US Environmental Protection Agency notified, for instance, of the risks of using the common pesticide "Chlorpyrifos" only after it had already been in use for over 35 years. It is unclear if every new study on this or that pesticide also considers the damage to man and to his environment, caused by the relevant pest. Humanity is determined to find a clever solution that will satisfy the authorities. What is clear is that, until it is found, we will have many intimate moments with the fly.

AN INTERNATIONAL DIET

The level of a local industry of a given country is judged, to a large extent, by the patents that it produces. Similarly, patents shed light on a nation's approach to many subjects. Therefore, if we wish to characterize the competency of a nation in any field, we can use its patents as an effective analysis tool.

An interesting example of this is food. A cursory nonscientific study reveals the following data:

After hundreds of years of beer production in European breweries, there is still room for innovation. Recently, beer manufacturer Heineken was granted a patent on a "METHOD OF FERMENTING WORT" (US 8,647,688).

Even if there is a complicated debate in relation to the quality and the taste of raw fish, there is apparently justification for technological progress there, too, because a Japanese company took the trouble to develop a "DEAERATED PACKAGED FROZEN SUSHI, PROCESS FOR PRODUCING THE SAME AND METHOD OF

COOKING," for which it was granted US Patent No. 8,133,517.

Pasta lovers know that human life is not long enough to taste all the varieties and kinds that have been developed throughout history. If we combine the number of pasta varieties with the varieties of sauces, we come to thousands of different pasta dishes. Nevertheless, an Italian company has seen fit to develop a new kind of "FILLED FOOD PRODUCT AND METHOD OF PRODUCING SUCH FOOD PRODUCT" and also, recently, to file a US patent application thereon (US 2015/0313264).

And from this gallery, the place of the Swiss is not vacant, as they work feverishly to develop "CHOCOLATE PRODUCTS" on which they were granted US Patent No. 5,985,341.

But what about the French? A quick review reveals that in recent years, no US patents were granted to any French company relating, for instance, to the production of wine or cheeses—two of the flagships of French cuisine. Only a handful of French patent applications were filed on the subject. This indicates stagnation in the French food industry, which apparently refuses to be renewed and adheres to its old (and good) recipes.

This trend is also evident in other fields—fashion, for instance. Fashion today is no longer what it used to be, and alongside the personal taste of the designer, there is a necessity for technological developments that will lower the price of the product and improve its quality. Shoes, for instance, are a complicated matter. A quick review of the progress in the shoe production field reveals that in the years 2014–2015, over 1,000 patents and patent applications were published that have as a subject the manufacturing of shoes or shoe-related inventions (such as soles or methods of manufacturing them). Of those, 862 patent documents are Chinese patent applications relating to all aspects of shoe manufacturing! It is not difficult to predict, therefore, that China will be the leading industrial country for shoe manufacturing in the near future and perhaps for many years to come.

This simple example works for everyday products with which every one of us is familiar and uses, and it is also valid for more advanced products. A simple analysis of the kind presented above allows us to know quite easily where to look for a partner, customer, or competitor for technological developments in a specific field. Of course, it is possible to focus the analysis from the national level to the individual level and, in this manner, to identify industries that deal intensively with technological development in the area that interests us. Since obtaining patents is an expensive, complicated, and lengthy process, it generally constitutes a true measure of the interest of their holders.

CHAPTER 23
Different Perspectives

Patent systems around the world do not all work in the same way. However, the internal logic of the patent system is generally preserved consistently in most countries.

A DIALOGUE BETWEEN DEAF PEOPLE

Patent applications that are filed with the patent authorities[49] in the different countries undergo a process that is called "examination," during which a professional examiner studies the invention, examines it according to the prior knowledge in the field (the "prior art") and the criteria set in the laws of his country, and discusses with the applicant his right to receive the requested monopoly[50] on his invention. The examination process is a dialogue in which the examiner presents to the applicant everything that he has found, while the applicant revises whatever requires revision and presents substantive arguments to persuade the examiner to withdraw rejections of claims, which, in his opinion, are unjustified.

This process, particularly in the United States and Europe, sometimes feels like a dialogue between deaf people, in which the

[49] **Reminder:** The generic term "patent authority" is used here to refer to the central patent office of a country, not to be confused with a patent law firm, which is also sometimes referred to as "patent office."

[50] A patent is a legal, state-sanctioned monopoly.

examiner ignores the answers that are given to him and staunchly insists on his arguments. Examiners are no different from other populations, and there may be examiners of low competence who do not understand the invention and will not understand it even if we make every possible effort to explain it to them. In these cases, we will generally have no other option, and we may have to appeal the rejections of the examiner to a higher instance.

However, before we decide that we are victims of an incompetent examiner, we should examine ourselves and ensure that we are not erring with a misguided feeling of entitlement. The applicants sometimes tend to forget that they are applying for a monopoly. The authority facing them is not required to grant them what they want automatically, and it will certainly not do so without a review to its satisfaction. The examiner facing us is working under guidelines and constraints set for him by the system and cannot invest infinite time in each patent application. Therefore, if we do not know how to properly appreciate what issues are bothering the examiner, and we do not clarify our answers to him in a persuasive manner, he will not accept our application.

There are applicants who regard the examiner as an unwarranted obstacle facing them and as someone who should be treated with hostility and disdain. An examiner who does not understand, they maintain, should be treated as an imbecile and his incompetence exposed before all. The more we do so, they believe, the faster the examiner will acknowledge his limitations and accept our patent application with no further argument, lest we humiliate him again with our superior technological ability. They are, therefore, very surprised when the examiner does not curl up out of shame and does not immediately grant a patent but again stands his ground as before. These applicants do not understand the rules of the game and have forgotten that the application, and not the examiner, is up for examination.

A patent application is not an intelligence test and not a showcase of the genius of the inventor. It is a technical–legal document that must explain technological details, which are sometimes hard to grasp, in the clearest manner. The simpler the inventor will make it for the examiner to understand, the better his invention will be appreciated by him. So, when the examiner comes and asks a question that demonstrates a lack of understanding of the invention, we must first ask ourselves where we have not been clear enough and how to better clarify the invention to him, before making futile comparisons between the professional competence of the inventor and that of the examiner.

It is important to know that the examiner is not our enemy. He fulfills his duty using the tools at his disposal, and it is our duty to help him attain the necessary level of understanding and not to criticize him for needing explanations that seem trivial to us. If we behave in this manner, and we come up against a dim-witted or unprofessional examiner, and our explanations are to no avail, it would then be warranted to appeal his rejections. However, it is important to bear in mind that filing an appeal against a final rejection of the examiner is generally a costly pleasure, in terms of time and money, and we should not be tempted to do so, except when there is no other choice.

THE BLESSING OF PUBLICATION

In most advanced countries, patent applications are published 18 months after their "effective date." For this purpose, the effective date (the priority date) is the date of the first application on which the patent application is based, which was filed in a country that is a party to the Paris Convention (which essentially involves all important countries with very few exceptions).[51]

The publication of the patent application brings much blessing to the applicant and to the industry. It prevents the phenomenon of "submarine patents," which were very common in the past in the United States when a patent application remained pending for a long time and there was no way of knowing of its existence before the patent was issued. During "the submergence" period, people working in the same field invested efforts and resources that sometimes turned out to be wasted because an emerged patent covered the fruits of its

[51] For more details on the Paris Convention, see Appendix B.

labor. The early publication of the patent application updates the information in the possession of the industry at an earlier time so that resources can be timely diverted to more productive directions.

The early publication is also a blessing for the applicants. First of all, it is a basic and fundamental condition to having "provisional protection" for an invention. The essence of this protection is that a holder of a patent that has been granted would be able to demand compensation from an infringer of his patent, which is due from the day of publication of his patent application. This is particularly important in relation to short-term inventions, such as in the Internet and telecommunications field, in which the use of the invention by the competitors may occur at a relatively early stage following exposure of the technology. A potential infringer, on the other hand, will have to take the patent application into account and decide whether he wishes to invest his time and money in committing infringing acts that, ultimately, could make him pay compensation from the first day of the infringement. And for someone who does not intend to willfully infringe, the early publication will afford the opportunity to avoid investing in a nonproductive direction.

A second blessing for the patent applicant is the raising of the entry threshold of competitors into his field of practice. Ignoring the existence of a relevant patent application, a competitor may make a significant investment in a development that will infringe the patent when issued. And although a patent may be granted eventually, quite often we witness a situation in which the competitor is too invested in the project to be able to simply give up. This competitor may find itself with its back to the wall and may be forced to engage in a patent war against its will in order to salvage its investment, which will be lost if the patent remains valid.

TEMPORARY GREED

The issuance of the above-referenced provisional protection also constitutes a "quieting of conscience" of the patent authority, which is generally the one responsible for delays in the examination of the patent application due to workload and for lack of resources. Granting this provisional protection constitutes a "consolation prize" for an applicant who was stuck in a long and inefficient examination. However, the protection provided to the applicant with the publication is not always valuable: a condition of taking advantage of this protection is that the granted patent claims will be identical in scope to those of the application as published. A further condition is that the infringer must be informed of the existence of the patent application. It is easy to fulfill the second condition, because all that this requires is that a letter be sent to the infringer, which draws his attention to the existence of the patent application,[52] but complying with the first condition is altogether another story.

Justice and logic require that if the claims of the application have been amended to such an extent that what seemed to be an infringement no longer infringes the resulting patent, the patentee has no recourse against what he originally viewed as an infringement. However, this condition opens a wider door, through which infringers may be able to claim immunity for their infringements during the period prior to the grant of the patent, because the patent claims have undergone extensive amendment and are not "essentially the same" as those that were originally published. That's why excessive greed on the part of the applicant might not pay off.

Quite often, we see patent applications with unreasonably broad claims, which will obviously be narrowed in the end to more reasonable and sensible claims. And, nevertheless, instinct drives us to begin with a broad claim and to narrow it later so as not to file an overly narrow claim at the outset. Filing a claim with the suitable breadth requires investing work and thought, which can sometimes be substantial. Therefore, a manufacturer of a reinforced window with eight different layers of glass joined with different polymeric materials on each layer will make life easier for himself and claim, for instance, "a reinforced glass window including a polymer," which is a definition that certainly will not exclude any element of his invention but that does not define the invention at all. This common practice may

[52] In Europe, for the preliminary protection to become available, translations of the claims have to be deposited in the patent offices of the relevant countries.

constitute a double-edged sword, if it turns out that the patent holder eventually needs provisional protection.

It could be argued that the court must only address the final form of the claim and determine whether the infringing act or product are still covered, and it does not matter what its form and breadth were at the time of the publication of the application. Perhaps, but such a sweeping determination would encourage the filing of unreasonably broad claims, whose whole purpose would be to intimidate the competitor in an unfair manner. In fact, a requirement of reasonability in a change that is made to a claim in the course of the examination, in order to be entitled to the provisional protection, is what may prompt applicants to file applications with reasonable claims in advance and to thereby fulfill the additional role of the early publication: presenting the current state of existing patent protection to the public in the most correct way. Therefore, courts may deem an extreme change in the breadth of the claim sufficiently good cause to deny the patent holder the benefit of provisional protection. To try to avoid this potential danger, it is not necessary to implement extreme measures; it is enough to invest thought when drafting a set of claims and draft it in a way that, even if broad, is within the realm of reason.

EQUIVALENTS

One of the central pillars of the patent system is the doctrine of equivalents. Simplistically, this is a doctrine that is intended to prevent a situation in which a seasoned patent infringer will "literally" circumvent the patent claims but will still carry out the essence of the invention. This doctrine is extremely important because it cannot always be foreseen which opportunities will enable the shrewd infringer "to outwit" the patent claims. The intent of the legislature is to give the owner of the invention a protection that is commensurate with the scope of his invention; therefore, it has to block creative possibilities of circumvention.

This doctrine was established firmly in rulings throughout the enlightened world. In Israel, the legislature outdid itself and established this principle in the law[53] so that there would be no doubt in the heart of the potential infringer that he will not profit from making an equivalent infringement. In this way, the world acted quietly and peacefully, until one clear day, the United States of America was stunned: a new blow landed on it, nicknamed *Festo*, which refers to a verdict of the Federal Court of Appeals in the matter of ***Festo Corporation v. SMC Corporation et al.***[54] Within the framework of this landmark case, the question was examined of whether a claim that was amended in the course of the examination of the patent application can be infringed by equivalents. The question related to a specific patent, but not to be confused—and knowingly—the court established a sweeping rule, according to which it would not be possible to rely on the doctrine of equivalents for a claim that was amended in the course of the examination. Since there is almost no claim that does not undergo some amendment in the course of the examination, this decision seemed to almost totally eliminate the doctrine of equivalents.

The reactions of the professionals in the United States were harsh, for the most part, and, in the words of one of the dissenting judges, *"Rather than promote technological growth, the majority's new rigid rule will effect a serious invasion of the patentee's security of receiving the full benefit of his invention and is likely to be a disincentive to early disclosure of new inventions and discoveries."*

This question was brought to the decision of the Supreme Court of the United States, which set aside the sweeping generalization of invalidation of the doctrine of equivalents that derived from the *Festo* ruling and restored the system to sanity by establishing a necessity to perform a substantive review on a case-by-case basis. Since the second *Festo* ruling, courts have been fiddling with the rules and with the conditions applicable to it, coming up with sometimes dissonant conclusions, but the fine details of this issue are outside the scope of this book and are too abstruse to make for good reading. They are, thus, better left to patent attorneys to juggle with.

---

[53] Section 49 (a) of the Patents Law.

[54] 234 F.3d 558 (Fed. Cir. 2000).

However, the overall conclusion that we can draw from this event, which shook the United States for some time, is that the patent system is built on sufficiently healthy foundations that do not allow extremely illogical situations to exist for very long. Temporary fads of the system are expected to eventually correct themselves, and the patent applicant must not despair and give up when he encounters them before having explored every possible way to deal with them.

ONLY A SMART PERSON IS ALSO CLEVER

In a landmark decision, the Enlarged Board of Appeal of the EPO addressed the question of the content of the right of priority granted to a patent application by its priority document.[55] This decision clarified questions that, at least at the fundamental level, should have been clear from the start, based on the basic principles of the patent system, but had not been internalized by everybody.

The priority right is the right on which we rely under the Paris Convention to claim a priority to an invention in various countries on the basis of an initial application that we filed on the same invention in another country no more than a year ago. Simplistically, the Paris Convention[56] establishes that our right to priority on an invention that was included in a patent application will be reserved to us for a year in all the member countries of the Union (which are most countries of the world). This basic convention is what allows us to postpone the processing of the patent application in other countries without losing our rights to our invention.

In the natural course of events, during the year that elapses from the filing of "the priority" application and until we rely on this right to file patent applications in other countries, changes may occur in the body of the application, both because our development plan has progressed and yielded additional information and for reasons of drafting and our wish to clarify and to improve the text of the application. Indeed, the Paris Convention establishes that the right of priority will be given to "the same invention," and when coming to

[55] Decision G02/98.

[56] See also Appendix B.

make changes, we must ascertain whether this involves only drafting changes, or perhaps we have added critical information that did not exist in the original text. Significant new information will not benefit from the right of priority but will only bear the date of our filing in the additional countries.

The question examined by the Board of the EPO was what will nevertheless benefit from the right of priority. A very limited rule was established in the decision, according to which the right of priority will only be acknowledged if the subject matter of the claim derives directly and unambiguously from the description of the original application (naturally while relying on the general knowledge in the field). To give a simple example, assume that we described in the original patent application a flowchart of a computer process without going into the details of its implementation. Subsequently, before filing the patent application in Europe, we prepared a more detailed description, in which we included all the subprocesses required for the practical execution of the basic process; this process will not benefit from the right of priority. There may, therefore, be a situation in which it will be found that the process that we described in the original application is unpatentable due to its generality (lack of sufficient description), and only a claim for the whole process has, in principle, a patentable nature. But, in the meantime, if we have published the detailed process during the time that elapsed between filing the priority application and filing the applications abroad, a claim for the detailed process may no longer be new and, therefore, we will not be able to obtain a patent on it. In this way, we would have lost from all sides: the process on which we have a right of priority is unpatentable, and the one that was potentially patentable is no longer novel and cannot be patented. This is not an uncommon situation with applicants who have decided to rely on what they deemed a bargain—that is, a provisional patent application for which they mistakenly believed that no detailed description was needed.[57]

As already explained, proponents of shortcuts might discover

57 For a detailed discussion of this matter, see also "Provisional Patent Application" in Chapter 6.

someday that the right of priority that they have claimed is devoid of content. The value of the priority right (and of any right obtained under a patent) is related to the content of the patent application. When an applicant is allowed to file an application devoid of content, he is allowed de facto to file an application that will not grant him any substantive right and that may even undermine his right to the invention.

It seems, unfortunately, that many have not understood the problems associated with devoting too little attention to the quality of the description of a patent application on which a priority right is based. The EPO, by its decision, sent us a reminder that to be clever, we must first be smart.

REGIONAL SOLUTIONS

Many patent applicants quite often debate whether to invest money and effort in an attempt to protect their invention in remote and less conventional countries, such as African and Asian countries. This dilemma usually exists when the patent applicant is in an early stage of the business development, and it is still unclear to him whether his invention justifies a major investment in protection in countries other than the "usual ones," such as the United States, European countries, and major countries in the Far East, such as Japan, China, and Korea. There is no magic solution to this dilemma, but the accession of many countries to the PCT[58] opened a convenient route for taking advantage of regional protections.

An example of regional protection is the patent application filed through the EPO. By filing one patent application, we can cover, at least temporarily, all countries of the European Common Market, as well as additional annexed countries. While, eventually, it will be necessary to complete a formal process in the various countries to be entitled to protection there, this will happen in the distant future, when we hope to know more about our product and its market and when we will be able to make a more intelligent decision regarding the

[58] See also Appendix C.

geography of our invention and its protection needs.

However, the European convention is not the only regional convention. If you expect that his product may sell well, for instance, in Congo, Chad, or Burkina Faso, or in other African countries, you can file a patent application under the OAPI convention, which incorporates fifteen African countries. Another African convention is the ARIPO,[59] which incorporates 11 countries, among them important ones, such as Kenya and Uganda. And if you need a patent that covers Tajikistan or Kazakhstan, you can try your luck through the Eurasian Patent, which incorporates nine countries, among them countries that are not at all trivial, such as Russia and Belarus.

Beyond the regional organizations that have acceded as members to the PCT, there are also other organizations that operate on the basis of reciprocity, such as the Union of South American Nations and Arab organizations, but many countries have no access to these.

It should be borne in mind that alongside the convenience of using regional organizations, there are also risks. The primary risk lies in that filing a centralized patent application could result in a rejection of the application and in a failure to obtain a patent in all the member countries of the organization. For instance, if a European patent application is filed and it is rejected by the EPO, we will not be able to obtain a patent in any of the countries of the European Union. If we have chosen the regional route, we cannot change our mind midway. Therefore, in some cases, we will choose, in addition to the regional route, to also file national patent applications in countries in which we have a special interest to increase our chances of being awarded a patent there. This route has its own complications, inasmuch as, in principle, it is not possible to be granted two patents for the same invention in the same country. However, with proper planning, it is generally possible to overcome these difficulties and to derive the maximum benefit from the existence of the two parallel options: the regional and the national routes.

From all the aforesaid, we can get the sense of at least one truth: when coming to plan international protection, we must not act in a

---

[59] African Regional Intellectual Property Organization.

mechanical and formulaic way, and we must thoroughly explore the wide range of options that are available to us.

CHINA GOES WESTERN

"China? It is impossible to protect patents in China!"

This is the immediate response you are likely to get if you dare to suggest consideration of the filing of a patent application in the People's Republic of China. It turns out that old stigmas are difficult to remove. However, the recognition of the necessity for a good intellectual property protection system is already firmly established at the highest levels of the Chinese government. This recognition, rooted in the structural changes in the Chinese economy, also finds a firm hold in the Chinese industry and commerce circles, which are working at an accelerated pace toward the modernization of their production systems, toward raising product quality, and particularly toward finding international markets for their products. Many Chinese entrepreneurs firmly understand that their approach to advanced technologies is becoming increasingly dependent on their country's intellectual property system.

We should add to this the outside pressure, mainly from the United States, aimed at adding China to the league of nations that recognize and protect intellectual property. All these have led China, since 1990, to instigate dramatic reforms of all the relevant laws. Furthermore, China has acceded to all the important international conventions, such as the Paris Convention and the PCT. As a result of its accession to the Agreement on Trade-Related Aspects of Intellectual Property Rights (TRIPS), which was signed within the framework of the WTO, China has also been working vigorously to complete legislative amendments deriving from the agreement. The reforms aim to give China a system of laws in all matters relating to the protection of intellectual property, which would not be inferior to that of any Western country.

The argument of the cynics that the changes are only cosmetic and that we should not depend on the Chinese legal system is no longer a serious one. In 2014, two of the top three PCT applicants were located in China. With 3,442 applications published, Huawei Technologies Co. Ltd. of China became the top PCT applicant. It also became the third company to have had more than 3,000 applications published in the space of one year. Qualcomm Inc. of the United States and ZTE Co. of China ranked second and third, respectively. For the first time, over 10% of the top 50 PCT applicants were from China. The Chinese are serious where IP is concerned, and they mean business.

All the signs, therefore, show that the government and the people in China have properly understood what not every industrialist in the Western world understands: even if anarchy in intellectual property sometimes leads to easy profits, for someone whose fleet-footedness allows him to benefit from the property of another, the enjoyment derived is short term and holds in store very serious harm to the development of international commerce and industry in the country. Undoubtedly, China still has a long way to go toward a Western-style intellectual property system in general and a patent system in particular. However, the Chinese nation is working to further this goal with its typical vigor, and those who discount this effort and its expected outcome will eventually lose the opportunity to take advantage of its fruits.

THE EUROPEAN PATENT OFFICE

Until the beginning of the millennium, the EPO was undoubtedly a very good office—perhaps the best in the world. This status stemmed not only from its high professional competence but also from the fair treatment of the EPO examiners toward the applicants and their no-nonsense and positive approach. These qualities stood out favorably, particularly in light of the inevitable comparison with what was being done in the US Patent Office, which operated and operates under a heavy load and with personnel quality problems. It is no secret that the relatively low level of the work received from the USPTO does not stem entirely from professional incompetence but is also caused by the desire to shorten examinations and to save time and effort. The adverse results of this situation are particularly apparent in the examination of international patent applications (PCT), in which it has happened that US examiners did not provide search reports in a timely manner (the same search that is supposed to be used by an examiner to prepare his opinion on the international application), thus failing to adhere to the time limits set forth in the PCT Convention.

All this, the optimists believed, would not happen in Europe, in a patent office that is managed in an exemplary "Teutonic" and orderly manner. Until one day, the EPO sent out a notification that "delays" were expected in the issuance of search reports of the office for international patent applications. *Well*, we said to ourselves, *everyone can have a bad moment, and surely this will pass.* And overall, we were pleased that the EPO chose to contact us directly and candidly and to inform us of its difficulties, instead of seeking ways to alleviate the work stress while compromising its quality. Our pleasure, however, was short-lived; we soon realized that reduced examination quality was here to stay.

There is reason to believe that the level of the EPO may rise again from its ashes, and we should hope that this will come to pass in the next few years. However, this appears to be the price of success of the European patent system, which has acquired popularity above and beyond all expectations and has steadily and rapidly enlarged its circle of users, and as long as the system expands, things may continue to stagnate.

Part VI: The Patent and Our Daily Lives

"Forth in thy name, O Lord, I go, My daily labor to pursue."

[Charles Wesley, Hymns and Sacred Poems *(1749)]*

This section looks at the patent system from the point of view of our daily lives.

CHAPTER 24
The Intertwining of Patents with Our Life Systems

Even someone who is not a "patent consumer" is affected by the patent systems in numerous ways, but we are generally unaware of the degree of involvement of these systems in different and sometimes highly important aspects of our lives. Below are some decidedly non-exhaustive examples.

TO INVENT OR NOT TO BE

The proper assessment of the importance of patents does not usually focus on one patent as a single factor but sees every patent as part of a whole array of a technological company's activity. This approach, which is important when we examine our own patent portfolio, should not divert our attention from the fact that a single patent of a competitor, which protects a key product, or a key element of an important product, could make it difficult for our company to function. It has happened again and again that a corporation announced that it would enter into bankruptcy proceedings (such as US Chapter 11) because of a verdict under which it was found liable for damages of millions for infringing a competitor's patent. Such a verdict may deal a heavy blow to the shares of the company. Although a verdict of this type in the first instance is subject to appeal and is not final, its consequences for the life of the company may prove to be critical and extreme. It may be assumed that the investors in the capital markets paid heed to the significant financial damages awarded in the verdict, but also understood that the value of the technology that the company used had become, at a minimum, doubtful, because most, if not all, of it apparently belongs to a competing company. This kind of verdict, therefore, has far-reaching consequences for the future of any company.

This being the case, how do we avoid getting into this kind of situation? The answer is not always simple, particularly in borderline cases, inasmuch as it cannot be known with certainty how a court will decide when there are differing opinions on the question of whether a product infringes a competitor's patent. The surest way, of course, is "to move farther from the boundary"—that is, not to deal at all with a product if there is even the slightest concern that it may infringe a patent. However, in real life, such an approach will sometimes lead us to a dead end, in which we will not be able to manufacture anything due to the multitude of patents in the field. Moreover, sometimes our opinion will be that a patent, which seemingly is an obstacle to our activity, should not be valid at all and was granted in error. Is it conceivable that we would be precluded from developing our activity due to a patent that is prima facie invalid? Of course not. But we must remember that a court may think otherwise.

The answer, if so, lies in a prudent risk management, which takes into account all the contingencies and the possible consequence of every situation and which does not blindly follow our tendencies and our absolute sense of justice. But it is surprising to discover to what extent risk management sometimes makes way for emotional policy, whose distance from the prudent analysis is too great for safety.

PATENTS AND WAR

Since the patent system, as stated, is directly linked to our other life systems, the events surrounding us impact what is being done in the patent field and are reflected through this field. It would not be surprising to discover that in wartime, a dwindling number of patent applications are filed. The decline in the overall economic activity in times of crisis, as well as the absence of inventors from their workplaces, is almost certainly the cause of a significant decline in the number of inventions that find their way to the patent office. However, a more interesting question is what long-term traces a war leaves on the level of technological progress.

The United States joined World War II in the latter part of 1941, following Japan's attack on Pearl Harbor. In each of the four years preceding the war—that is, 1936–1940—more than 60,000 new patent applications were filed in the United States. In 1941, this number already fell to 52,339, but this decline can be attributed to the fact that the world had already been busy with the war that the United States had only joined in the month of December, and this also impacted commercial activity in the United States. During the course of 1942 and 1943, the number of applications fell to approximately 45,000 per year, but surprisingly, this number began to rise again in 1944 to 54,190 and, in 1945, reached 67,845. It should be noted that during the years in question, the influence of foreigners on the statistics was very minor (1,000–4,000 patent applications a year), so the behavior described above properly reflects the national behavior in the United States. Although the war ended in 1945 (in the last quarter of the year), its effects were still highly evident inasmuch as many soldiers had not yet been discharged, and this is without taking the death of many potential inventors into account. One possible explanation for these figures is that after the initial period of shock from the war, the inventive ability of the residents recovered and even increased.

Another interesting question is whether the inventions for which the patent applications were not filed during the war were lost. From a statistical perspective, it can be said that this was absolutely not the case. Immediately after the war (in 1946), the number of patent applications jumped to the astonishing level of 81,056. In the subsequent years, a high but dwindling level was maintained (75,443, 68,740, 67,592, and 67,264 patent applications in 1947–1950, respectively) and only in 1951 did the number of applications filed reach the prewar level—that is, 60,438. Since 1952, a steady increase was recorded again.

It seems, therefore, that US soldiers took their inventions with them and dealt with them after their return from the war. The average number of patent applications per year over a decade was 62,551—exactly the level before the world war and immediately after. Therefore, overall, over this decade, the war had no effect on the level of inventiveness of the warring nation, as reflected in the number of inventions for which patent applications were filed.

It turns out that also under the most difficult conditions, man does not stop thinking productive thoughts and does not lose his inventive ability. And thank goodness for that.

THE LOVE BOX

Some believe that the subject of a granted patent should not be restricted, nor should the issuance of a patent be prevented, simply because it is preposterous or impossible to carry out. The proponents of this approach believe that we should let natural selection take its course, inasmuch as a worthless and foolish patent will not come to fruition and its memory will fade quickly. "Who is harmed by a preposterous patent?" they ask.

The answer is simple, and the reasons for alarm are self-evident. The patent system must maintain a high degree of seriousness, both from the technological aspect and with regard to its objectives. This system is essential for regulating our lives, and it deals with momentous issues and with matters of great economic importance. It is not a playground for people with peculiar ideas. The patent system regulates the production and marketing of almost every product, such as pharmaceuticals, satellites, computer systems, and nearly every item that comes to our table, warms our bodies and our homes, and allows us to move from place to place. Any trivialization of this system is detrimental to one of the delicate and important systems of our lives. Just as it is inconceivable to use the justice system in a disrespectful manner, or the medical system for entertainment purposes, so we should not allow any exception from minimal rules of logic and respect for the patent system.

For the sake of illustration, let us consider US Patent No.

4,194,629, which was issued in 1980 and is titled "LOVE BOX." Below is an abstract of the patent objectives:

> *"A box for use as a token between lovers for assuring their love to each other; the box includes an instruction sheet that states the box is filled with love and no matter how often it is opened, it can never be emptied; and to get a little love, the box should be opened for a short time, while to receive all the person's love it should be left open all the time; the box including* [sic] *a case and a removable cover."*

United States Patent [19] **Ledman et al.**

[11] **4,194,629**
[45] **Mar. 25, 1980**

[54] LOVE BOX

[76] Inventors: **Dale A. Ledman,** c/o George Spector, 3615 Woolworth Bldg., 233 Broadway; **George Spector,** 3615 Woolworth Bldg., 233 Broadway, both of New York, N.Y. 10007

[21] Appl. No.: **887,860**

[22] Filed: **Mar. 17, 1978**

[51] **Int. Cl.**² **B65D 73/00**
[52] **U.S. Cl.** **206/573;** 40/313
[58] **Field of Search** 40/312, 313, 539, 542, 40/459, 475, 448, 491, 508, 573; 206/459, 45.13, 573

[56] **References Cited**

U.S. PATENT DOCUMENTS

1,414,682	5/1922	Zautner	40/313
1,450,477	4/1923	Allworth	206/45.13
1,568,982	1/1926	Lengsfield	40/312
2,595,973	5/1952	Neugass	40/542
2,622,955	12/1952	Kramer	206/45.13
2,657,793	11/1953	Goldshine	206/45.13
2,675,911	4/1954	Thurston	206/45.13
2,684,757	7/1954	McCarthy	206/45.13
3,418,740	12/1968	Gray	40/313
3,822,781	6/1974	Braginetz	206/45.14

FOREIGN PATENT DOCUMENTS

14332	of 1899	United Kingdom	40/313
1005574	9/1965	United Kingdom	40/312

Primary Examiner—Herbert F. Ross

[57] **ABSTRACT**

A box for use as a token between lovers for assuring their love to each other; the box including an instruction sheet that states the box is filled with love, and no matter how often it is opened, it can never be emptied; and to get a little love, the box should be opened for a short time, while to receive all the person's love it should be left open all the time; the box including a case and a removable cover.

1 Claim, 5 Drawing Figures

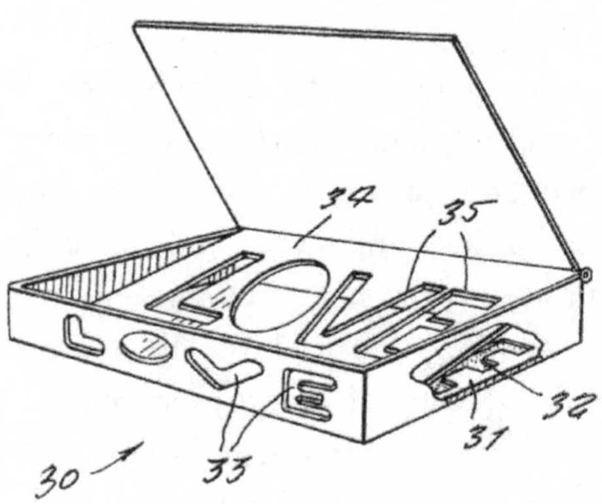

Fig. 24-1: US Patent No. 4,194,629– "Love Box"

This patent evokes rueful reflections about the dreadful failure that enabled it to be granted. What appears to be a mistake of the examiner on the substantive level, in his determining that "the invention" was patentable, is not particularly worrisome, inasmuch as patents that should not be issued are sometimes issued by mistake. What is worrisome is that the examiner and his superiors did not sense the foolishness of granting it, particularly because it would be hard, to say the least, to prove that it has any utility and that it actually works as described. This failure could only be the result of applying dry rules in a mechanical and thoughtless manner—a characteristic that could lead to disastrous consequences in any system.

However, we can also find comfort in the existence of this patent for two reasons: first of all, the patent was granted in 1980, and since then, the global patent system has not collapsed, which indicates its soundness, and second, a mass granting of foolish patents has not begun.

CHAPTER 25
Questions of Morality

In all the previous chapters, an emphasis has been placed on the significance of the patent as a commercial tool. We examined the objectives and the capabilities of the patent in our battle against our competitors to gain an advantage over them. So, how does morality come into it? What does this have to do with the patent system, you may ask? The answer is that the advantage can (and should) be a fair advantage and that there is no contradiction between honestly obtaining a commercial and economic advantage and not trampling the natural and proprietary rights of another—reflections on something that transforms the patent into a work tool that is not only strong but also just.

BOUNDARIES OF THE PATENT

A patent is a right with a defined scope. As the area of a plot on which we build a home is defined and finite, so are the maximum boundaries of a patent. It is true that sometimes our vision does not see the exact boundary, and the scope of the patent appears somewhat blurry in the eyes of someone whose everyday work does not involve patents, but at any time, it is possible to verify and evaluate the patent boundaries and to ascertain its value. These boundaries sometimes change, following the discovery of a patent or prior publication that was previously unknown to us, but this change can only shrink the area included within its boundaries and never expand its scope.

Notwithstanding the above, we sometimes encounter patent holders who do not understand the limited scope of their patent and consequently build heaven and earth on unverified assumptions and on their desire to see in the patent something that is not there. This is similar to a contractor who plans to construct a building but has not bothered to ascertain the boundaries of the plot that he owns with the accuracy necessary to avoid constructing on the area belonging to another.

This situation usually evolves gradually. First, the inventor thinks, for instance, of an original solution for efficiently boiling water and invents a new teakettle that solves the boiling problems of the contemporary teakettles. His teakettle is fairly successful and sells in nice numbers, but suddenly, it becomes clear to the owner of the invention that a serious setback has occurred: the public is still purchasing teakettles of the old variety and even new versions of the old teakettles. At this stage, the patent holder resents that the competitors have found a way to "circumvent" his patent and feels that there is no justice in the world, because he is unable to prevent, through his patent, the sale of all kinds of teakettles. The patent holder has, therefore, moved from a stage in which he hoped to obtain modest exclusivity with a patent on his innovative teakettle, so that he may maintain the commercial advantage that it provides him over less sophisticated teakettles, to a stage in which the boundaries of the patent and its significance have become blurred to the extent that he has forgotten his original goals and aspirations.

It is sometimes difficult to explain to a patent holder a simple fact of life: someone who works outside the boundaries of the patent is not "circumventing" it, but he is simply not infringing it; he is doing something else. The patent is only intended to protect the invention claimed in it. A patent holder suffering from this kind of blurring of vision might construct schemes and make investments that have no basis. It is very important to always remember and memorize the commercial objectives of the patent and not to lose a sense of proportion with regard to them. Even if, in many cases, basic patents can be obtained that block broad technological areas, this result cannot usually be achieved when involving new uses and products that are based on existing technologies. In these cases, greater effort must be invested in identifying the objectives, before filing the patent application, and in maintaining a proper, realistic, and up-to-date vision regarding the boundaries of the patent. An entrepreneur who acts in this manner will be able to correct distortions and block loopholes before it is too late and will not wake up one morning to discover, by complete surprise, that the plot on which he has constructed his factory does not belong to him.

THE PARASITES WHO LIVE AT OUR EXPENSE

There are those who treat patent infringers with infinite forgiveness, and there are also those who view them as "clever guys" who fight the patent holders as though they were evil and he, the infringer, some kind of modern Robin Hood. This forgiving attitude stems from a misunderstanding of the severity of the act. Many people do not understand the nature of the property rights embodied in a patent and are not accustomed to treating them as "real rights." The patent infringer is not a heroic figure but a person who puts his hand into the pocket of another and robs his property. As there is no room for admiration toward a daring bank robber or a train robber, so there should be no admiration for a patent infringer; rather, he should be seen for what he is: a thief who steals the property of others.

It is human nature that we tend to be more forgiving toward someone who steals the property of others rather than our own property. If so, let us see why a patent infringer harms every one of us. There are several levels on which we should see ourselves as harmed. First, the infringer is acting against the law and, therefore, harms us at the basic level at which every citizen is harmed by damage to the rule of law. Moreover, patent infringement undermines the objective of the patent system: promoting R&D and promoting the welfare of us all. Modern R&D requires more and more resources, and without resources, R&D companies will not be able to develop new products that are required for the advancement and welfare of society. Patent infringement impairs the ability of the company that made the investment to recoup it and to generate the profit required for new investments. The immediate result is a slowdown in the progress and the pace of R&D, which, in some cases, may come to a complete halt due to a lack of resources. It is difficult for a single person to see the complete picture of the global needs of R&D, and, therefore, patent laws were created that are intended to protect him and society.

The patent infringer is not Robin Hood; he is not a romantic train robber either: he is a parasite. Just like any parasite, he detects a body that has invested extreme effort and immense resources, hoping to see blessing and profit from his investment, and attempts to rob him of his profits without investing anything. The parasite has many ways to justify his actions to himself and to others. He alludes to the massive profits of the patent holder, as though they were profits that had not been made honestly and are, therefore, theirs for the taking. He relies on "his shrewdness" in finding ingenious ways to infringe the patent, as though it makes him immune from the law. And when all other arguments fail, he explains to us that his actions are purely in the interest of the public and the state.

We are the ones who pay for the consequences of the parasitic action of the infringer. We have to pay a higher price than necessary for new developments to guarantee the developing company against loss of profits due to the infringements of its patents. We benefit less from R&D results, whose pace is slowed down. Ultimately, it is our money that finds its way into the pocket of the infringer, who will not invest one cent in R&D from which we may see any blessing or benefit. Eventually, also, the infringer is harmed by his infringement, just as any common parasite, inasmuch as his weakened prey will provide him with less and less sustenance. We cannot stand by and think that patent infringement only concerns the patent holder and is none of our business. At the end of the day, those standing on either side of the patent law barricade are the parasite and us.

SIZE DOES MATTER

In 1985, Harvard University filed a patent application on "the OncoMouse," a mouse whose properties were modified through genetic engineering by inserting an Oncogene into his genome so that it would develop a susceptibility to cancer. In August 2000, the Canadian court of appeals decided that a patent should be granted for the mouse and, thereby, Canada joined the enlightened world, and particularly the United States, Europe, and Japan, which had already understood that there is no escape from granting patents on higher forms of life.

There is no doubt that there is reluctance in the world to give exclusivity through patents on life forms. Weighty moral questions prompt, in this context, honest dilemmas by the legislators. Those sowing panic speak of patents that will determine ownership of human beings, organs grown for transplants, and life itself.[60] However, these voices originate, for the most part, in a misunderstanding of the essence of the matter. It has long been accepted by most of those who deal with these matters, for instance, that a transgenic bacterium is an object worthy of patent protection. This is a lower form of life on which genetic manipulations were carried out in the laboratory that created a new bacterium, whose properties differ from the original one. The main key to patentability of the transgenic bacterium is in the intervention of the hand of man, who took a microorganism from nature, altered it according to his will, and obtained a different result than that intended by the Creator. And how does the transgenic mouse differ from the transgenic bacterium? In patent terms, it does not differ at all. The difference, apparently, is in the fact that, for most of the accusers, a mouse is a tangible living creature, while the bacterium is perceived as something virtual because it is not visible to the naked eye. The difference is therefore primarily in size.

However, we must always bear in mind the objective of the patent system: it is designed to promote R&D and to give developers an economic reason to invest their time, their effort, and their money

---

[60] Excellent movies, such as *The Island*, add fuel to the fire.

into developing technologies that can benefit mankind. There is no doubt that a mouse (or another higher form of life) that was created by the hand of man, which can be used to study diseases and to find medications to treat them, has great importance to humanity, and this is no trivial matter. The author of these lines does not know how to engineer mice for useful purposes and so, most probably, neither does the reader of these lines. Engineering mice requires extensive knowledge, many years of human investment and large financial investments. Does this not deserve fair compensation? Why is it clear to us that an ultrasonic device for medical testing deserves to be granted a patent, but an OncoMouse does not? In terms of patents, there is no difference between these developments, and both of them are patent worthy. And those who cling to the letter of the law as the horns of the altar to attempt to delay the admission of higher forms of life into the range of inventions on which a patent should be granted are waging a hopeless fighting retreat in the course of which all they will accomplish is to slow down progress to some degree.

A central argument of some of the opponents of this type of patent is that encouraging the development of transgenic animals is fraught with dangers to humanity by creating species that have undergone uncontrolled modifications, the consequences of which cannot be known. To them, it should be said that this is being done every day with microorganisms and in a controlled manner. In principle, it could have been feared that creating an antibiotic-resistant transgenic bacterium would constitute a great danger to human life, but, in fact, these studies are conducted in a responsible, controlled manner and without disastrous results, and there is no reason to think that this would not also be the case with regard to higher forms of life.

In his amazing book,[61] the great British writer John Wyndham tells of God-fearing people who hunt mutants and destroy deformed animals or any genetically modified crop. They also hunt humans if their genetic heritage has caused even the slightest difference in their appearance. Those who fear the advancement of genetic research on animals are somewhat similar to the people in the story who murmur

---

[61] John Wyndham, *The Chrysalids*.

mystical slogans denouncing the mutation without considering the root and the nature of the difference. Hopefully, we will cease being afraid and start investing in understanding the tremendous advantages that can benefit mankind.

A Last Word

If you got this far, you have acquired a fair understanding of how the patent system works. You know about its dynamic, ever-changing complexity and have also glimpsed its ailing branches, which must be treated, sooner or later, by the relevant governments, who typically awake to those needs with much delay and often with little understanding.

What I do hope you have definitely gleaned from the pages of this book is that patents are not a dry, monolithic subject but are, instead, a multifaceted tool with which you can work and, yes, as the title of the book indicates, even have fun.

I started telling tales of patents to the general public at the turn of the century with a view to educate (and, perhaps, also to entertain a little, because entertaining reads make for better learning), and I wrote this book with the same goal in mind. So, if you find that reading it has enriched you a little, please tell others about it. Also, leaving a review for others to see would help them find it and I, for one, would certainly appreciate it. Popular review links are conveniently found at **kfirluzzatto.com/fun-with-patents-reviews**. Thank you.

Kfir Luzzatto, February 2016.

Meet the Author

Kfir Luzzatto was born and raised in Italy and acquired his love for the English language from his father, a former US soldier and WWII veteran, a voracious reader, and a prolific writer. Kfir has a PhD in chemical engineering and manages the well-known Israeli patent law firm *Luzzatto & Luzzatto*. He is a recipient of the prestigious Landau Award for Research and has been granted several patents for his own inventions.

Over the years, Kfir has advised small start-ups and multinational companies alike. He considers himself lucky to have had the opportunity to defend patents to many important products, some of which—Voltaren, Prozac, and Viagra, to mention but a few—will ring a bell for the reader.

Kfir has published extensively in the professional and general press over the years, including a weekly "Patents" column that he wrote for *Globes* (Israel's financial newspaper). His nonfiction book, ***The World of Patents***, was published in 2002 by Globes Press. He also writes fiction and is the author of numerous short stories and six novels.

Kfir's professional web site is www.luzzatto.com, and his literary one is www.KfirLuzzatto.com. Follow him:

on Twitter: @KfirLuzzatto

on Facebook: https://www.facebook.com/KfirLuzzattoAuthor.

Appendix A

Patent Application for “BIOLOGIC ALARM SYSTEMS”

BIOLOGIC ALARM SYSTEM

FIELD OF THE INVENTION[62]

[0001] The present invention relates to alarm systems. More particularly, the invention relates to an alarm system that uses biologic apparatus to generate an alarm.

BACKGROUND OF THE INVENTION[63]

[0002] Alarm systems have become a necessity for virtually every household. However, many home owners cannot afford to purchase expensive, advanced electronic systems and, as a result, their homes remain exposed to burglary and, generally, to malicious intruders.

[0003] Although many different alarm systems exist on the market, a need still exists for a relatively inexpensive alarm system that is simple to implement and which maintains a high level of intrusion detection.

SUMMARY OF THE INVENTION[64]

[0004] The biologic alarm system of the invention comprises a living animal provided with:

(a) a main body;

(b) hind and fore legs and hind and fore feet;

---

[62] This section of the specification briefly identifies the subject of the invention.

[63] The background section explains the current state of the art and introduces the need for the invention. It should be kept as short as possible and should not be used to make an extensive review of all the publications in the field.

[64] The summary sets forth the invention in its various aspects. It is directly related to the claims and in many patent documents is essentially identical to the claims as originally filed. However, as the claims are amended in the course of the examination differences may exists between the summary and the claims, which are often substantial.

(c) at least two auditory sensors;

(d) at least one olfactory sensor;

(e) noise generation apparatus;

wherein the noise generation apparatus is suitable to be activated as the result of a potential intrusion detection performed by either or both of said auditory and olfactory sensors.

[0005] In one embodiment of the invention the biologic alarm system comprises a dog.

[0006] In another embodiment of the invention the auditory sensors comprise ears and in yet another embodiment the olfactory sensor comprises a nose.

[0007] In one particular embodiment of the invention the noise generation apparatus of the invention comprises a bark generator.

[0008] The biologic alarm system of the invention therefore provides an efficient and inexpensive alarm system, which can be easily implemented.

[0009] It is another object achieved by the invention, to provide an alarm system that is sensitive to even minor noises and which is capable of being activated by unknown approaching individuals.

[0010] The above and other objects and advantages of the invention will be easily understood through the following illustrative description of a preferred embodiment, with reference to the appended drawing.

BRIEF DESCRIPTION OF THE DRAWINGS[65]

[0011] In the drawings:

[0012] Fig. 1 is a perspective view of an alarm system, according to one embodiment of the invention.

---

[65] This section helps the reader to navigate the drawings. In some patents we can find a large number of drawings and the list in this section allows us a quick view of their relevance. Therefore, the description of each figure is as concise as possible.

DETAILED DESCRIPTION OF AN EMBODIMENT OF THE INVENTION[66]

[0013] The biologic alarm system of the invention consists of a dog, provided with intrusion detection apparatus and with alarm generation apparatus, which will be described in greater detail below.

[0014] Generally speaking and with reference to Fig. 1, a dog is generally indicated by numeral 1. The dog of the invention is provided with a main body, 2, which is connected to a tail 3, forefeet 4a and 4b (also referred to as "paws") and hind feet, 5a and 5b. While tail 3 is only of limited importance, inasmuch as it is only used to provide visual indication of the state of the alarm system, hind feet 5a and 5b and forefeet 4a and 4b, each connected to hind legs or to fore legs, respectively, are provided for the purpose of allowing the system to move from one suspect location to another, thereby permitting a better sensing of a potential intrusion, when one is suspected.

[0015] The most important part of the alarm system is the head 6, which houses two types of intrusion sensors, namely, noise sensors, which are located symmetrically on both sides of head 6 (but of which only one sensor 7, also referred to as "ear" is shown), and olfactory intrusion sensor 8 (also referred to as "nose"). Both types of sensors are extremely sensitive and may detect a potential intruder at great distance, even when the intruder moves outside the perimeter that is secured by the biologic alarm system.

[0016] The alarm generation system 9 is housed in the throat, which is integrally connected to head 6. When one or both of intrusion sensors 7 or 8 detect a potential intrusion, the alarm generation system is activated and a loud alarm noise alerts that an unauthorized person is in the vicinity of the house and may be a security hazard.

[0017] The biologic alarm system of the invention is very easy to operate as it only requires minimal maintenance, such as a daily

[66] Also called "Detailed Description of the Invention" or "Detailed Description of Preferred Embodiments of the Invention" (an old title, nowadays almost no longer in use). This is where the invention is described in great detail, making reference to the figures and explaining alternative embodiments. This is an extremely important section because it provides support for the claimed subject matter and, therefore, it is often tediously long and detailed.

supply of dog food and some fresh water. Moreover, in contrast to prior art alarm systems, the biologic alarm system of the invention is mobile and can be easily moved from one house to another, or even taken on a trip with its owner. Accordingly, the system of the invention provides round-the-clock and year-long protection to its owner.

[0018] The above description of a preferred embodiment of the invention was provided for the purpose of illustration and is not meant to limit the invention in any way. Many modifications and improvements can be provided to the invention. For instance, instead of the spaniel of Fig. 1, dogs of many other breeds can be used. Moreover, other biologic apparatus can be used, such as, for example, lemurs, hyenas and wolves, all without exceeding the scope of the invention as claimed in the appended claims.

What is claimed is:[67]

1. A biologic alarm system, comprising a living animal provided with:

(a) a main body;

(b) hind and fore legs and hind and fore feet;

(c) at least two auditory sensors;

(d) at least one olfactory sensor;

(e) noise generation apparatus;

wherein the noise generation apparatus is suitable to be activated as the result of a potential intrusion detection performed by either or both of said auditory and olfactory sensors.

2. The biologic alarm system of claim 1, which comprises a dog.

3. The biologic alarm system of claim 1, wherein the auditory sensors comprise ears.

[67] This is where we define the monopoly that we want the patent to give us when we draft a patent application and, in the case of a granted patent, this is the monopoly that was actually granted to us. When reading a patent document it is important to ascertain whether the document we are reading is a granted patent or merely a patent application, for which the claims represent wishful thinking that may or may not materialize after the application is examined.

4. The biologic alarm system of claim 1, wherein the olfactory sensor comprises a nose.

5. The biologic alarm system of claim 1, wherein the noise generation apparatus comprises a bark generator.

ABSTRACT [68]

A biologic alarm system comprises a living animal provided with (a) a main body; (b) hind and fore legs and hind and fore feet; (c) at least two auditory sensors; (d) at least one olfactory sensor; and (e) noise generation apparatus; wherein the noise generation apparatus is suitable to be activated as the result of a potential intrusion detection performed by either or both of said auditory and olfactory sensors.

[68] The abstract is used in the printed publication of both the patent and the patent application to provide a bird's eye view of what the invention is about. It typically reflects the contents of the broadest claim.

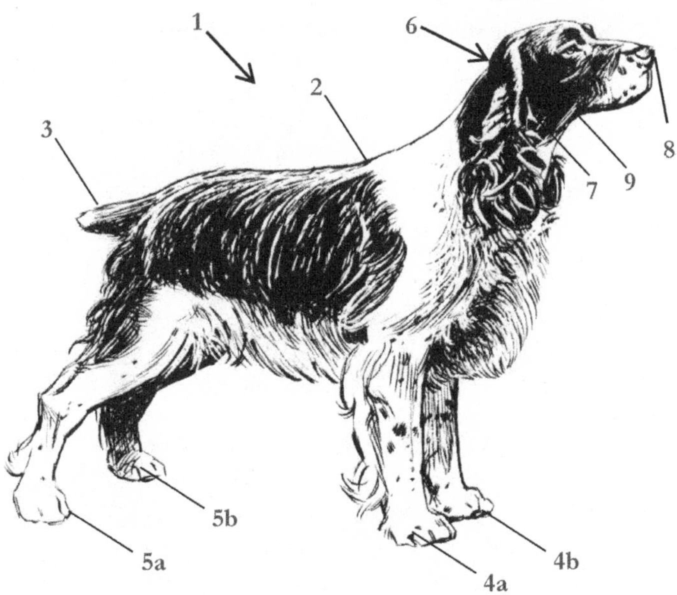

Fig. 1

Appendix B

Excerpts from the Paris Convention for the Protection of Industrial Property

PARIS CONVENTION
FOR THE PROTECTION OF INDUSTRIAL PROPERTY
of March 20, 1883,
as revised at Brussels on December 14, 1900,
at Washington on June 2, 1911,
at The Hague on November 6, 1925,
at London on June 2, 1934,
at Lisbon on October 31, 1958,
and at Stockholm on July 14, 1967,
and as amended on September 28, 1979

(Selected Articles)

Article 1
Establishment of the Union; Scope of Industrial Property

(1) The countries to which this Convention applies constitute a Union for the protection of industrial property.

(2) The protection of industrial property has as its object patents, utility models, industrial designs, trademarks, service marks, trade names, indications of source or appellations of origin, and the repression of unfair competition.

(3) Industrial property shall be understood in the broadest sense and shall apply not only to industry and commerce proper, but likewise to agricultural and extractive industries and to all manufactured or natural products, for example, wines, grain, tobacco leaf, fruit, cattle, minerals, mineral waters, beer, flowers, and flour.

(4) Patents shall include the various kinds of industrial patents recognized by the laws of the countries of the Union, such as patents of importation, patents of improvement, patents and certificates of addition, etc.

Article 2
National Treatment for Nationals of Countries of the Union

(1) Nationals of any country of the Union shall, as regards the protection of industrial property, enjoy in all the other countries of the Union the advantages that their respective laws now grant, or may hereafter grant, to nationals; all without prejudice to the rights specially provided for by this Convention. Consequently, they shall have the same protection as the latter, and the same legal remedy against any infringement of their rights, provided that the conditions and formalities imposed upon nationals are complied with.
(2) However, no requirement as to domicile or establishment in the country where protection is claimed may be imposed upon nationals of countries of the Union for the enjoyment of any industrial property rights.
(3) The provisions of the laws of each of the countries of the Union relating to judicial and administrative procedure and to jurisdiction, and to the designation of an address for service or the appointment of an agent, which may be required by the laws on industrial property are expressly reserved.

Article 3
Same Treatment for Certain Categories of Persons as for Nationals of Countries of the Union

Nationals of countries outside the Union who are domiciled or who have real and effective industrial or commercial establishments in the territory of one of the countries of the Union shall be treated in the same manner as nationals of the countries of the Union.

Article 4
A to I. Patents, Utility Models, Industrial Designs, Marks, Inventors' Certificates: *Right of Priority*
G. Patents: *Division of the Application*

A.

(1) Any person who has duly filed an application for a patent, or for the registration of a utility model, or of an industrial design, or of a trademark, in one of the countries of the Union, or his successor in

title, shall enjoy, for the purpose of filing in the other countries, a right of priority during the periods hereinafter fixed.

(2) Any filing that is equivalent to a regular national filing under the domestic legislation of any country of the Union or under bilateral or multilateral treaties concluded between countries of the Union shall be recognized as giving rise to the right of priority.

(3) By a regular national filing is meant any filing that is adequate to establish the date on which the application was filed in the country concerned, whatever may be the subsequent fate of the application.

B. Consequently, any subsequent filing in any of the other countries of the Union before the expiration of the periods referred to above shall not be invalidated by reason of any acts accomplished in the interval, in particular, another filing, the publication or exploitation of the invention, the putting on sale of copies of the design, or the use of the mark, and such acts cannot give rise to any third-party right or any right of personal possession. Rights acquired by third parties before the date of the first application that serves as the basis for the right of priority are reserved in accordance with the domestic legislation of each country of the Union

C.

(1) The periods of priority referred to above shall be twelve months for patents and utility models, and six months for industrial designs and trademarks.

(2) These periods shall start from the date of filing of the first application; the day of filing shall not be included in the period.

(3) If the last day of the period is an official holiday, or a day when the Office is not open for the filing of applications in the country where protection is claimed, the period shall be extended until the first following working day.

(4) A subsequent application concerning the same subject as a previous first application within the meaning of paragraph (2), above, filed in the same country of the Union shall be considered as the first application, of which the filing date shall be the starting point of the period of priority, if, at the time of filing the subsequent application, the said previous application has been withdrawn, abandoned, or refused, without having been laid open to public inspection and

without leaving any rights outstanding, and if it has not yet served as a basis for claiming a right of priority. The previous application may not thereafter serve as a basis for claiming a right of priority.

D.

(1) Any person desiring to take advantage of the priority of a previous filing shall be required to make a declaration indicating the date of such filing and the country in which it was made. Each country shall determine the latest date on which such declaration must be made.

(2) These particulars shall be mentioned in the publications issued by the competent authority, and in particular in the patents and the specifications relating thereto.

(3) The countries of the Union may require any person making a declaration of priority to produce a copy of the application (description, drawings, etc.) previously filed. The copy, certified as correct by the authority which received such application, shall not require any authentication, and may in any case be filed, without fee, at any time within three months of the filing of the subsequent application. They may require it to be accompanied by a certificate from the same authority showing the date of filing, and by a translation.

(4) No other formalities may be required for the declaration of priority at the time of filing the application. Each country of the Union shall determine the consequences of failure to comply with the formalities prescribed by this Article, but such consequences shall in no case go beyond the loss of the right of priority.

(5) Subsequently, further proof may be required.

Any person who avails himself of the priority of a previous application shall be required to specify the number of that application; this number shall be published as provided for by paragraph (2), above.

E.

(1) Where an industrial design is filed in a country by virtue of a right of priority based on the filing of a utility model, the period of priority shall be the same as that fixed for industrial designs.

(2) Furthermore, it is permissible to file a utility model in a country by virtue of a right of priority based on the filing of a patent application, and vice versa.

F. No country of the Union may refuse a priority or a patent application on the ground that the applicant claims multiple priorities, even if they originate in different countries, or on the ground that an application claiming one or more priorities contains one or more elements that were not included in the application or applications whose priority is claimed, provided that, in both cases, there is unity of invention within the meaning of the law of the country.
With respect to the elements not included in the application or applications whose priority is claimed, the filing of the subsequent application shall give rise to a right of priority under ordinary conditions.

G.

(1) If the examination reveals that an application for a patent contains more than one invention, the applicant may divide the application into a certain number of divisional applications and preserve as the date of each the date of the initial application and the benefit of the right of priority, if any.

(2) The applicant may also, on his own initiative, divide a patent application and preserve as the date of each divisional application the date of the initial application and the benefit of the right of priority, if any. Each country of the Union shall have the right to determine the conditions under which such division shall be authorized.

H. Priority may not be refused on the ground that certain elements of the invention for which priority is claimed do not appear among the claims formulated in the application in the country of origin, provided that the application documents as a whole specifically disclose such elements.

I.

(1) Applications for inventors' certificates filed in a country in which applicants have the right to apply at their own option either for a patent or for an inventor's certificate shall give rise to the right of priority provided for by this Article, under the same conditions and with the same effects as applications for patents.

(2) In a country in which applicants have the right to apply at their own option either for a patent or for an inventor's certificate, an applicant for an inventor's certificate shall, in accordance with the

provisions of this Article relating to patent applications, enjoy a right of priority based on an application for a patent, a utility model, or an inventor's certificate.

Article 4*bis*

Patents: *Independence of Patents Obtained for the Same Invention in Different Countries*

(1) Patents applied for in the various countries of the Union by nationals of countries of the Union shall be independent of patents obtained for the same invention in other countries, whether members of the Union or not.

(2) The foregoing provision is to be understood in an unrestricted sense, in particular, in the sense that patents applied for during the period of priority are independent, both as regards the grounds for nullity and forfeiture, and as regards their normal duration.

(3) The provision shall apply to all patents existing at the time when it comes into effect.

(4) Similarly, it shall apply, in the case of the accession of new countries, to patents in existence on either side at the time of accession.

(5) Patents obtained with the benefit of priority shall, in the various countries of the Union, have a duration equal to that which they would have, had they been applied for or granted without the benefit of priority.

Article 4*ter*

Patents: *Mention of the Inventor in the Patent*

The inventor shall have the right to be mentioned as such in the patent.

Article 4*quater*

Patents: *Patentability in Case of Restrictions of Sale by Law*

The grant of a patent shall not be refused and a patent shall not be invalidated on the ground that the sale of the patented product or of a product obtained by means of a patented process is subject to restrictions or limitations resulting from the domestic law.

Article 5

A. Patents: *Importation of Articles; Failure to Work or Insufficient Working; Compulsory Licenses*

B. Industrial Designs: *Failure to Work; Importation of Articles*

C. Marks: *Failure to Use; Different Forms; Use by Co-proprietors*

D. Patents, Utility Models, Marks, Industrial Designs: *Marking*

A.

(1) Importation by the patentee into the country where the patent has been granted of articles manufactured in any of the countries of the Union shall not entail forfeiture of the patent.

(2) Each country of the Union shall have the right to take legislative measures providing for the grant of compulsory licenses to prevent the abuses which might result from the exercise of the exclusive rights conferred by the patent, for example, failure to work.

(3) Forfeiture of the patent shall not be provided for except in cases where the grant of compulsory licenses would not have been sufficient to prevent the said abuses. No proceedings for the forfeiture or revocation of a patent may be instituted before the expiration of two years from the grant of the first compulsory license.

(4) A compulsory license may not be applied for on the ground of failure to work or insufficient working before the expiration of a period of four years from the date of filing of the patent application or three years from the date of the grant of the patent, whichever period expires last; it shall be refused if the patentee justifies his inaction by legitimate reasons. Such a compulsory license shall be non-exclusive and shall not be transferable, even in the form of the grant of a sub-license, except with that part of the enterprise or goodwill which exploits such license.

(5) The foregoing provisions shall be applicable, mutatis mutandis, to utility models.

B. The protection of industrial designs shall not, under any circumstance, be subject to any forfeiture, either by reason of failure to work or by reason of the importation of articles corresponding to those which are protected.

C. –

.

.

.

Article 5*bis*

All Industrial Property Rights: *Period of Grace for the Payment of Fees for the Maintenance of Rights*;
Patents: *Restoration*

(1) A period of grace of not less than six months shall be allowed for the payment of the fees prescribed for the maintenance of industrial property rights, subject, if the domestic legislation so provides, to the payment of a surcharge.
(2) The countries of the Union shall have the right to provide for the restoration of patents which have lapsed by reason of non-payment of fees.

Article 5*ter*

Patents: *Patented Devices Forming Part of Vessels, Aircraft, or Land Vehicles*

In any country of the Union the following shall not be considered as infringements of the rights of a patentee:
(i) the use on board vessels of other countries of the Union of devices forming the subject of his patent in the body of the vessel, in the machinery, tackle, gear and other accessories, when such vessels temporarily or accidentally enter the waters of the said country, provided that such devices are used there exclusively for the needs of the vessel;
(ii) the use of devices forming the subject of the patent in the construction or operation of aircraft or land vehicles of other countries of the Union, or of accessories of such aircraft or land vehicles, when those aircraft or land vehicles temporarily or accidentally enter the said country.

Article 5*quater*

Patents: *Importation of Products Manufactured by a Process Patented in the Importing Country*

When a product is imported into a country of the Union where there exists a patent protecting a process of manufacture of the said product, the patentee shall have all the rights, with regard to the imported product, that are accorded to him by the legislation of the country of importation, on the basis of the process patent, with respect to products manufactured in that country.

.

.

.

Article 11

Inventions, Utility Models, Industrial Designs, Marks: *Temporary Protection at Certain International Exhibitions*

(1) The countries of the Union shall, in conformity with their domestic legislation, grant temporary protection to patentable inventions, utility models, industrial designs, and trademarks, in respect of goods exhibited at official or officially recognized international exhibitions held in the territory of any of them.
(2) Such temporary protection shall not extend the periods provided by Article 4. If, later, the right of priority is invoked, the authorities of any country may provide that the period shall start from the date of introduction of the goods into the exhibition.
(3) Each country may require, as proof of the identity of the article exhibited and of the date of its introduction, such documentary evidence as it considers necessary.

Article 12

Special National Industrial Property Services

(1) Each country of the Union undertakes to establish a special industrial property service and a central office for the communication to the public of patents, utility models, industrial designs, and trademarks.
(2) This service shall publish an official periodical journal. It shall publish regularly:
(a) the names of the proprietors of patents granted, with a brief designation of the inventions patented;

(b) the reproductions of registered trademarks.

.

.

.

Article 28

Disputes

(1) Any dispute between two or more countries of the Union concerning the interpretation or application of this Convention, not settled by negotiation, may, by any one of the countries concerned, be brought before the International Court of Justice by application in conformity with the Statute of the Court, unless the countries concerned agree on some other method of settlement. The country bringing the dispute before the Court shall inform the International Bureau; the International Bureau shall bring the matter to the attention of the other countries of the Union.

(2) Each country may, at the time it signs this Act or deposits its instrument of ratification or accession, declare that it does not consider itself bound by the provisions of paragraph (1). With regard to any dispute between such country and any other country of the Union, the provisions of paragraph (1) shall not apply.

(3) Any country having made a declaration in accordance with the provisions of paragraph (2) may, at any time, withdraw its declaration by notification addressed to the Director General.

Article 29

Signature, Languages, Depositary Functions

(1)

(a) This Act shall be signed in a single copy in the French language and shall be deposited with the Government of Sweden.

(b) Official texts shall be established by the Director General, after consultation with the interested Governments, in the English, German, Italian, Portuguese, Russian and Spanish languages, and such other languages as the Assembly may designate.

(c) In case of differences of opinion on the interpretation of the various texts, the French text shall prevail.

(2) This Act shall remain open for signature at Stockholm until

January 13, 1968.

(3) The Director General shall transmit two copies, certified by the Government of Sweden, of the signed text of this Act to the Governments of all countries of the Union and, on request, to the Government of any other country.

(4) The Director General shall register this Act with the Secretariat of the United Nations.

(5) The Director General shall notify the Governments of all countries of the Union of signatures, deposits of instruments of ratification or accession and any declarations included in such instruments or made pursuant to Article 20(1)*(c)*, entry into force of any provisions of this Act, notifications of denunciation, and notifications pursuant to Article 24.

The full text of the Paris Convention can be viewed on the website of the World Intellectual Property Organization (WIPO) at http://www.wipo.int/treaties.

Appendix C

Excerpts from the Patent Cooperation Treaty (PCT)

PATENT COOPERATION TREATY (PCT)
Done at Washington on June 19, 1970,
amended on September 28, 1979,
modified on February 3, 1984,
and on October 3, 2001
(Selected Articles)

The Contracting States,

Desiring to make a contribution to the progress of science and technology,

Desiring to perfect the legal protection of inventions,

Desiring to simplify and render more economical the obtaining of protection for inventions where protection is sought in several countries,

Desiring to facilitate and accelerate access by the public to the technical information contained in documents describing new inventions,

Desiring to foster and accelerate the economic development of developing countries through the adoption of measures designed to increase the efficiency of their legal systems, whether national or regional, instituted for the protection of inventions by providing easily accessible information on the availability of technological solutions applicable to their special needs and by facilitating access to the ever expanding volume of modern technology,

Convinced that cooperation among nations will greatly facilitate the attainment of these aims,

Have concluded the present Treaty.

INTRODUCTORY PROVISIONS

Article 1
Establishment of a Union

(1) The States party to this Treaty (hereinafter called "the Contracting States") constitute a Union for cooperation in the filing, searching, and examination, of applications for the protection of inventions, and for rendering special technical services. The Union shall be known as the International Patent Cooperation Union.

(2) No provision of this Treaty shall be interpreted as diminishing the rights under the Paris Convention for the Protection of Industrial Property of any national or resident of any country party to that Convention.

Article 2
Definitions

For the purposes of this Treaty and the Regulations and unless expressly stated otherwise:

(i) "application" means an application for the protection of an invention; references to an "application" shall be construed as references to applications for patents for inventions, inventors' certificates, utility certificates, utility models, patents or certificates of addition, inventors' certificates of addition, and utility certificates of addition;

(ii) references to a "patent" shall be construed as references to patents for inventions, inventors' certificates, utility certificates, utility models, patents or certificates of addition, inventors' certificates of addition, and utility certificates of addition;

(iii) "national patent" means a patent granted by a national authority;

(iv) "regional patent" means a patent granted by a national or an intergovernmental authority having the power to grant patents effective in more than one State;

(v) "regional application" means an application for a regional patent;

(vi) references to a "national application" shall be construed as references to applications for national patents and regional patents, other than applications filed under this Treaty;

(vii) "international application" means an application filed under this

Treaty;

(viii) references to an "application" shall be construed as references to international applications and national applications;

(ix) references to a "patent" shall be construed as references to national patents and regional patents;

(x) references to "national law" shall be construed as references to the national law of a Contracting State or, where a regional application or a regional patent is involved, to the treaty providing for the filing of regional applications or the granting of regional patents;

(xi) "priority date," for the purposes of computing time limits, means:

(a) where the international application contains a priority claim under Article 8, the filing date of the application whose priority is so claimed;

(b) where the international application contains several priority claims under Article 8, the filing date of the earliest application whose priority is so claimed;

(c) where the international application does not contain any priority claim under Article 8, the international filing date of such application;

(xii) "national Office" means the government authority of a Contracting State entrusted with the granting of patents; references to a "national Office" shall be construed as referring also to any intergovernmental authority which several States have entrusted with the task of granting regional patents, provided that at least one of those States is a Contracting State, and provided that the said States have authorized that authority to assume the obligations and exercise the powers which this Treaty and the Regulations provide for in respect of national Offices;

(xiii) "designated Office" means the national Office of or acting for the

State designated by the applicant under Chapter I of this Treaty;

(xiv) "elected Office" means the national Office of or acting for the State elected by the applicant under Chapter II of this Treaty;

(xv) "receiving Office" means the national Office or the intergovernmental organization with which the international application has been filed;

(xvi) "Union" means the International Patent Cooperation Union; (xvii) "Assembly" means the Assembly of the Union;

(xviii) "Organization" means the World Intellectual Property Organization; (xix) "International Bureau" means the International Bureau of the

Organization and, as long as it subsists, the United International Bureaux for the

Protection of Intellectual Property (BIRPI);

(xx) "Director General" means the Director General of the Organization and, as long as BIRPI subsists, the Director of BIRPI.

CHAPTER I
INTERNATIONAL APPLICATION AND INTERNATIONAL SEARCH

Article 3
The International Application

(1) Applications for the protection of inventions in any of the Contracting

States may be filed as international applications under this Treaty.

(2) An international application shall contain, as specified in

this Treaty and the Regulations, a request, a description, one or more claims, one or more drawings (where required), and an abstract.

(3) The abstract merely serves the purpose of technical information and cannot be taken into account for any other purpose, particularly not for the purpose of interpreting the scope of the protection sought.

(4) The international application shall: (i) be in a prescribed language;

(ii) comply with the prescribed physical requirements;

(iii) comply with the prescribed requirement of unity of invention; (iv) be subject to the payment of the prescribed fees.

Article 4
The Request

(1) The request shall contain:

(i) a petition to the effect that the international application be processed according to this Treaty;

(ii) the designation of the Contracting State or States in which protection for the invention is desired on the basis of the international application ("designated States"); if for any designated State a regional patent is available and the applicant wishes to obtain a regional patent rather than a national patent, the request shall so indicate; if, under a treaty concerning a regional patent, the applicant cannot limit his application to certain of the States party to that treaty, designation of one of those States and the indication of the wish to obtain the regional patent shall be treated as designation of all the States party to that treaty; if, under the national law of the designated State, the designation of that State has the effect of an application for a regional patent, the designation of the said State shall be treated as an indication of the wish to obtain the regional patent;

(iii) the name of and other prescribed data concerning the applicant and the agent (if any);

(iv) the title of the invention;

(v) the name of and other prescribed data concerning the inventor where the national law of at least one of the designated States requires that these indications be furnished at the time of filing a national application. Otherwise, the said indications may be furnished either in the request or in separate notices addressed to each designated Office whose national law requires the furnishing of the said indications but allows that they be furnished at a time later than that of the filing of a national application.

(2) Every designation shall be subject to the payment of the prescribed fee within the prescribed time limit.

(3) Unless the applicant asks for any of the other kinds of protection referred to in Article 43, designation shall mean that the desired protection consists of the grant of a patent by or for the designated State. For the purposes of this paragraph, Article 2(ii) shall not apply.

(4) Failure to indicate in the request the name and other prescribed data concerning the inventor shall have no consequence in any designated State whose national law requires the furnishing of the said indications but allows that they be furnished at a time later than that of the filing of a national application. Failure to furnish the said indications in a separate notice shall have no consequence in any designated State whose national law does not require the furnishing of the said indications.

Article 5
The Description

The description shall disclose the invention in a manner sufficiently clear and complete for the invention to be carried out by a person skilled in the art.

Article 6
The Claims

The claim or claims shall define the matter for which protection is sought. Claims shall be clear and concise. They shall be fully supported by the description.

Article 7
The Drawings

(1) Subject to the provisions of paragraph (2)(ii), drawings shall be required when they are necessary for the understanding of the invention.

(2) Where, without being necessary for the understanding of the invention, the nature of the invention admits of illustration by drawings:

(i) the applicant may include such drawings in the international application when filed,

(ii) any designated Office may require that the applicant file such drawings with it within the prescribed time limit.

Article 8
Claiming Priority

(1) The international application may contain a declaration, as prescribed in the Regulations, claiming the priority of one or more earlier applications filed in or for any country party to the Paris Convention for the Protection of Industrial Property.

(2)(a) Subject to the provisions of subparagraph (b), the conditions for, and the effect of, any priority claim declared under paragraph (1) shall be as provided in Article 4 of the Stockholm Act of the Paris Convention for the Protection of Industrial Property.

(b) The international application for which the priority of one or more earlier applications filed in or for a Contracting State is claimed may contain the designation of that State. Where, in the international application, the priority of one or more national applications filed in or for a designated State is claimed, or where the priority of an international application having designated only one State is claimed, the conditions for, and the effect of, the priority claim in that State shall be governed by the national law of that State.

Article 9
The Applicant

(1) Any resident or national of a Contracting State may file an international application.

(2)

.
.
.

Article 10
The Receiving Office

The international application shall be filed with the prescribed receiving Office, which will check and process it as provided in this Treaty and the Regulations.

.
.
.

Article 12
Transmittal of the International Application to the International Bureau and the International Searching Authority

(1) One copy of the international application shall be kept by the receiving Office ("home copy"), one copy ("record copy") shall be transmitted to the International Bureau, and another copy ("search copy") shall be transmitted to the competent International Searching Authority referred to in Article 16, as provided in the Regulations.

(2)

.

.

.

Article 15
The International Search

(1) Each international application shall be the subject of international search.

(2) The objective of the international search is to discover relevant prior art. (3) International search shall be made on the basis of the claims, with due

regard to the description and the drawings (if any).

(4) The International Searching Authority referred to in Article 16 shall endeavor to discover as much of the relevant prior art as its facilities permit, and shall, in any case, consult the documentation specified in the Regulations.

(5)(a)

.

.

.

Article 16
The International Searching Authority

(1) International search shall be carried out by an International Searching Authority, which may be either a national Office or an intergovernmental organization, such as the International Patent Institute, whose tasks include the establishing of documentary search reports on prior art with respect to inventions which are the subject of applications.

(2)

•

•

•

Article 18
The International Search Report

(1) The international search report shall be established within the prescribed time limit and in the prescribed form.

(2) The international search report shall, as soon as it has been established, be transmitted by the International Searching Authority to the applicant and the International Bureau.

(3) The international search report or the declaration referred to in Article 17(2)(a) shall be translated as provided in the Regulations. The translations shall be prepared by or under the responsibility of the International Bureau.

Article 19
Amendment of the Claims before the International Bureau

(1) The applicant shall, after having received the international search report, be entitled to one opportunity to amend the claims of the international application by filing amendments with the International Bureau within the prescribed time limit. He may, at the same time, file a brief statement, as provided in the Regulations, explaining the amendments and indicating any impact that such amendments might have on the description and the drawings.

(2) The amendments shall not go beyond the disclosure in the international application as filed.

(3)

•

•

•

Article 21
International Publication

(1) The International Bureau shall publish international applications.

(2)(a) Subject to the exceptions provided for in subparagraph (b) and in Article 64(3), the international publication of the international application shall be effected promptly after the expiration of 18 months from the priority date of that application.

(b) The applicant may ask the International Bureau to publish his international application any time before the expiration of the time limit referred to in subparagraph (a). The International Bureau shall proceed accordingly, as provided in the Regulations.

(3) The international search report or the declaration referred to in

Article 17(2)(a) shall be published as prescribed in the Regulations.

(4)

.

.

.

Article 27
National Requirements

(1) No national law shall require compliance with requirements relating to the form or contents of the international application different from or additional to those which are provided for in this Treaty and the Regulations.

(2)

.

.

.

Article 29
Effects of the International Publication

(1) As far as the protection of any rights of the applicant in a designated State is concerned, the effects, in that State, of the international publication of an international application shall, subject to the provisions of paragraphs (2) to (4), be the same as those which the national law of the designated State provides for the compulsory national publication of unexamined national applications as such.

(2) If the language in which the international publication has been effected is different from the language in which publications under the national law are effected in the designated State, the said national law may provide that the effects provided for in paragraph (1) shall be applicable only from such time as:

(i) a translation into the latter language has been published as provided by the national law, or

(ii) a translation into the latter language has been made available to the public, by laying open for public inspection as provided by the national law, or

(iii) a translation into the latter language has been transmitted by the applicant to the actual or prospective unauthorized user of the invention claimed in the international application, or

(iv) both the acts described in (i) and (iii), or both the acts described in (ii) and (iii), have taken place.

(3) The national law of any designated State may provide that, where the international publication has been effected, on the request of the applicant, before the expiration of 18 months from the priority date, the effects provided for in paragraph (1) shall be applicable only from the expiration of 18 months from the priority date.

(4) The national law of any designated State may provide that

the effects provided for in paragraph (1) shall be applicable only from the date on which a copy of the international application as published under Article 21 has been received in the national Office of or acting for such State. The said Office shall publish the date of receipt in its gazette as soon as possible.

Article 30
Confidential Nature of the International Application

(1)(a) Subject to the provisions of subparagraph (b), the International Bureau and the International Searching Authorities shall not allow access by any person or authority to the international application before the international publication of that application, unless requested or authorized by the applicant.

(b) The provisions of subparagraph (a) shall not apply to any transmittal to the competent International Searching Authority, to transmittals provided for under Article 13, and to communications provided for under Article 20.

(2)(a)

.
.
.

CHAPTER II
INTERNATIONAL PRELIMINARY EXAMINATION

Article 31
Demand for International Preliminary Examination

(1) On the demand of the applicant, his international application shall be the subject of an international preliminary examination as provided in the following provisions and the Regulations.

(2)(a)

.

.

.

Article 33
The International Preliminary Examination

(1) The objective of the international preliminary examination is to formulate a preliminary and non-binding opinion on the questions whether the claimed invention appears to be novel, to involve an inventive step (to be non-obvious), and to be industrially applicable.

(2)

.

.

.

Article 35
The International Preliminary Examination Report

(1) The international preliminary examination report shall be established within the prescribed time limit and in the prescribed form.

(2) The international preliminary examination report shall not contain any statement on the question whether the claimed invention is or seems to be patentable or unpatentable according to any national law. It shall state, subject to the provisions of paragraph (3), in relation to each claim, whether the claim appears to satisfy the criteria of novelty, inventive step (non-obviousness), and industrial applicability, as defined for the purposes of the international preliminary examination in Article 33(1) to (4). The statement shall be accompanied by the citation of the documents believed to support the stated conclusion with such explanations as the circumstances of the case may require. The statement shall also be accompanied by

such other observations as the Regulations provide for.

(3)(a)

.

.

.

Article 38
Confidential Nature of the International Preliminary Examination

(1) Neither the International Bureau nor the International Preliminary Examining Authority shall, unless requested or authorized by the applicant, allow access within the meaning, and with the proviso, of Article 30(4) to the file of the international preliminary examination by any person or authority at any time, except by the elected Offices once the international preliminary examination report has been established.

(2) Subject to the provisions of paragraph (1) and Articles 36(1) and (3) and 37(3)(b), neither the International Bureau nor the International Preliminary Examining Authority shall, unless requested or authorized by the applicant, give information on the issuance or nonissuance of an international preliminary examination report and on the withdrawal or nonwithdrawal of the demand or of any election.

.

.

.

Article 41
Amendment of the Claims, the Description, and the Drawings, before Elected Offices

(1) The applicant shall be given the opportunity to amend the claims, the description, and the drawings, before each elected Office within the prescribed time limit. No elected Office shall grant a patent, or refuse the grant of a patent, before such time limit has

expired, except with the express consent of the applicant.

(2) The amendments shall not go beyond the disclosure in the international application as filed, unless the national law of the elected State permits them to go beyond the said disclosure.

(3) The amendments shall be in accordance with the national law of the elected State in all respects not provided for in this Treaty and the Regulations.

(4) Where an elected Office requires a translation of the international application, the amendments shall be in the language of the translation.

Article 42
Results of National Examination in Elected Offices

No elected Office receiving the international preliminary examination report may require that the applicant furnish copies, or information on the contents, of any papers connected with the examination relating to the same international application in any other elected Office.

.
.
.

Article 45
Regional Patent Treaties

(1) Any treaty providing for the grant of regional patents ("regional patent treaty"), and giving to all persons who, according to Article 9, are entitled to file international applications the right to file applications for such patents, may provide that international applications designating or electing a State party to both the regional patent treaty and the present Treaty may be filed as applications for such patents.

(2) The national law of the said designated or elected State

may provide that any designation or election of such State in the international application shall have the effect of an indication of the wish to obtain a regional patent under the regional patent treaty.

.

.

.

Article 49
Right to Practice before International Authorities

Any attorney, patent agent, or other person, having the right to practice before the national Office with which the international application was filed, shall be entitled to practice before the International Bureau and the competent International Searching Authority and competent International Preliminary Examining Authority in respect of that application.

The full text of the Patent Cooperation Treaty can be viewed on the website of the World Intellectual Property Organization (WIPO) at http://www.wipo.int/treaties.

Index

Made in the USA
Coppell, TX
01 June 2020

26810128R00163